Praise for *Re:Align*

'Jonathan Trevor has succeeded in writing an authoritative and highly compelling exposition about strategic realignment – a mission critical matter for every type of enterprise, whether social, governmental or commercial. *Re:Align* is a must read for any serious student or practitioner of leadership.'

Lord Victor Adebowale CBE, former CEO, Turning Point and Chancellor of the University of Lincoln

'In *Re:Align*, Jonathan Trevor continues to share why connecting core purpose, strategy and organization enable businesses to overcome disruption and improve performance. *Re:Align* articulates a framework that enables us to better bridge these critical components to seamlessly navigate our teams into in the rapidly changing future.'

Dame Angela Ahrendts, former SVP, Apple Retail & CEO, Burberry

'As someone who is often resistant to accepting advice from business books for even my own strategies, it is no small feat that Jonathan Trevor's book, *Re:Align*, has commanded my attention and that, more importantly, I have learned immensely from it.'

John Crabtree OBE, Lord Lieutenant of West Midlands and Chair of the 2022 Commonwealth Games Organizing Committee

'This new edition carries timely observations on making the best out of disruption and the unexpected. Senior leadership teams eager to improve their performance will find this book provides a clear pathway to diagnosing problems and making choices for action to deliver sustainable change.'

Dame Sandra Dawson, Professor Emerita, University of Cambridge

'*Re:Align* is essential reading for any business leader looking to improve performance and realise the enduring purpose of their enterprise. While refreshingly acknowledging that there is no "one size fits all" approach, Trevor unveils tangible insights into how companies can perform to their full potential.'

David Mills, CEO, Ricoh Europe

'Today's C-suites are well-advised to heed Jonathan Trevor's distinctive wisdom and method. More and more, we see business leaders caught out by inconsistency and gaps between their beliefs and their behaviour. If you want to build a thriving company in our increasingly complex and unpredictable world, you have to take a holistic approach to your company's values, strategy and structures. Greater alignment can undoubtedly help secure lasting success.'

***Paul Polman, CEO Unilever (2009–19) and co-author of* Net Positive**

'Align has been my bedside companion, and my institutional guardian angel, for the last two years. *Re:Align* offers a swathe of new insights on dealing with strategic change at the enterprise level. As a worthy successor to *Align*, *Re:Align* is essential reading for strategic leaders in both public and corporate sectors.'

Lt Gen Sir Nicholas Pope, Former Deputy Chief of the General Staff, British Army, Chair of the Service Charities Federation

'Dr Jonathan Trevor's *Re:Align* vividly demonstrates not only strategic alignment's power to clarify the strategic priorities we should be focusing on but, more importantly, the unhelpful distractions we should be letting go of.'

Trent Smyth, Executive Director, The Chief of Staff Association

'*Re:Align* is an invaluable compass in an unpredictable and ever-more dynamic global environment, and allows business leaders to understand their organizations better and plot their future with confidence.'

Hajime Watanabe, CEO, Development Bank of Japan

Praise for the first edition, *Align*

'A unique blend of practical insights and academic research make this a definitive guide to enterprise alignment. *Align* is a core read for every business leader.'

Dominic Barton, Global Managing Partner Emeritus, McKinsey & Company

'When the business community finds the right balance between customers, employees, communities and shareholders, society as a whole benefits. The key to this is alignment, and Jonathan Trevor's book provides a unique insight into why holistic management has become so crucial.'

Sergio Ermotti, CEO, UBS Group AG

'The success of any enterprise is highly dependent upon the effective alignment of its various elements. *Align* is the essential guide for any business leader looking to master this process.'

Ning Tang, CEO and founder, CreditEase

'A tour de force. Jonathan Trevor argues powerfully that the alignment of purpose, strategy and organization are the bedrock of successful performance. He provides a wealth of examples and sets out the questions which leaders need to ask if they are to overcome disruption and intense competition.'

Lord Richard Wilson GCB, former Cabinet Secretary and former Head of the Home Civil Service

Re:Align.

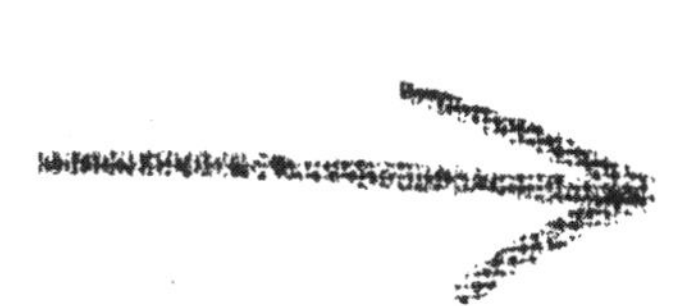

A leadership blueprint for overcoming disruption and improving performance

JONATHAN TREVOR

BLOOMSBURY BUSINESS
LONDON • OXFORD • NEW YORK • NEW DELHI • SYDNEY

BLOOMSBURY BUSINESS
Bloomsbury Publishing Plc
50 Bedford Square, London, WC1B 3DP, UK
29 Earlsfort Terrace, Dublin 2, Ireland

BLOOMSBURY, BLOOMSBURY BUSINESS and the Diana logo are trademarks of Bloomsbury Publishing Plc

First published in Great Britain 2022

A catalogue record for this book is available from the British Library

Library of Congress Cataloguing-in-Publication data has been applied for

ISBN: 978-1-3994-0059-6; eBook: 978-1-3994-0060-2

2 4 6 8 10 9 7 5 3 1

Typeset by Deanta Global Publishing Services, Chennai, India
Printed and bound in Great Britain by CPI Group (UK) Ltd, Croydon CR0 4YY

Dedicated to my wife, Clara. The person to whom I seek to align in all things; and realign howsoever she requires me to.

CONTENTS

LIST OF FIGURES

INTRODUCTION

The first edition of this book, *Align: A Leadership Blueprint for Aligning Enterprise Purpose, Strategy and Organization*, was published in late 2019. Pleasingly, it was well received: it was a *Financial Times* business book of the month, a finalist for the 2020 Business Book Awards and featured in the press as a must-read for CEOs and senior leaders. Much more importantly, it struck a chord with a lot of people. The kind notes I received from folk out of the blue suggested the book was raising awareness of the importance of *strategic alignment*. It was helping readers to influence their organizations positively by applying its concepts and frameworks. *Align* seemed to be making a difference, which was always my hope.

This type of positive impact is central to my abiding interest in *alignment* and the enduring purpose behind my work as a business school professor – to help enterprises of any description to function and perform better. I am fascinated by organizational theory and practice. It may not be particularly rock 'n' roll, as interests go, but I have been hooked ever since my first undergraduate lecture on the subject. It was as if the lights in the lecture theatre went up by 50 per cent when I was first introduced to classical theories of management, such as Weber and bureaucracy, scientific management, human relations theory and other more recent works. As all good theory should, the subject's appeal was to help me understand the confusing world around me better.

Studying business and management helped me to make sense of the stories of work-related satisfaction and frustration my parents shared with me throughout my childhood, and which I now observe in my career and those around me. It helped me to make sense of what I read in the news concerning matters of national and international importance, such as the civil unrest of the UK miners' strike in 1984 or the banking crisis of 2008, and why these events occur and why they matter. In short, it helped explain why the world was the way it was. Observing then the dwindling attendance of my classmates at lectures, it was (and still is) baffling to me why more people were not – and are not now – more interested in the subject.

Organizations, or *enterprises* as they are referred to in this book, are central to all our lives. Take you as an example, dear reader. In all likelihood, you were carefully brought into this world by the best of efforts of an enterprise in the form of a hospital and its staff. You were, or perhaps are being currently, educated by enterprises in the form of schools, colleges and universities. You will spend the majority of your adult waking life working for enterprises, whether employed or self-employed. Your retirement is secured financially by the success of enterprises, whether privately or publicly funded. And yes, inevitably, you will be buried by an enterprise, whether you like it or not. Whether commercial, governmental or social in nature, enterprises form a vital part of the human experience at every stage of our lives and are essential to our economic and social well-being, both collectively and personally. So, shouldn't we really care about how to make them function as best as possible?

What, then, is the secret sauce of a high-performing enterprise? There are two competing schools of thought in management literature. It is a raging debate between – and stick with me on this – *universalists* and *contingency theorists*. Put simply, universalists contend that enterprises function best when they adopt universally applicable management practices, which always produce superior results regardless of context. Whether you are a large or a small business, domestic or international, governmental or commercial, a manufacturer or a bank, these off-the-shelf 'best practices' are suitable for all occasions.

You will have encountered numerous examples of best practice – they often dominate management discussions (*'What's best practice in this area?'* or *'What does such and such company do?'*, for instance). They are prescribed everywhere and by everyone, from management gurus in slick books (not at all like this one, honest) to frighteningly expensive glossy management journals and jargon-heavy blog posts by the ever-swelling ranks of business influencers and executive coaches.

Best practice evangelists would have you believe that the biggest management challenge is simply one of effective implementation of standard practice.

If only it were so simple. Sadly, it is not.

Contingency theorists, of which I am firmly one, reject notions of universal best practice. There is no one-size-fits-all approach to management. For us, the best management practice is the one that best fits – or *aligns* – to the unique context of each enterprise. And every enterprise is different. In other words, what is best depends solely upon specific requirements and the context in which it is being applied. By implication, there is no standard recipe, instruction manual or efficient shortcut for how to strategize and organize for success. This presents a considerable leadership challenge. Leaders must exercise careful judgement in choosing, from a vast array of options, that which might fit their particular situation best, based upon the best available information, and mindful of the consequences of choosing poorly. The quality of decision-making by leaders becomes a major factor – perhaps the most important one – in explaining why some enterprises do well and many others do poorly.

The academic world is prone to fads and fashions in the same way as any other social field, and especially so in business and management. Contingency theory used to be all the rage, but it has fallen out of favour in published research, and universalists have taken the hill, for now at least. And yet, in my work with companies, most leaders subscribe to contingency theory intuitively, even if they do not use scholarly jargon. They understand that choosing how to align all the moving parts of their enterprise, including its business strategy and the way in which it is organized, to best support the fulfilment of its enduring purpose – its *raison d'être* – is a critical performance condition.[i]

Their challenge always is to understand better their increasingly complex world and make better forward-looking decisions. What they don't understand fully, perhaps, is the nature of the contingencies they face – how the choices about the core elements of their enterprise all fit together and the critical importance for their enterprise's performance that they do.

So far so good, until …

ALIGN DISRUPTED; RE:ALIGN

Shortly after the publication of *Align*, in mid-February 2020, I facilitated a workshop of senior executives from leading blue-chip companies. We had gathered in Munich to address a common question arising in part from the book: what does the future of work look like, and how aligned are we as enterprises to embrace it? There followed an imaginative discussion centred around the promise of artificial intelligence, machine learning, gig economy, networks, platform business models and so on. The talks were optimistic and painted a picture of the long-term transformation to a better way of working through innovation, experimentation and learning. Our gazes were fixed firmly on the future and all of the exciting possibilities it offered.

As I write the introduction to this new edition just over a year later, in the summer of 2021, it is profoundly humbling to reflect that despite our forward-looking best efforts, we had absolutely no idea about what was coming down the line, even in the immediate term. None of us predicted that within just a few weeks, we would all be confined to working from home on an indefinite basis. Nor did we know that non-essential shops and retail would close; that international travel would slump by up to 90 per cent; that millions of employees would be put on state-financed furlough or find themselves out of work.

We didn't foresee that government emergency spending would thrust many countries into levels of national debt not witnessed since the end of the Second World War and that every industry globally would be scrambling to cope with the fallout of a public health crisis unprecedented in living memory. How could we have known that family members would not be allowed to visit each other or even see dying relatives because of legally enforced lockdown measures? How could we have even conceived of the horror that, within a year, almost 3 million lives would be lost to a novel disease for which there was no immediate remedy available?[1] I refer to just some of the events associated with the

[1]Source: John Hopkins University, national public health agencies, as reported by the British Broadcasting Corporation, April 2021.

Covid-19 global pandemic, of course, and which is still ongoing – raging in fact – at the time of writing.

Were we naive as a group not to see the coming crisis? Perhaps. But if we were, then so was everyone else. There is some small comfort in this but also a serious warning. There is so much that we take for granted. Disruptions like Covid-19 challenge us to reflect on our taken-for-granted assumptions and, when required to, choose a different path in response, if we can.

The first few months of the pandemic were a roller coaster for me, as I am sure they were for you too. Closure of the Oxford campus and offices where I work meant all teaching and meetings had to transition to Zoom, Teams or other such platforms. It was a mad scramble to adjust. A month on from the onset of the global pandemic, what we were dealing with became a bit clearer. Self-evidently, a return to 'normal' in the short or even medium term was fantasy. Long-standing plans were set aside. A book tour of Asia, the Middle East and the Americas was postponed indefinitely. Scheduled client work evaporated. Research fieldwork was abandoned. Contacts went quiet. I could not blame them; keeping heads above the water was everyone's priority.

Following quiet months kept busy with teaching and writing, company contacts started to come up for air bit by bit. Conversations resumed. There was a hunger for learning and reflection to make sense of what was going on. For some, the desire simply was to learn about how others were coping. For others, it was to reflect upon the latest tips and tricks for remote working, virtual team tactics and so on. For a small subset, the desire was for something more fundamental, stemming from the realization that in this crisis there were opportunities. As the famous saying goes, *'Don't let a good crisis go to waste'*. This sentiment is certainly not meant to make light of the sheer awfulness of the pain and suffering of Covid-19. However, in the context of the business environment, the unprecedented disruption represented an opportunity for the far-sighted to introduce fundamental organizational changes that would not otherwise be possible – or even palatable – in so-called normal times.

From these more strategic conversations emerged the notion of *strategic realignment*: the act of not merely reacting to disruption in the short term but treating it as an opportunity to proactively transform the core elements that make up every enterprise to be a better fit for the future business environment. In other words, to emerge from an episode of disruption stronger than before, more vital than ever. While many enterprises hunkered down waiting for the storm to pass, some chose not to wait until the pandemic was over to introduce significant, long-term changes intended to secure them an advantage in the future.

What also became readily apparent was that highly aligned enterprises responded better to pandemic-related disruption when compared to their poorly aligned peers. A common observation was that Covid-19 had massively accelerated the pace of changes already underway. Digital transformation is an obvious example. Highly aligned enterprises were better able to respond quickly to these changes. They proved more resilient when challenged on the fundamentals of their business, whether that was the business of commerce, government or nonprofit.

Alignment is analogous to fitness, and the fittest stand the best chance of survival in any environment, all other things being equal. In my conversations with leaders, the major question soon became: how can we realign our business to survive the current crisis *and* thrive in the (post-pandemic) long-term future? Strategic realignment offered a means of turning a negative into a positive, of turning adversity into an advantage.

The contents of *Align* helped to frame these conversations and considerations. Its frameworks and concepts provided the underpinning logic by which leadership teams could strategize in a structured, engaging and inclusive way. I suddenly became busy helping colleagues, clients and collaborators to apply strategic alignment thinking to envision how they might realign their businesses, or significant parts of them, for long-term advantage. From those interactions, and the kind encouragement of my editor at Bloomsbury, the idea for a new realignment-oriented edition of the book was born.

This book is about strategic realignment as the means of overcoming disruption and securing high performance on a sustainable basis. It is a perspective on what makes enterprises perform well (alignment) and how they can transform to maintain their advantage in the context of a fast-changing business environment (realignment). At the same time, and if it isn't a bit too 'meta', this new edition is itself a response – realignment – to the first edition having been disrupted by the global pandemic.[2] By the time you read this, I hope that the level of disruption posed by Covid-19 is a memory and no longer a lived experience. But the lessons should remain because there will be other disruptions, which are themselves mere punctuations in our ever-more dynamic business environment.

The Covid-19 global pandemic is treated in this book as one source of disruption. There are many others that leaders need to consider in their thinking – everything from the introduction of new technologies to geopolitics. Given all of these persistent drivers of change to the business environment, strategic realignment must become a core competency for all enterprises and leaders if they are to stand a chance of succeeding in future. This is a book, then, about how enterprises might respond better to change and disruption in general – whether major or minor, short-term or long-term – in purposeful, thoughtful and practical ways to secure and maintain a high state of alignment.

To acknowledge this refocusing, this edition of the book has a new title. It is intended to do what it says on the tin: *Re:Align: A Leadership Blueprint for Overcoming Disruption and Improving Performance*.

THE PURPOSE OF THIS BOOK

I have had the privilege of teaching terrific undergraduate, graduate and executive students in the classroom. I have worked as an advisor to enterprises big and small, operating in all sectors around the world. My research, much of which is in collaboration with leading subject specialists at other universities and institutions, has sought to shed light on how enterprises function in the contemporary and future operating environment, what form they might take and how they are best led for value.

I am sorry to say there are thousands of enterprises globally that are operating below their potential simply because they are not well

[2]For reference, the Cambridge Dictionary defines 'meta' as: '*Of something that is written or performed referring to itself or to something of its own type.*'

aligned or fail to realign to reflect the new realities of their changing business environment. In my experience, the best companies are the ones in which their leaders regularly ask critical questions of each other, approach decision-making in a strategic, structured and systematic way, and use evidence to inform and defend their choices to all concerned for maximum engagement. I would argue that many enterprises struggle and will continue to do so because their leaders are not strategic in their consideration of alignment as a factor determining their performance and competitiveness.

With this book, I have sought to explore one issue: how can leaders make better choices to align and realign their enterprise to overcome disruption and improve performance on a sustainable basis. The purpose of such a line of enquiry is to provide leaders with a blueprint to help them to ask the right questions, convene better conversations with their teams and make the best possible alignment and realignment choices. The blueprint is the focus of this book, but it is not intended to prescribe 'the answer' to every business and management situation its readers might encounter.

Unlike prescriptive best practice, it will not tell anyone what to think or what to do. Its goal is to offer you, the reader, regardless of your remit, a leadership perspective on *how to think* strategically about your enterprise and its alignment. The purpose is to: (1) improve its alignment and, by extension, its performance; and (2) adapt to the changing business environment and overcome disruption by realigning your enterprise to ensure it remains fit for purpose over time. Great upheaval provokes change and stimulates creativity, resulting in new ways of doing things. Even today's highly successful companies are likely to struggle in the future if they lack an effective and practical means of conceptualizing the alignment of changing strategic and organizational requirements. A highly aligned enterprise is the ideal *state* that all enterprise leaders should aspire to; strategic realignment is the *process* of achieving it and maintaining it. Both are matters of strategic concern. Hence this book refers to them as *strategic alignment* and *strategic realignment*.

This leadership perspective is essential because the *'Best-aligned [enterprises] are the best performing'*, now and always, but only by design.[ii] Some enterprises even emerge from severe disruption stronger than they were previously. This is because their leaders imaginatively and courageously envision how to realign their enterprise to thrive in the longer-term future.[iii] In this time of disruption, or any other, a likely cause of failure for many of today's enterprises will be if they attempt to maintain or return to the status quo.

Strategic alignment (and realignment) should be a matter of concern for all leaders because even a marginal increase in the performance of an enterprise can make a dramatic difference – not simply to the bottom line but also to the lives of customers, communities and employees. What would a 1 per cent increase in productivity mean for your enterprise in terms of profitability, for example? How about 10 per cent? Or consider the difference a 10 per cent increase in the productivity of a hospital would mean for the improved efficiency and quality of patient care? While such thoughts are all well and good in theory, the obvious question is *how?* This is where this book seeks to make a contribution in a thoughtful and practical way.

HOW TO READ THIS BOOK

Bridging academic research and practical application, this book is written for the benefit of practitioners, regardless of role, sector or seniority. Packed with practical examples and key concepts, it is hoped that it is relevant to all those who wish to lead their enterprises for value, in whatever form that may take, whether they are seasoned executives, aspiring high-potential leaders, functional specialists or students of business and management. If you've already read the first edition, *Align*, thank you very much. A lot is new here, and I hope it makes it a worthwhile visit for a second time around. If you haven't read the first edition (for shame), then please do not worry. *Re:Align* builds upon the first edition, and the same fundamental concepts are still contained within, albeit updated.

You can read this book conventionally from start to finish or, if you prefer, dip into individual chapters if they are of special interest.

- The first chapter provides a general introduction to the concept of strategic alignment.

- The second chapter delves into detail about the process of strategic realignment, which is essential to overcome disruption and sustain performance over the long term.
- The following five chapters focus on individual links of the *enterprise value chain* – how we think about the construction of any enterprise in alignment terms – and covers each in depth:[ii]
    - Chapter 3: *Enterprise Purpose* – the enduring *raison d'être* of an enterprise;
    - Chapter 4: *Business Strategy* – strategy choices about how to fulfil the enduring purpose;
    - Chapter 5: *Organizational Capability* – the capabilities required to implement the chosen strategy well;
    - Chapter 6: *Organizational Architecture* – the resources required to develop strategically valuable organizational capability;
    - Chapter 7: *Management Systems* – the functional management systems required to deliver high performance in line with stated ambitions.

Each chapter contains several standard sections. Section 1 describes a fictionalized and anonymized case study inspired by real-life events, written in the form of a vignette, to set the scene for the chapter overall. Section 2 introduces the chapter topic, including concepts and essential insights. In Chapters 2 to 7, Section 3 identifies the *leadership challenge* of achieving a state of high alignment for that particular link in the enterprise value chain. Section 4 in Chapters 4, 5 and 6 makes reference to the book's golden thread – the *Strategic Alignment Framework*, which is introduced in Chapter 2 as a sense-making device and central feature of the blueprint by which to meet the challenge and make better choices about enterprise fundamentals. Section 5 in Chapters 2, 4, 5 and 6 outlines the *leadership opportunity* to lead the process of strategic realignment. Each chapter concludes with insights, findings and examples from the practical application of the frameworks to a variety of different enterprise settings.

Many of the real-world examples and case studies referenced in the book are anonymized to protect research subjects and client confidentiality. However, the very best illustrative case study that I can offer you is your own enterprise. When reading this book, I encourage you to pause, reflect and apply the thinking to your situation at every stage. I very much hope that you do and that it helps you understand your world a little better so that you can indeed ask good questions, have better conversations and make the best choices possible. Above all, I hope it helps you, the reader, to lead your enterprise and that you, in turn, can help others. If the Covid-19 global pandemic has taught us anything, it is that we are all in it together. Stay safe, as we say now, and best of luck.

JT

1

INTRODUCTION TO STRATEGIC ALIGNMENT

SECTION 1.1 A FAMILIAR STORY?

I had spent two days shivering in an overly air-conditioned and nondescript conference room with the company's executive board members. I was facilitating a workshop to address fundamental questions about the company's corporate purpose, strategy and organizational design. As a business school professor consulting to the company's senior leadership, it was not an easy task. For a start, nobody wanted to be there. For many of the senior managers, it must have felt like another distraction from the day job. But I knew that the company's CEO had become increasingly frustrated with his top team – with good reason. The future of the company looked uncertain.

On the face of it, the company was performing well. Over 25 years, it had become a major player in its region and the second-largest competitor in its home country market. The fact that the company had achieved such stellar growth was rightly a source of great pride. But the company was still feeling the effects of the global recession some years earlier. Making money had become harder, and investors were unsympathetic. As a start-up challenger to the old order back in the day, the company had been the first to introduce novel technological innovations. They were no longer a differentiator 20 years later.

At the same time, the company's customers had become increasingly sophisticated and were willing to take their custom elsewhere. Rather than off-the-shelf products and services, they expected greater choice and personalization. And they preferred a one-stop shop for their needs. There were more competitors than ever before. Interestingly, the leadership team still thought of competitors in terms of the usual suspects – other established companies in its industry. However, there was a sense that, elsewhere in the world, there were new and disruptive entrants to the marketplace. 'Digital' was a word much bandied around but little understood, especially regarding how the company might respond to it as either an opportunity or a threat.

The CEO used to have all the answers to the company's challenges – he had built a highly successful career on it. He was hugely popular among staff and enjoyed a reputation as a canny operator and a generous and charismatic boss. His 'walkabouts' of the company's offices were celebrated by staff. The sharing of selfies with the 'big boss' on Facebook was not uncommon. But now, it was obvious that he could not have all the answers, and he turned to his top team for help. He wanted to create a vision for the long-term future while also delivering the short-term results demanded by investors.

His executives were woefully unprepared for this task. It was clear that they only came together for strategic discussions as a *committee* of direct reports – not as a team. When questioned, nobody seemed to understand in any detail what was happening outside of the company. This was concerning as the company operated in one of the most competitive markets in its sector. Individually, they struggled to look beyond their own areas of responsibility and think of the company and its direction as one enterprise. A competitive atmosphere prevailed at executive board meetings – someone doing poorly made the others look better by comparison, or so they thought. While they had a shared interest in the balance sheet, there was no unified sense of purpose.

To compound matters, day-to-day firefighting was taking up the lion's share of executive focus; there was neither the time nor the appetite to have conversations about the future. As a result, the company lacked a coherent and well-understood vision and strategy for the future, or even the very near future. There may have been frenetic activity all around, but there was very little progress.

In lieu of a long-term strategy, the company responded to its challenges by doubling down on its existing business model. This meant pushing its lines of business even harder, minimizing costs and squeezing every ounce of 'juice' out of its assets. This included its people. The strategic focus was not on innovation but on execution – doing the same as it always had, just better. Practically, attempts were made to be more efficient at allocating resources, controlling performance and beefing up operational governance. This 'bureaucratic intensification' process was accompanied by buzzwordy statements about becoming more innovative, more joined-up and, in particular, more agile. Words and deeds, however, were inconsistent and confusing.

From an external perspective, it was hard to say what differentiated the company from its competitors. It wasn't more innovative than any other enterprise. Nor, if truth be told, was it any more efficient. It was running in the same race as its competitors and doing so in the same way. Despite the burning need for competitive differentiation, ideas about how the company might be better aligned to changing customer needs and stand apart from competitors remained elusive.

Even if the executive board had wanted to pursue a different business strategy, there would have been significant barriers to implementation. Organizationally, the company resembled a 'hub-and-spoke' type structure. This was not intentional; rather, it had emerged naturally over time. As it had grown, the company had diversified into new product areas and markets. As it did so, it set up teams to mine opportunities in new markets as best they could. Inevitably, multiple specialist teams branched off into several separate business lines. Over time, these had come to form the bulk of the company's easy-to-forget organizational chart.

The hub-and-spoke structure had worked well when the company was small and straightforward. It permitted each business line a good deal of freedom to respond to customer and competitor pressures in its area. The engagement had been high, especially at the coalface – staff were highly invested in making their bit of the business work.

The downside was that each business line had evolved to be a stand-alone unit. Sure, there was a standard corporate logo and strapline (although no one could remember it easily), but there was little in the way of day-to-day collaboration between staff in different business lines. Obvious synergies were not exploited. Staff were incentivized to maximize the performance of their area, but no more than that. In the past, this hadn't mattered much. The company had grown fast precisely because its various parts were performing well and maturing into serious market players in their own right. But today, it meant the company was incredibly siloed.

In practice, this meant that service lines pursued different priorities, and the left hand didn't know what the right hand was doing. Turf wars between different lines of business and geographies were commonplace. Individuals guarded their client relationships jealously and didn't share opportunities with colleagues in other departments for fear of losing control or diluting their bonus. It felt like the various departments within the company were battling each other rather than external competitors.

The siloed structure was a problem for customers too. Customers wanted to interact with a single touchpoint to have easy access to the full range of the company's offerings. In reality, the same customer dealing with two different parts of the company would be treated as a separate customer in each case and experience two very different ways of working.

In the early days, when the company was much smaller and less complex, the CEO had been able to be everywhere all the time, or at least that is how it had seemed. At the time, there was little consistency of management style across the company, but it didn't matter, as long as he could intervene from the top. The CEO's job had been to corral his best performers to go out, beat rivals to the punch and stake the company's claim.

Today, however, the market had matured. The company's growth had abated. It was being held back by the same structure that had once supercharged its growth. As it had grown, it had become much more complex: hundreds of employees had become thousands; a handful of business activities had become a diverse portfolio; one or two locations now extended to a major regional presence with multiple offices; and limited business relationships with local institutions now formed a complex web of international partnerships. Misalignment between the company's different lines of business, functions and hierarchical levels made achieving meaningful organizational change all the more challenging.

The view from staff in middle ranks, those closest to the customer, was that the executive board needed to 'self-disrupt'. They should realign the company proactively and not wait until forced to do so under crisis conditions. Even if they had wanted to, it was obvious to me that the company's top executives didn't know how to approach the realignment conversation. They lacked a blueprint to think strategically about aligning their enterprise and realigning it over time. They didn't know which questions to ask, which conversations to have and which choices to make to give the company the best possible future.

It didn't help that investor pressure for short-term results was so high. The more the company struggled, the more investors panicked and ramped up the pressure for quarterly results. This distracted the executives even more from devoting time to longer-term strategic considerations, which jeopardized future performance. It was a vicious cycle. A breakthrough was required, but in the absence of meaningful joined-up direction from the top, the status quo persisted.

I spent about three months at the company, on and off, asking 'dumb' questions and trying to encourage people to develop robust answers to overcome disruption and improve performance. I must have sounded like a broken record, and I certainly felt as if I was bothersome. My engagement came to a natural conclusion, and I moved on to new things and a new academic role. In the six months following my departure, I learned that the company had failed to meet its targets, and investors were not happy – profits had taken a double-digit dip.

Within nine months, the CEO had been summarily removed from his group position, despite more than 25 years of stellar service. The company's chairman replaced him as an interim measure until a new successor could be found. Several of the executive board recruited originally by the CEO also left, although some had survived. The last I heard, the company's chairman was still holding the reins – and not by choice.

As I reflect now, it's sobering to think that all of the reasons why the company was not performing were internal. Sure, the external environment was changing, but that was a challenge for everyone, including competitors. The only thing holding back the company was, well, the company itself.

SECTION 1.2 STRATEGIC ALIGNMENT

Does any of this real-life inspired story sound familiar? In my experience, the company illustrated in the previous section is far from unusual. Most leaders I work with know intuitively that aligning the core elements of their enterprise, including its strategy and how it is organized, is critical to its performance.[ii] They express this innate knowledge using informal language such as *'We need joined-up thinking'* or *'We need to get our ducks in a row'*. The problem is that operationally they lack a robust system of thought – or blueprint – to help them to do so. They are not alone. Thousands of enterprises globally are operating below their potential because they are poorly aligned. This book aims to change that.

While the concept of *alignment* – or 'fit' and 'congruence' as it is also known – is not new, part of the problem is that it means different things to different folk.[3] For example, employee relations and human resources specialists see alignment as synonymous with employee engagement, demonstrated in enhanced employee effort and positive behaviour. For strategy folk, alignment is implementation by another name. Indeed, there is an entire field dedicated to 'strategy execution' as a sub-discipline of strategic management. For software engineers, alignment is how well different 'stacks' of code speak to each other. More widely, chiropractors use the term in their practice, as do mechanics when replacing the wheels on a car, to describe what is essentially the same thing, as far as I can tell.

It is vital for us to align (no pun intended) behind a standard definition to get the most out of this book. For our purposes, the concept of alignment goes to the heart of how we define the 'work organization', or enterprise, as it is referred to here. Regardless of shape, size, sector or location, all enterprises can be thought of as *groups of people acting together to fulfil a common aim*. Implicit within this definition are four key assumptions:

[3]See for example seminal academic works by Tushman, M. & Nadler, D. 'Designing organizations that have good fit: A framework for understanding new architectures'. In Gerstein M., Nadler, D. & Shaw, R. (eds.) (1992). *Organization Architecture*. Jossey-Bass, San Francisco; and Lawrence, P.R. & Lorsch, J.W. (1967). 'Differentiation and integration in complex organizations'. *Administrative Science Quarterly*, pp. 1–47.

1. All enterprises are defined first and foremost by a common interest, which is articulated in the form of an overall aim or a purpose (the terms are used interchangeably in this context).
2. The people employed by an enterprise (including contractors and those of partners) are a means to fulfilling its ends, and therefore need to be capable of doing so as directed.
3. To fulfil the common purpose, these people need to be organized to co-operate effectively and produce a value greater than the sum of their individual efforts.
4. The more people are united – or aligned – behind an enterprise's purpose, the more likely they are to work hard, demonstrate commitment and loyalty, and behave in a way that is considered strategically desirable.

Highly aligned enterprises are typically the most purposeful, customer-aligned, capable and resilient competitors in any field. They experience the highest employee engagement scores and the strongest commitment to stated enterprise values.[iv]

The definition above sets out the essential criteria for how to think about a modern enterprise and what determines its performance. All enterprises are systems consisting of many moving parts (including people as just one form of resource). These need to exist in some form of functioning equilibrium – or in a state of alignment, we might say – to be effective. Management literature on alignment has long drawn inspiration from the physical world to frame its debates.[v] Biological systems, such as the human body, are considered healthy when they are homeostatic – for example, when temperature and fluids are well balanced and operating stably within required limits.

Biological systems achieve a state of equilibrium – or fitness – through an evolutionary process of variation, selection and retention over time. However, unlike physical systems, enterprises can be *designed* with fitness in mind because they are *socially constructed* (more on this in Chapter 2: Strategic Realignment). In other words, it is within the power of any enterprise's leadership to design their enterprise to be highly aligned and, by extension, high performing. It is simply a matter of choice.

While this is all well and good in theory, the definition discussed above is an idealized version of how enterprises work. In reality, enterprises are complex social entities, and many can be better described as *groups of people acting together to achieve their various aims*. This definition introduces a valuable critical perspective on why some enterprises perform better than others. Unlike the first definition, it recognizes that people working within enterprises may be more or less aligned to the common purpose. Different groups might co-operate more or less effectively with an associated negative impact on enterprise performance.

For example, conflicting interests, priorities and assumptions – or misalignment – within enterprises can be individual in scope (e.g. an individual employee may be dissatisfied in their work for a variety of reasons) or collective (e.g. a group of employees may be in conflict with their employer over terms and conditions of their employment). Poor alignment may also be the product of an absence of clarity over the enterprise's strategic direction and priorities. This can result in employees working towards the wrong aims despite having the best of intentions. Alignment is a crucial determinant of productivity, performance and competitive advantage. Put simply, better-aligned enterprises do better than their poorly aligned peers.

To apply these ideas practically, consider the following questions for your own enterprise or another with which you are familiar. Use a scale of one to five to conduct an assessment of your chosen case, with one being very poor and five being very good:

1. How clear and motivating is the enterprise's purpose?
2. How capable are the enterprise's people of performing its purpose as directed?
3. How well organized are the enterprise's people to ensure effective co-operation?
4. How unified are individuals and groups within the enterprise behind its common purpose?

How did you evaluate the enterprise out of a total of 20? Why did you give the scores you did? Is there one factor that is of particular concern? Where does your overall score place your chosen enterprise on the diagram illustrated in Figure 1.1?

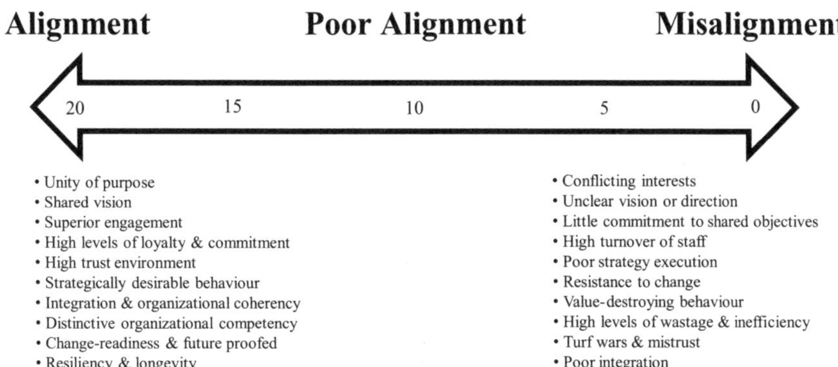

FIGURE 1.1 Alignment, poor alignment and misalignment (Source: adapted from Trevor, J. (2013). 'From New Pay to the *New*, New Pay?'. *WorldatWork Journal*, *22*(1), pp. 19–28.)

The closer an enterprise is to the left of the spectrum (and a score of 20), the higher-performing it is likely to be, all other things being equal. The right-hand side is beset with harmful conflict in the form of conflicting priorities, interests, assumptions and behaviour. All of these drain the enterprise of its resources and diminish opportunities for value creation.[vi] When asked the same questions, do members of your team share the same opinions as you? How about colleagues more widely in the enterprise? The results also answer a fifth and final question indirectly – how capable is the enterprise's leadership? A low score implies there is room for improvement.

Two key considerations help to set the scene for what follows in the remainder of this book. The first is that alignment – the arrangement of all of these elements – is a critical but often overlooked variable in securing enterprise performance. Indeed, it is often the most significant factor in explaining the difference between the success of some companies and the failure of others. So why then do we not give alignment more attention in our thinking? In truth, securing alignment is a complex process and easily overwhelming for hard-pressed executives under immense pressure to deliver short-term results. Securing enterprise-wide alignment involves having tough conversations and making even tougher decisions, the results of which are rarely ever immediately appreciable.

The second is that, even if they are mindful of its importance, I would argue that many leaders simply do not know *how to think* about the alignment of their enterprise as a matter of strategic concern. Nor do they know how to improve and maintain alignment over time as a result of their decision-making. As noted at the beginning of this section, this book provides a blueprint to address this gap in the leadership tool kit. This is essential because alignment within complex enterprises does not occur by accident or by chance – it is the result of choice alone.

Arguably the greatest responsibility of every leadership team is to align their enterprise to improve its performance as much as possible and, subsequently, to realign it over time as required to ensure it remains fit for purpose in the constantly changing business environment. Alignment and realignment are matters of strategic importance. This is the essence of *strategic alignment*, the focus of this chapter, and *strategic realignment*, which is the focus of the next.

What is strategic alignment?

Consider the example of the global fast-food retailer McDonald's – a leader in its market for decades. It succeeds by maximizing economies of scale and selling as much of its product as possible, as efficiently as possible. It serves over 70 million customers every day and generates more than $20 billion in revenues annually.[vii] Its 1.3 million employees working on the front line sell more than 75 hamburgers a second in 34,000 restaurants located in more than 120 countries worldwide.[viii] It is highly attuned to the preferences of its loyal customer base and can precisely match predictable demand with predictable supply. Operating at scale is made possible by offering only standardized and straightforward products to market.[ii] Standard menus limit variation to maximize scalability and minimize waste.

Standardization is also reflected in the design of its operations and approach to workforce management, including its working culture. This varies little across the world. The McDonald's 'playbook' defines what 'good' looks like for performing virtually every single task in each front-line role (think restaurants). Front-line work is deliberately highly routinized, with staff performing tasks according to strictly prescribed standards of work intensity, quality and safety. The company's restaurant-based culture emphasizes formalization, close co-operation teamwork, error-avoiding behaviour and rule following.[(ibid)] All of this is necessary to maintain tight control over such a large operation and achieve operational excellence on a consistent basis. McDonald's is a finely calibrated machine – an engine firing smoothly on all cylinders all of the time. And it works. It is not by accident that McDonald's is consistently ranked as one of the most powerful brands globally. Its logo, the golden arches, is the most recognized symbol in the world.[ix]

ARM Ltd, on the other hand, is a company that you might never have heard of but is likely to have had a major impact on your life.[i] ARM microprocessors power the vast majority of the world's smart devices – these range from phones, tablets, computers to the ever-expanding Internet of Things. Over 180 billion (approximately 95 per cent) of the world's smart devices use ARM-designed chips.[x] The ARM story is closely connected to cutting-edge research in the 'Silicon Fen' ecosystem based around the University of Cambridge, UK. Right from the get-go, ARM's innovation capability has lain at the heart of its success. Unlike McDonald's, ARM is small by design. It employs 6,500 people based chiefly at its headquarters in Cambridge. Its staff adhere to a common purpose and a robust set of shared values. These are intended to enable collaboration between technical and market-facing teams, high levels of technical autonomy and to reduce barriers to creative problem solving.[i]

ARM is a knowledge economy company. It produces cutting-edge designs for ever-more powerful and efficient (for which read improved battery life) microprocessors. Unlike McDonald's, much of the knowledge it relies upon to power its innovation capability does not reside within the company. ARM leverages a network of thousands of external partners (think other companies, researchers).[(ibid)] They work in fields ranging from software and hardware design to original equipment manufacturing, product development, systems integration, distribution and training.[xi] Its partner ecosystem enables it to source and integrate new knowledge in artificial intelligence, infrastructure, security and other disciplines vital to its business.[xii]

If McDonald's resembles a superbly machined engine, ARM resembles an organic network. Perhaps a human brain is an appropriate metaphor – consisting of thousands of different actors (cells) sharing connections (synapses). Through these, knowledge is created, exchanged and integrated to create a whole company (mind) that's considerably more valuable than the sum of its individual parts.[xiii] At the time of writing (in 2021), the US graphics chip designer, Nvidia, has offered $54 billion to buy ARM from its Japanese parent company, Softbank. The stated goal of the acquisition is to power Nvidia to become the *'Premier computing company for the age of artificial intelligence'*.[xiv] The acquisition is not without controversy and is not yet completed.[xv] However, it demonstrates how a company – ARM – that started with a small team of engineers working out of a converted turkey barn in Cambridge just 30 years ago has become *'A driving force in the global semiconductor industry'*.[xvi]

On the face of it, McDonald's and ARM are two highly successful companies that seem to share very little in common. It would be wrong to conclude this because the source of their success is the same – the strength of their alignment. Both companies are guided by a clear long-term purpose that is well understood and highly valued inside and out. Both companies share a laser-like focus on their chosen business strategies and propositions to market, whether business-to-consumer in the case of McDonald's or business-to-business in the case of ARM. They both have clearly articulated strategic priorities that provide a high level of focus and clear direction for employees and partners alike.

Both companies have also invested heavily in becoming distinctively capable – whether for superior execution in the case of McDonald's or superior innovation in the case of ARM – in ways that their competitors cannot emulate easily. Both companies are organized purposefully to support the implementation of their chosen strategy, including the form of their organizational culture, structure, processes, people and technology. Both companies use sophisticated human resources, information technology and operations management systems to elicit high levels of performance from their critical resources. Finally, and perhaps most importantly, the leadership of both companies treat the alignment of all of these facets of their enterprise as a matter of strategic concern. They evaluate what works well and what could work better on a frequent basis. And they do not seek to copy what works for others but to develop home-grown solutions that best fit their particular circumstances over the short *and* long term.

This is strategic alignment in practice: the purposeful arrangement of the key elements that form the make-up of every enterprise – including its approach to market and how it is organized – '*To best support the fulfilment of its long-term purpose*'.[i] A strategic alignment perspective views every enterprise as a value chain, consisting of its *business strategy*, *organizational capability*, *culture*, *structure*, *work processes*, *people* and *management systems*.[ii] All of these enable it to perform its *purpose* more or less well according to how well aligned they are. As a value chain, '*The enterprise is only as strong as its weakest link*'.[(ibid)]

Strategic alignment, then, encompasses virtually every aspect of business and management, from an enterprise's *raison d'être* (its purpose) through to its performance (how well it fulfils its purpose) and all things in between, and at all levels. This includes the enterprise level (i.e. the whole enterprise) and its individual divisions/business lines, teams and individual employees. Strategic alignment thinking also applies to one-off activities of strategic importance. For instance, a survey by the Project Management Institute indicates that enterprises that '*Align their [enterprise-wide project management office] to strategy report 38 per cent more projects meet their original goals and business intent and 33 per cent fewer projects are deemed failures*'.[xvii] Whether commercial, governmental or nonprofit, highly strategically aligned enterprises are more:

- *purposeful*: with explicit values and priorities behind which to align the enterprise;
- *customer aligned*: sensitive to customers' changing preferences and needs;
- *differentiated*: by being capable in distinctive and difficult-to-emulate ways;
- *focused*: with a well-understood strategic direction and image of 'what "good" looks like';
- *productive*: above the industry average for output and efficiency relative to inputs;
- *resilient*: durable and change-ready in the face of all forms of disruption;
- *engaging*: leading to high performance, commitment and loyalty among their people.

On the other hand, poorly aligned enterprises experience sub-par performance. They are more vulnerable to the ravages of the competitive marketplace, whether competing for market share (in commercial markets) or competing for resources (in the case of the public and nonprofit sectors). According to research by the Economist Intelligence Unit, 90 per cent of respondents in a sample of 500 senior executives of major corporations reportedly fail to implement all of their strategic goals due to misalignment between strategy and execution. What's more, 53 per cent report that a lack of appropriate organizational capability leaves their enterprise unnecessarily vulnerable to competition and disruption.[xviii]

All other things being equal, strategic alignment is one of the most critical factors explaining why some enterprises thrive and others struggle or fail. It is an untapped source of advantage worthy of significant leadership attention. How, then, should we think about alignment as a matter of strategic concern?

SECTION 1.3 THE STRATEGICALLY ALIGNED ENTERPRISE VALUE CHAIN

Asking clients or executives in my classes to describe their enterprise is fascinating. It reveals how they think and what they prioritize in their roles, either consciously or unconsciously. Most describe either their industry (*'We're in consumer electronics'*), some version of their balance sheet (their important financial activities) or draw an organizational chart illustrating various boxes connected by wires, resembling an engineering schematic (which is precisely what it is). The problem is that viewing enterprises through these partial lenses can result in disjointed decision-making, conflicting priorities, incoherent messaging and confusion.

Illustrated by Figure 1.2, Section 1.3 reviews an important framework – the *enterprise value chain* – derived from my collaboration with Dr Barry Varcoe.[4] It is intended to help leaders to ask good questions, have better

[4]For additional insights and examples, refer to Trevor, J. & Varcoe, B. (2017). 'How aligned is your organization?'. *Harvard Business Review*. 7 February. Harvard Business School Publishing.

External Enterprise Environment

Internal Enterprise Environment

Leadership Challenge	*What is our enduring enterprise purpose and how can we make it as meaningful as possible?*	*Which business strategy best fulfils our enterprise purpose in our dynamic business environment?*	*Which organizational capabilities are critical to implementing our chosen business strategy?*	*Which organizational architecture will make us capable in strategically desirable ways?*	*Which management systems will maximize performance in line with our stated ambitions?*
	Enterprise Purpose	**Business Strategy**	**Organizational Capability**	**Organizational Architecture**	**Management Systems**
Leadership Opportunity		**Choose the ideal form of our:** • Product/service offering(s)? • Market(s)? • Customer proposition? • Competitor differentiation? • Branding?	**Choose the ideal form of our:** • Organizational capability? • Core competency? • Diversity of capability?	**Choose the ideal form of our:** • Core people? • Core organization structure? • Core organizational culture? • Core processes? And our: • Technologies? • Organizational shape & size?	**Choose the ideal form of our:** • HR system? • IT system? • Workplace? • Finance system? • Procurement system? • Operations system?

'The enterprise value chain is only as strong as its weakest link'

FIGURE 1.2 The strategically aligned enterprise value chain (Source: adapted from Trevor, J. & Varcoe, B. (2017). 'How aligned is your organization?'. *Harvard Business Review*. 7 February. Harvard Business School Publishing; Copyright © Jonathan Trevor and Barry Varcoe 2016.)

joined-up conversations and make together the best possible choices to be strategically aligned.

The universal linkages (or elements as they have been referred to previously) that form the make-up of every enterprise's value chain are, in order:

1. ***Enterprise purpose***: Enterprise purpose is the enduring *raison d'être* of any enterprise.[ii] It is the idealistic reason why the enterprise exists and why it is maintained through thick and thin. It should convey aspirations for the positive impact the enterprise wishes to have on the world and why anyone outside the enterprise itself should care. Consider for your enterprise:
   - What is your enduring enterprise purpose? What do you do as an enterprise, and why does it matter?
   - To whom should your purpose matter? Who are your stakeholders, and which matter to you most? How well do they understand the purpose? How much do they value it, and is it manifest in their motivation and behaviour?

The more its purpose is valued by others outside of the enterprise itself – be they customers, investors, regulators, governments or the general public – the greater the potential for its impact in the long term. Enterprise purpose is the focus of Chapter 3.

While an enterprise's purpose is the *enduring* north star to which all things should be aligned, all other links in the value chain are *dynamic*.[i] They should change in step with the changing external environment. The first dynamic link is the enterprise's business strategy:

2. ***Business strategy***: Its business strategy is how an enterprise intends to fulfil its purpose in the market(s) in which it is competing for an advantage. The fundamentals of an enterprise's business strategy should include: first, the choice of the enterprise's offerings to market in the form of products and services; second, the ideal strategic approach to align to customer or stakeholder demand and gain a

competitive edge; and third, how to differentiate from the best efforts of competitors, whether competing for market share or resources.[ii] The obvious goal for decision-makers is to match known and nascent market demand as much as possible. Multiple lines of business within diversified enterprises may each require a different strategic approach. A primary criterion for all decision-making should be how well an enterprise's chosen offerings to the market support the fulfilment of its enduring enterprise purpose.[(ibid)] Consider for your enterprise:

- Which products and services do you offer to the external market to fulfil your enterprise purpose? How much are they in demand? Which are priorities for growth? Given what you know about emerging opportunities and threats in the external market, which should you continue to offer, start offering or even stop offering in, say, the next five to 10 years?
- For each of these offerings, which mode of competitive differentiation – the choice between efficiency or innovation, for example – will give you the best chance of aligning to customer requirements and standing apart from competitors?
- How should you articulate your strategy choices as a compelling customer proposition *and* a coherent strategic narrative and set of priorities for your people?

Your answers to these questions define the first principles of your business strategy – how you define the successful implementation of your enterprise's purpose in the short, medium and longer term. An enterprise's business strategy is expressed typically as vision statements, priorities, planning and measures. Business strategy is the focus of Chapter 4.

Even the best-formulated business strategy is merely a set of good intentions unless it can be implemented. In your quest to strategically align your enterprise, you also need to consider changing the fundamentals of its organizational capabilities, architecture and management systems.

3. ***Organizational capability***: Organizational capability refers to the abilities, competencies and powers required to implement an enterprise's chosen business strategy.[(ibid)] At the most basic level, organizational capability refers to the possession of general or industry-specific know-how – the functional knowledge needed to run a business day to day. However, functional knowledge alone is rarely a compelling differentiator in a competitive marketplace because it is easy to acquire. To secure sustainable competitive advantage, enterprises need to develop organizational capability that is as distinctive as – and aligned to – their differentiated business strategy.[xix]

   For example, to implement a synergy-based business strategy, diversified enterprises need to realize the potential for 'cross-value' between complementary lines of business. This could include sharing valuable customer insights, cross-fertilizing innovative practices, pooling resources and co-creating new market offerings. Alternatively, suppose customer-centricity is the basis for competitive differentiation. In that case, an enterprise needs to be capable of customer agility, the configuring and reconfiguring of its market offerings to match its customers' changing preferences as closely as possible.[ii] Critical trade-offs also need to be carefully considered when choosing which organizational capability to develop. It is tough to be efficient and flexible simultaneously.[xx] The implication is that enterprise leaders must choose wisely which organizational capability (or capabilities in diversified businesses) to develop for the long term in line with strategy requirements. Consider for your enterprise:

   - What does your enterprise need to be capable of organizationally to implement its chosen business strategy? Is it superior efficiency, as it is for McDonald's, or is it superior flexibility and innovation, as it is for ARM? Which should you prioritize for development?
   - How capable are you at the current time? What are your competitors capable of doing? How can you develop a

distinctive capability – your enterprise's core competence – that is difficult for peers to emulate or acquire?

- How diverse are your organizational capability requirements? As per your business strategy, does your enterprise need to be capable of implementing only one thing (i.e. for a single line of business) or many different things (i.e. for multiple different lines of business)?

Your answers to the questions above define your organizational priorities and set the criteria for how you should organize your enterprise – its organizational architecture. Organizational capability is reviewed in Chapter 5.

4. ***Organizational architecture***: If organizational capability represents the *function* (the why) of how you organize your enterprise the way you do, then your organizational architecture is the actual *form* it takes (its shape). Form follows function, and organizational architecture combines an enterprise's core organizational components: its core organizational *culture*, core organizational *structure*, core work *processes* and core *people*.[ii] When configured appropriately, they support the development of strategically valuable organizational capability.[(ibid)]

   There are many different forms of each of these core organizational components. For example, organizational structure can be hierarchy or network based, flexible or steady state, open or closed. Organizational culture can be individualistic or collectively oriented; internally or externally focused; controlling or empowering. Leaders must design their organizational architecture appropriately by carefully selecting the ideal form of each core organizational component in line with their organizational capability requirements.[(ibid)] Enterprises seeking to secure a market advantage through innovation, for example, value people characteristics such as individual creativity, a focus on long-term performance and a willingness to take risks. Alternatively, enterprises pursuing a cost-containment strategy are likely to value employee cost-consciousness, proficiency against prescribed standards and error-reducing behaviour much more. Consider for your enterprise:

- To develop your enterprise to be distinctively capable, which is the best design of organizational architecture for you?
- Which form of each core organizational component – your core organizational structure, culture, work processes and people – should you select ideally, and how do you integrate them to be as complementary as possible?

Your answers to the questions above define your organizational design priorities. Organizational architecture is the focus of Chapter 6.

5. ***Management systems***: Management systems are the functional policies, procedures and practices used to achieve desired performance from an enterprise's resources. Most corporations express their management systems as specialized functions, such as human resources, finance, operations, information technology and estates. Like the organizational architecture they support, each management system should be designed with the enterprise's strategic requirements in mind.[(ibid)]

   Consider just one aspect of an enterprise's human resource system (itself just one functional management system of many) – its approach to employee performance management. Performance management systems can be designed to emphasize individual, team or overall company performance (or a combination of all three). Measures can be primarily qualitative or quantitative (or both); objectives can be set in advance or assessed retrospectively; an appraisal can be performance focused or developmental (or both). Leaders must choose between these various options when designing their system to generate superior performance.

   Additionally, whichever form of performance management system is selected, it should complement how the enterprise intends to manage other aspects of its human resources. This can include employee reward, development, progression, recruitment and communication. To meet this challenge, functional leaders, such as human resource department specialists, need to be strategic and cross-functional in their outlook and decision-making, as do their peers in other functions. To manage your enterprise's resources, consider:

- How well do your functional strategies and systems (e.g. human resources, information technology) support enterprise performance in line with the enterprise's organizational architecture requirements?
- What could you change about how you manage your people, your information technology, your finances or your operations for the better?

Management systems are the focus of Chapter 7.

Every question posed above represents a strategic choice. Your combined answers describe your enterprise at its core – either how *it is* currently or how *it should be* ideally. In a strategically aligned enterprise, there is no difference between the two.

Form follows function in the enterprise value chain, and it is the vital role of leadership to ensure their enterprise's value chain is as aligned as it possibly can be by selecting the appropriate form of each linkage. For instance, an enterprise's business strategy is deemed effective to the extent that it supports the fulfilment of the enterprise's enduring purpose.[(ibid)] Organizational capabilities are considered strategically valuable depending upon how well they support the implementation of the enterprise's chosen business strategy. Investments in resources, including human and technological, are desirable if they support the development of strategically valuable organizational capabilities. Management systems are effective if they mobilize desired levels of performance from the enterprise's core organizational components (e.g. its people and other resources).[(ibid)]

The problem is that leaders often focus on one link at a time, creating the potential for poor alignment or even harmful misalignment within their enterprise.[i] What matters for performance is how well all links of the enterprise value chain *align* and support the fulfilment of enterprise purpose overall.[(ibid)] This is the meaning of a strategic perspective on alignment – strategic because it is a purposeful, systematic and joined-up attempt to improve and maintain enterprise performance and advantage over time.

Building upon self-reflection of the previous section, consider further for your own enterprise:

1. *How aligned is your enterprise value chain?* How well does your chosen business strategy support your enterprise's enduring purpose? Equally, how capable organizationally is your enterprise of implementing its intended business strategy?[(ibid)] If not, why not? What are the potential barriers to alignment in your enterprise? And what are the consequences for performance and value? Is there a particular link that is of greater concern than the others? Where should you focus your attention to improve alignment? Who should be involved in that conversation? Do your customers, for example, think the same way that you do? How about your external business partners?
2. *If the enterprise value chain is only as strong as its weakest link, who is responsible for aligning it?* The obvious answer I hear all the time is: *'The CEO and the Board, of course!'* However, a limitation of relying upon the enterprise's most senior leaders is one of 'bounded rationality' – there is simply too much to consider in today's complex business environment for an individual or small group to make good choices.[xxi] Should the answer be 'everybody', then? The limitation here is that everybody can quickly become 'nobody', with accountability for securing alignment becoming too diffuse to be anything other than ineffectual.[ii] There is no easy answer to the question, but, in my experience, highly participative decision-making serves enterprises best, especially when operating under conditions of high uncertainty.
3. *How capable is your leadership of strategically aligning your enterprise?* Whoever they are, are your enterprise leaders

> mindful of the importance of alignment? Do they assume responsibility for strategic alignment within your enterprise, and, additionally, do they possess the skills and knowledge to achieve it? The most capable enterprise leaders I have worked with are 'multi-everything': 'multi-stakeholder' in their sense of accountability; 'multi-disciplinary' in their knowledge; 'multi-level' in their thinking; 'multi-phased' in their short-, medium- and long-term planning; and 'multinational' in their environment scanning.[xxii] Who are the enterprise leaders where you work, and do they understand what is required of them? How can you develop your enterprise's leadership capability further? Finally, and critically, how aligned is your leadership team? A poorly aligned team cannot hope to lead a highly aligned enterprise.

So far, we have focused on what strategic alignment is and *how to think* to 'get it right' in the quest for enhanced performance and competitiveness. There is another side to the alignment challenge. What about when we 'get it wrong'? In other words, what are the risks of misalignment?

SECTION 1.4 IF ALIGNMENT EQUALS PERFORMANCE, THEN MISALIGNMENT EQUALS RISK

The company in Section 1.1 provides a real-life inspired story of a misaligned enterprise. Its leaders were not asking the right questions, not sharing in joined-up strategic conversations, not acting in concert to lead the company as one enterprise. Its business strategy did not reflect the new realities of customers' changing preferences or competitors' capabilities, nor was it organized to be distinctive or easily differentiated. The company lacked focus and had lost sight of how it was trying to succeed in the marketplace or how it should be organized.

The global bank Barclays provides another example of the risks posed by poor alignment. Like others in its industry, it has been the subject of numerous punitive fines over the past decade for poor business practices.[5] It is tempting to assume a few bad apples or rogue employees were the cause of Barclays' well-documented woes.[i] However, an independent review commissioned by Barclays in 2013 speaks to a systemic leadership failure to manage the company's organizational culture: *'We believe that the business practices for which Barclays has rightly been criticized were shaped predominantly by its cultures, which rested on uncertain foundations. There was no sense of common purpose in a group that had grown and diversified significantly in less than two decades.'*[xxiii] To improve enterprise-wide governance and performance (in other words, become better aligned), today Barclays is dramatically reducing its headcount, its range of banking activities and global presence to focus on retail and investment banking in the UK and the US.[xxiv]

Alignment is a two-sided coin, but if alignment equals performance, then the converse – misalignment – does not necessarily equal poor performance. Misalignment creates *unnecessary risk* and value-destroying enterprise behaviour in the form of dysfunction, wasted effort, reckless conduct and misallocated resources.[xxii] For example, attempts to generate a culture of inter-departmental collaboration will fail utterly if a hierarchical organizational structure frustrates attempts by employees to connect with those outside of their individual line of business or function. Equally, poorly selected management systems (e.g. human resources and information technology systems) introduce harmful friction into the engine room of the enterprise by creating incentives or working practices that run counter to strategic goals or the enterprise's values. A strategic approach to alignment is how an enterprise's leaders can maximize performance and at the same time minimize unnecessary risk.

[5]Examples include violation of the International Emergency Economic Powers Act (fines of $298 million in 2010), Payment Protection Insurance mis-selling (Barclays agreed to put aside £1 billion for compensation to mis-sold customers in 2011), settlement with UK and US authorities over illegal manipulation of foreign exchange rates (LIBOR and Euribor, fines of $450 million in 2012) and a fine from the US Justice Department for conspiring to fix foreign currency rates ($710 million in 2015) (source: www.corp-research.org/barclays). These, and other fines, continue to hit profits (source: www.telegraph.co.uk/business/2018/10/22/serious-fraud-office-presses-case-get-criminal-charges-reinstated/).

So why do so many enterprises struggle to secure alignment? Out of many potential reasons, three stand out. Put bluntly, the first is poor leadership. This is often due to performance pressure, being time poor or even just lacking awareness and understanding of the contingencies at play.[ii] An enterprise's leadership can become tempted or even blinded by the siren song of best practice prescriptions and end up adopting strategies, practices and systems that are a poor fit for their own purposes. Or, more operationally, they fail simply to communicate their vision for their aligned enterprise in ways that are meaningful and engaging for their stakeholders, be they customers, investors or employees. Research by Gallup indicates that only about four in 10 employees (41 per cent) understand what their company stands for and what makes it different from competitors.[xxv]

I've encountered struggling leadership teams in all sectors. Often it is because they do not devote sufficient time to discussing matters of strategic importance, which resonates with broader research on executive focus.[xxvi] Figure 1.3 presents results from a survey of leaders from 80 different enterprises about how often they talk about strategic alignment within their teams. The results are startling, if not surprising. These data indicate that some respondents do not discuss strategic alignment at all. If they do, it is on a yearly or monthly basis in the majority of cases. By contrast, a significant proportion of the same

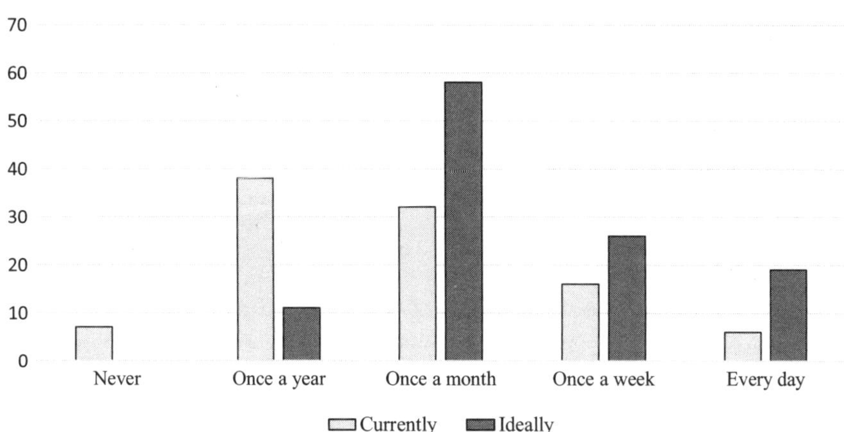

FIGURE 1.3 Time spent talking about strategic alignment within teams (Source: Oxford IEDP Survey, April 2021.)

respondents believe that the alignment of their enterprise's purpose, strategy and organization should be a monthly, weekly or even daily conversation ideally.

The implication is that leaders do not discuss strategic alignment nearly as often as they think they should. This matters for two reasons. First, in the absence of strategic direction, it is all too easy to mistake activity for progress, which it is not, of course.[ii] Second, failing to lead strategically creates the potential for poor alignment or even misalignment within the enterprise.

So why are these conversations not occurring as frequently as they should? In my experience, many senior leaders are too often drawn into operational matters and spend the lion's share of their time reacting (not leading), firefighting and problem solving.[(ibid)] How often do you talk about strategic alignment with your team? Is it as often as you should? If not, why not? And what can you do to create the opportunity to discuss it more frequently and avoid the inevitable distractions that will crop up down the line?

Furthermore, the business environment is considerably more complex than it ever has been. A hundred years ago (and covered in more detail in Chapter 2), the prevailing logic of the enterprise was scale and simplicity. Typically, businesses focused on one market and the offering of one type of standardized product. Good management practice was to reduce the enterprise and all of its moving parts, including its people, to the simplest possible form and then manage it mechanistically in the most efficient and standard way possible. Repetition and routine were prized organizational qualities, and change was not on the agenda – *'If it ain't broke, don't fix it'*, or so the logic went. Elements of this thinking still apply today, but the business environment is considerably more challenging in the demands it places upon enterprises of all shapes and sizes and in all sectors.

Globalization and free trade have opened significant opportunities for established players in new markets and vice versa. Investor pressure for high returns is evident in the highly performance-leveraged incentives paid to their executives, and if companies are not growing, often the market view is that they are failing. Not only is constant expansion gruelling, but it can also lead to excessive risk-taking. The quest for growth and competitiveness has driven many enterprises to diversify their offerings and the markets in which they operate. The two-dimensional matrix of product and geography (i.e. multiple products offered in different markets) is a common feature of many multi-divisional and multinational enterprises. It can become extraordinarily complex because each line of business and geography imposes different and constantly changing requirements for success.[(ibid)]

Growth-fuelled complexity also presents enterprise leaders with so-called 'wicked problems' for which there are no obvious or easy solutions. These problems are difficult to solve because of incomplete or contradictory information, competing viewpoints and entanglement with other problems.[xxvii] Even the most capable leadership teams can be caught off guard by the operational complexities of the modern enterprise. All enterprises, and especially complex ones, are prone to entropy – the loss of energy in the form of failed capital expenditure (including human, social and technological capital in addition to financial capital). For example, complex multinational companies are the most prone to misalignment and dissipate energy the most quickly in the absence of active management. Complex enterprises are the most at risk of disintegration and the performance penalties described by the second definition of work organization mentioned earlier in the chapter – individuals and groups working together to achieve their *various* aims.

Third, the business environment is also considerably more dynamic than it was – and that change is not episodic but a constant. Product, service and business model innovation has come to the fore as quality and cost offer less and less scope for competitive differentiation in mature markets. Today's products and services are not expected to remain the same if they are to stand out from the offerings of competitors and appeal to fickle customers. More widely, the introduction of digital technology is speeding up the pace of change in every industry, both in terms of customer buying behaviour – their preferences and needs – and how enterprises themselves operate. Along the entire enterprise supply chain, from upstream development of new products and services to downstream delivery, digital transformation is changing radically the ways in which we go about our respective businesses in every field.

From an alignment perspective, constant change poses two challenges. First, while an enterprise's purpose doesn't change generally, its strategy and organization should if they are to keep pace with the changing business environment.[ii] Constant change can make aligning all of the individual linkages of the enterprise value chain feel like an impossible game of Whac-A-Mole.[6] Second, enterprises tend to maintain the same trajectory unless steered purposefully in a different direction by their leaders. This is what academics refer to as 'path dependency', and it explains the persistence of established customs and practices even when they no longer make sense. This is especially true when leaders are required to make strategic decisions with uncertain outcomes. In the absence of knowing what is best for the future, managers often seek to maintain the status quo and, sooner or later, fall foul of changes in the business environment for which they are poorly equipped to respond. Inevitably, even the best-aligned enterprises *will* become misaligned over time if they fail to keep pace with their changing environment.

Consider the classic example of Xerox. In the 1970s, the company was the undisputed market leader in the supply of photocopiers. Like 'Hoover' for vacuuming, 'Xerox' entered the lexicon as a verb to describe the act of photocopying documents. In addition to its core business in print, Xerox also invested in developing new technologies via its Palo Alto Research Center. In 1973, it stole a march on competitors in the emerging personal computing market with the invention of the Xerox Alto. Complete with a graphics-based user interface and scrolling mouse, the Xerox Alto is a strong contender for the title of the world's first modern personal computer (PC).[xxviii]

However, Xerox failed to exploit its new technology, and others were quick to capitalize upon Xerox's *'dithering'* (as it was described by Steve Jobs), including Bill Gates at newly founded Microsoft and Jobs at Apple.[(ibid)] As Jobs described further: '*Xerox could have owned the entire*

[6]For the uninitiated, Wikipedia describes Whac-A-Mole as an amusement arcade game *'In which players use a mallet to hit toy moles, which appear at random, back into their holes'* (https://en.wikipedia.org/wiki/Whac-A-Mole).

computer industry, could have been the IBM of the nineties, could have been the Microsoft of the nineties.'[(ibid)] Fast-forward three decades, and today (in 2021), Apple and Microsoft vie for the title of the world's most valuable company, each with a market capitalization of over $2 trillion.[xxix] By comparison, Xerox's market capitalization stands at $4.5 billion.[xxx]

Why did Xerox fail to capitalize upon its initial technological advantage and become a leader in the most lucrative market of the late 20th century? Research on Xerox indicates the answer may be a phenomenon referred to as the 'competency trap'.[xxxi] This is where an enterprise's people are prevented from responding effectively to external threats and opportunities because they are limited to their existing knowledge and competence (or 'organizational capability' to use the language of the enterprise value chain). What made an enterprise successful in the past will not always guarantee success in future, but it is difficult to abandon what is known and proven. Where Xerox failed to embrace its new market opportunity, competitors moved quickly to gain a long-lasting advantage.

SECTION 1.5 REALIGN TO OVERCOME DISRUPTION AND IMPROVE PERFORMANCE

While it is true to say that change is a constant in today's business environment, we do experience episodes of extreme change – or disruption – in our environment, which have the potential to turn our economies, industries, enterprises and everyday lives upside down. The Covid-19 global pandemic is one such example. It has had a profound impact on us all, but it has disrupted individual industries and enterprises in different ways, with some finding opportunities and others only challenges.

For example, many technology companies have gone from strength to strength, especially collaboration platforms such as Zoom, streaming services such as Netflix and online retailers such as Amazon. Amazon's profits more than tripled in the period between March 2020 to March 2021 from $2.5 billion to $8.1 billion.[xxxii] Technology company, and Google's parent, Alphabet, saw its net profit leap by 162 per cent in the first three months of 2021. This was due to advertising revenues increasing by more than a third as more people than ever used its search, streaming and online services during the pandemic.[xxxiii]

Products and services that can be bought online and consumed at home also exploded in the age of lockdown. The exercise equipment manufacturer, Peloton, saw an increase in sales revenues of 172 per cent during 2020.[xxxiv] It did this by combining its standardized exercise products with personalizable gym instruction delivered via its proprietary streaming service. Its challenge has been to meet demand, which, by some accounts, it has struggled to do.[xxxv]

The retail and leisure sector, on the other hand, has been hard hit, with many companies, including major chains, going out of business due to a collapse in footfall, despite government support. The global travel industry has been similarly beleaguered since the beginning of the pandemic. In March 2020, the number of scheduled international flights originating from the US was down 72 per cent on the previous year, down 81 per cent in the UK and down 90 per cent in China.[xxxvi]

The international airline British Airways (BA) responded with aggressive cost cutting to overcome industry-wide disruption. It announced early on in the pandemic that it intended to reduce its headcount by 12,000 (out of 42,000) to weather the Covid-19 storm. It was far from alone. One of its UK-based competitors, Virgin Atlantic, laid off a third of its workforce in 2020. At the same time, the crisis spurred many airlines to find innovative solutions to the shortfall in passengers. The Japanese airline ANA was among the first to introduce an innovative 'Common Pass' digital health passport to accommodate Covid-19 travel restrictions.[xxxvii] To stay connected, it also offered a range of digital services to its loyalty club members, including bespoke media content and entertainment services, to enjoy 'on the ground' during pandemic-related air travel restrictions.

The implication is that to stand a chance of succeeding in the future, today's enterprises and their leaders must be capable of *strategic realignment* – rearranging their enterprise to fit the changing environment better, as a matter of course. This is true whether they are trying to improve alignment in the face of increased complexity, adapt an already aligned enterprise to keep pace with the changing business environment or overcome disruptive events as severe as Covid-19.

In conclusion, this chapter has put forward a few key points, which are summarized as follows:

1. Alignment is essential to the performance of every enterprise and should be treated as a matter of strategic concern.
2. Every enterprise is a value chain consisting of universal linkages, which can only be as strong as the weakest link.[ii]
3. Alignment equals performance, whereas misalignment introduces unnecessary risk in all aspects of an enterprise's operations.
4. Alignment is secured due to the quality of leaders' choices for every link of the enterprise value chain.[xxii] Strategies and organizational designs that work for one enterprise will not work for another.
5. Finally, even the best-aligned enterprises will become poorly aligned, or even misaligned, over time, given that change and disruption are now a constant in today's dynamic business environment. Realignment is the remedy.

This last point is especially true when disruption renders the enterprise status quo unviable. Strategic alignment might be considered an optimal *state* of enterprise equilibrium – the enterprise at its most fit and, by extension, most high performing. Strategic realignment is the *process* of transforming the enterprise to become more aligned or to adapt it to remain fit for purpose in a changing business environment. In other words, strategic alignment is the *what to do to do better*, and strategic realignment is the *how to do better*.

Both should be of the highest strategic importance for enterprises' leaders and central to their role. The next chapter outlines a powerful thought process, frameworks and guiding examples for how to realign your enterprise to overcome disruption and improve performance.

2

STRATEGIC REALIGNMENT

SECTION 2.1 NECESSITY IS THE MOTHER OF ~~INVENTION~~ REALIGNMENT

'Popular Brand Tobacco' (PBT) enjoyed a storied past. It had been a major player in the international tobacco market for over 150 years. From European roots, by the mid- to late-20th century, it had expanded to become one of only four genuinely global players. Like its global competitors, the PBT product portfolio consisted of dozens of local cigarette brands and a handful of international brands. Irrespective of brand, PBT products were known for their quality and smoothness, and its cigarettes were the gold standard in every local market. For decades, PBT had been highly profitable and was today still a cash-rich business that rewarded shareholders with solid performance and stable growth. Pedigree, tradition and excellence were near-sacred qualities at the company. PBT was a family, and its strong roots meant stability and consistency.

Even in the 21st century, the company retained a traditional feel. At its grand headquarters (HQ), executives enjoyed the use of a silver-service dining room with magnificent city views. HQ felt very much like the company's central administration – the head, not the beating heart – for PBT was a highly decentralized company. The company had depended upon a long-standing policy of dispatching highly talented expatriates worldwide to establish operations in high-potential emerging markets to secure its continued growth. Its many territories and locations operated largely independently of each other. They relied heavily upon their own resources and local leadership to promote sales in their markets, albeit within guidelines set by HQ. It had been a remarkably successful strategy.

Its growth in emerging markets had been a godsend, as PBT had been facing existential threats to its established markets for some time. Landmark rulings in highly publicized legal proceedings brought much attention to the health risks associated with smoking. Smoking had become indelibly linked to poor health. Worse still, some critics claimed that the tobacco industry had long known of the health risks posed by consuming their highly addictive products. The alleged implication was that the industry had put profits before people. The tide of public opinion had been turning against the industry for some time. It was not uncommon to hear it referred to as a *'sin industry'*. Companies in other controversial industries kept a watchful eye.

The consequences for tobacco companies were obvious. Cigarettes had become a guilty pleasure, and smoking was declining year on year. It was no accident: successive governments, especially in PBT's mature markets, taxed the sale of any form of tobacco product to discourage consumption. The price of a pack of cigarettes had increased by hundreds of per cent in just a matter of years. Newly introduced laws now prevented smoking in public or enclosed spaces, including bars and restaurants. Industry regulation also required cigarette packaging to be bland by design and feature shocking images of the medical consequences of smoking. Tobacco firms were banned from advertising on television or in public spaces. Concerns over corporate social responsibility and a fear of their reputations being damaged caused many institutional investors to abandon the industry, regardless of positive financial returns. Even recruitment was a challenge as top talent sought roles in less controversial industries.

All in all, it had made for an incredibly hostile business environment over the past 40 years and a core market in terminal decline. Changing sentiment within the social, regulatory and political environments had led people to smoke less. Some asked if there was even a future for the industry. PBT had been grappling with these challenges for years, of course. Still, the pace and scope of disruption was accelerating.

A fundamental realignment of the company was required: from *'Soup to nuts'* as one of the company's executives described it.[7] In practice,

[7] *'Soup to nuts'* refers to the first and last course of European banquet meals traditionally.

this meant reviewing every link of the company's value chain – from its stated purpose as a company to its strategy for succeeding in the marketplace and how it was organized to implement its chosen strategy.

Following a lengthy review and with much fanfare, PBT relaunched itself with a new purpose: a shift from producing the best-in-class tobacco products to a focus instead on lifestyle and health. Its stated mission became to eradicate harmful cigarettes by replacing them with scientifically proven low-risk alternatives. Under its new purpose, PBT was a 'lifestyle business' and not a tobacco company.

Branding shifted away from traditional channels, such as the sponsorship of male-centric motorsport. It focused instead on web-based advertising to a diverse range of marketing 'personas' – the types of people PBT hoped would be loyal customers in future. Young, healthy and wholesome, they were all a far cry from the iconic cigarette-smoking heroic white-straight-male that had once dominated its product advertising.

The most obvious tangible change was to introduce a new line of products to replace cigarettes. 'PowerPacks', as they were called, looked and operated nothing like the traditional cigarette stick. The sleek integrated mouthpiece and charging unit resembled a mobile phone more than anything. Like a mobile phone, it was a customizable fashion accessory, available in different colours and pouches to suit individuals' preferences. And like e-cigarettes or vaping pens, the power packs were non-disposable battery-powered units. They still relied upon nicotine chemically but used a proprietary flavoured gel instead of tobacco, which posed fewer health risks, or so the science said.

The power packs were said to represent the best of both worlds – the flavour of tobacco with the reduced risks of cigarette alternatives. They were a technological solution to a public health problem. PBT was betting on PowerPacks as a new and differentiated product in a highly disrupted market.

Organizationally, the realignment of the company required a shift in shape and size. At its peak, PBT had employed tens of thousands of people around the world. It was still large, but it would be leaner in future, with fewer people employed in regional super hubs as opposed to local country offices, as before. Where PBT had been decentralized, with a loose group structure and high levels of local autonomy, it was likely to be highly centralized in the future. Its new products were designed and produced centrally to one global standard. Its many brands were becoming an overall global brand: the PowerPack.

This approach wasn't simply more efficient; it's that the one standardized unit of production – the PowerPack – was highly customizable from a customer perspective. PBT had created an app to complement its physical product, through which 'users' (never 'smokers') could access an exclusive range of complementary lifestyle 'experiences'. It was a very different proposition from the standard pack of 20 cigarettes.

Radically new capabilities were required to support its new proposition. Recruitment activity focused on hiring technologists and scientists. A younger crowd generally, few of the new hires had any experience of the tobacco industry, and it didn't seem to matter, to the chagrin of 'legacy' staff. PBT's offices were revamped as part of the relaunch. Formal offices with a civil service feel were replaced with bright and breezy open-plan offices, resembling a technology start-up. Bright colours, informality, flexible working, little obvious hierarchy – all of these developments were welcome.

However, it was a difficult transition for many of PBTs long-standing staff, who still referred to superiors as Mr or Mrs. Despite the travails of the industry, they were proud of PBT and its history. Many had stayed at the company for more than 25 years and were fiercely loyal. Their emotional connection was a double-edged sword. It could quickly become vocal resistance if mismanaged. Merely changing the product was the easy bit.

In candid moments, senior managers complained that trying to realign PBT was like trying to fix an aircraft in mid-air. The short-term performance demands of the market meant that PBT couldn't afford to land to make repairs or implement significant changes (and stop making a profit, in other words). It was still heavily reliant on its traditional products during its transition. At the same time, unless it made significant changes to how it went about its business, it would not have a long-term future. The vision for PBT was bold, but the change had to be incremental. As PBT's CEO said: '*Treading the fine line between short-term survival and longer-term innovation is what keeps me up at night.*'

Time will tell if the strategic realignment was successful. But by attempting to realign its business to overcome unavoidable disruption in its environment, PBT had at least given itself a fighting chance of having a future.

SECTION 2.2 STRATEGIC REALIGNMENT

The previous chapter concluded with a warning that poor performance and value-destroying dysfunction is inevitable if enterprises fail to adapt to their increasingly complex, dynamic and disrupted business environment. The urgent priority for many leadership teams must be to review each dynamic link of their enterprise's value chain and choose the most appropriate form of business strategy, or design of the organization, or both, to best fit the requirements of their changing marketplace. This is a process I refer to as *strategic realignment* (and hence the title of this new edition). Inevitably such a *process* results in a change to the enterprise's status quo, whether major or minor. Still, strategic realignment is essential to secure a *state* of high alignment, maintain it over time and, critically, overcome disruption in the business environment.

In the context of a changing external environment, the primary goal for enterprise leaders is to transform their enterprises to be capable of meeting new opportunities and threats. There is a strong pedigree of thinking in this area. The extraordinary work of Charles Darwin is perhaps best remembered for the principle of natural selection. This is the process whereby individual species' genomes interact with their environment to produce variation (or mutation) over time. Successful variations are passed down over successive generations, resulting in evolution.[xxxviii] Less successful variations are eventually weeded out.

Crucial to biological success is the degree to which individual species can evolve through selective variation to fit their changing environment – the fittest survive, in other words.[8] The same principle applies to markets and enterprise behaviour. As noted in the book's introduction, alignment is analogous to fitness, meaning that those species that best 'fit' – or align to – the requirements of their environment are the strongest.

[8]The honour of coining the term *'Survival of the fittest'* goes to Herbert Spencer in 1864 and not Charles Darwin, as many assume. Source: Spencer, H. (1864). *The Principles of Biology* (two vols). London: Williams and Norgate. *System of Synthetic Philosophy*, *Volume 2*.

And since the environment is constantly changing, realignment – or 'variation' to use Darwin's language – is essential to success if individual enterprises are to survive and thrive.

Environmental change can take different forms, and it impacts different individuals, teams, divisions, enterprises and industries in different ways and to different degrees. For instance, change can be constant or episodic; minor or major; short term or long term in impact. While change is a constant, there are periods of upheaval in our environment that are highly disruptive in their impact. The Covid-19 global pandemic is one such example but by no means the only one. Sources of change and disruption in every social sphere, including political, economic, social, technological and legal drivers of change, quickly render many established strategies and ways of working obsolete. Realignment is the remedy. To put it in the words of business professor, Leon C. Megginson[9]: '*It is not the strongest of the species that survives, nor the most intelligent, but the one most responsive to change.*'[xxxix]

However, the principles and laws of the 'physically constructed' world of biological entities can only take us so far because enterprises are 'socially constructed'. In their most basic form, companies, charities and government agencies (one might also add institutions) are subjective ideas that exist only because people collectively accept them. Enterprises do not occur naturally, nor do they obey natural laws completely. Only people bring companies, government departments, institutions and charities into life and sustain them over time through their actions. Mindful of this crucial distinction between the physically and socially constructed worlds we inhabit, we must compare natural selection with *artificial selection*. As the name would suggest, there is no intentionality behind natural selection. It is a naturally occurring process that is blind to the outcome. On the other hand, artificial selection is an intentional process – it involves people selecting (choosing) which qualities and traits are worthy of being preserved over time because they fit the changing environment best, and deselecting those that do not.

[9]Like the term *'Survival of the fittest'*, the quote *'It is not the strongest of the species that survives, nor the most intelligent, but the one most responsive to change'* is often attributed to Charles Darwin in error, or so the Internet tells me.

Artificial selection is a vital aspect of the human experience and key to our success as a species. It involves exercising careful judgement if choices are to be considered successful ones. Such considerations resonate closely with the concept of human *agency*. This is our unique ability as a species to act of our own accord to choose, in this context, the form and function of the enterprises we rely upon to live well as individuals, families, communities and society at large. Without wishing to sound overly dramatic in a humble business book, the acts of strategic alignment and strategic realignment are, in the broadest sense, essential expressions of what makes us human. We can choose to do better by our own hand. It is a privilege gifted to no other species. What a weight of responsibility!

We often use emotive language to describe our attempts at realignment, especially in recent times when the lines between politics, business and society have become increasingly blurred. The United Nations' Sustainable Development Goals are an example of a proposed realignment of how businesses and society operate to reduce inequality, improve environmental sustainability and safeguard human rights, among other outcomes. More recently, a key phrase to emerge during the Covid-19 global pandemic, aside from *'You're on mute'*, of course, was *'Build back better'*. Whether in politics or business, or the intersection of both, the idea is that the Covid-19 disruption presents leaders with an opportunity to do things differently in future. It is a line in the sand from which to realign to something better than before, but only if we choose to do so and, critically, actually make good choices.

In the context of business and management, strategic realignment is akin to the process of artificial selection. Enterprise leaders should intentionally seek to realign the current form of their enterprise by selecting a different form that is a better fit for the requirements of their future business environment. The quality of leaders' choices determines the outcome of the realignment process. Poor choices, such as betting on the wrong product or selecting the wrong organizational structure, will eventually render an enterprise unfit and therefore prone to deselection in competitive markets (or, to put it bluntly, going out of business).

The tobacco company illustrated in this chapter, PBT, sought a fundamental realignment of its entire value chain to overcome disruption in its business environment stemming from predominantly political and social forces (i.e. changing attitudes to smoking). This included: its purpose (i.e. its *raison d'être*); strategy (i.e. a bet on a new customer proposition) and new products (i.e. technical innovation in the form of the PowerPack and proprietary gel technology); and organizational change (i.e. a move to a more centralized organizational structure, new employee roles and skills).

For another example, we might explore the ambitious strategic realignment of the energy and petrochemical company Royal Dutch Shell plc. Shell announced ambitious plans in 2020 to reduce the carbon intensity of fossil fuels it refines and sells by 45 per cent by 2035. It also plans to reduce its net emissions to zero by 2050 (this includes customers using its products). From a historical peak of oil production in 2019, this planned reduction represents a major strategic realignment of Shell's previous hydrocarbon-based business model. As part of a new long-term strategy to ensure its products are *'Low or no-carbon'*, Shell is focusing intensively on the development of alternative fuel sources, such as renewables, biofuels and hydrogen.[xl] A key aspect of the strategy is to accelerate the development of hydrogen as a fuel alternative. Clean-burning hydrogen offers enormous environmental benefits if it can be produced and distributed safely and cheaply.

Shell's existing production (think refineries) and forecourt infrastructure mean the company can plan for ambitious growth in the emerging hydrogen market, including energy for home heating and not simply mobility and transportation. Other aspects of its strategic pivot include increasing the number of electric vehicle charging points available on its forecourts from 60,000 to 500,000 by 2025. Shell executives' financial remuneration will also be linked to company performance against reduction targets.[xli]

In an additional challenge to the status quo, and an example of legal disruption, in 2021, a Dutch court ordered Shell to accelerate its plans to cut greenhouse gas emissions, bringing the target of 45 per cent forward to 2030.[xlii] Nonetheless, like PBT in Section 1, short-term financial performance requires Shell to continue to produce fossil fuels, which form the majority of its revenues at the time of writing.[(ibid)] The future of Shell is a radical departure from its current state and in a relatively short time frame. Still, strategic realignment is a phased process of moving from one state of equilibrium, as a petrochemical company, to another, as a renewable energy company.

Or consider the example of the 'self-disruption' of electronic component manufacturer, Foxconn. Foxconn is perhaps best known as a key supplier to Apple Inc. For over a decade, Foxconn has played a leading role in manufacturing virtually every iteration of the wildly popular iPhone. There is an excellent chance you might be reading this book on a Foxconn-manufactured Apple device. Apple updates its range of devices yearly, which requires a very close relationship between product design and development (performed by Apple) and product manufacturing (performed by Foxconn and other parts suppliers) within an extremely tightly managed global supply chain.

The symbiotic relationship between Apple and Foxconn, as a key supplier, has propelled the manufacturer to become a market-leading player globally in electronic component manufacturing (and its key customer to become one of the most valuable companies in the world). However, in addition to extending its established core market, Foxconn is also leveraging its success in consumer electronics to capitalize upon growth opportunities in new and fast-developing markets – the highest profile of which is the electric car market. Three key technologies are set to dominate the automotive industry in future: (1) plug-in hybrid electric vehicles (EV); (2) 48-volt EVs; and (3) battery EVs.[xliii] Plug-in hybrid EVs are predicted to more than double in sales in the next few years, from approximately 14 million units in 2021 to more than 30 million units by 2025.[(ibid)]

To stake a claim in one of the world's fastest-growing markets, Foxconn founded in 2020 an industry alliance with other companies, called MIH, to act as *'A complete software and hardware platform for making electric cars'*.[(ibid)] This new proposition to market is radically different from Foxconn's established modus operandi. It makes a great deal of sense when one considers that success in electric car-making requires many of the organizational competencies for which Foxconn is already a market leader. These competencies include its agile manufacturing capability and ability to deliver to very short product life cycles (i.e. accommodating technical innovation and bringing it to market quickly) as well as technical excellence in electronics and battery technology (and not just automotive technology).[(ibid)]

Its scale and established market presence has enabled Foxconn to quickly assemble a dream team of partners in its alliance to bring disruption to the electric car market from a standing start.[xliv] MIH already boasts 1,200 member companies, ranging from software developers (including ARM discussed in Chapter 1) to carmakers and also customers like Apple, who have automotive ambitions of their own.[(ibid)]

It is thought that Foxconn will exploit its massive existing operational infrastructure – it employs more than 1 million workers in China alone – to move quickly to design, manufacture and sell its electronic car offerings at scale. The pivot towards electric cars is a major strategic realignment of Foxconn's business strategy. It is intended to exploit the transferability of its core competence (i.e. organizational capability) in electronic component manufacturing excellence to quickly establish a competitive edge in a growing but already intensely competitive EV global market.

Like the notion of alignment reviewed in Chapter 1, realignment is not a new concept. It relates closely to business transformation and change management, both staples of MBA programme curricula and business books. It is a vast topic. And yet, despite all the attention it is given as a major management concern, most change management initiatives fail to meet their objectives in practice. The management consultancy McKinsey reports that 70 per cent of change programmes fail because of a combination of a lack of management commitment and employee resistance to change.[xlv]

These findings resonate with my experience. For instance, when I ask leaders to rate how capable their enterprise is of implementing their chosen business strategy, they respond with a range between 40 per cent and 60 per cent. When I ask about the effectiveness of the actual strategy itself (and not its implementation), the results are more positive, with a rating of between 70 per cent and 90 per cent. The implication is that internal factors, such as poorly aligned (or even misaligned) organizational culture, structure, processes and people, are often the weakest link in the enterprise value chain.[i]

Not only does poor 'internal' alignment limit enterprise performance, but an enterprise's people, culture, structure and processes are also often the hardest organizational components to realign – they are roadblocks to positive change if mismanaged. Reformulating an enterprise's business strategy is relatively more straightforward than changing its organizational culture because strategizing is essentially a desktop exercise. Strategically realigning an enterprise's organizational capability, architecture and systems is where the rubber truly hits the road. It requires the most amount of attention from the enterprise's leaders at all levels.

Unlike change management initiatives, which are often intentionally limited in scope, strategic realignment emphasizes the fundamental transformation of all aspects of the enterprise value chain over the short, medium and longer term. Moreover, strategic realignment cannot be piecemeal. To be capable organizationally of implementing a new business strategy requires a realignment of an enterprise's organizational architecture (its people, structure, culture and processes) and management systems. To get a sense of this thinking in practice, consider for your enterprise:

- How well does your business strategy align with, say, emerging technologies?
- Are you capable of responding to emerging opportunities and threats?
- What should you change organizationally if you are to avoid your existing capabilities limiting your business strategy options?
- Do you possess the human capital (people) you require to innovate in future?
- Do your management systems bring out the best of your most talented staff or limit their potential and performance?
- What are the consequences of failing to realign to the new realities of your ever-changing business environment?

It is also important to consider: how often should an enterprise realign? The slightly unhelpful but honest answer is that *it depends* on the pace and scope of change to its business environment. There is no hard and fast rule, but there is a general pattern we can observe. The noted management author, Charles Handy, offers an appealing metaphor to help leaders think about the nature and frequency of change – or 'strategic realignment' to use our preferred term. Illustrated in Figure 2.1, Handy uses the mathematical concept of the sigmoid curve to describe a cycle in which a company, say, makes an initial investment of financial and human capital (at point A in the diagram) and the ratio of input to output (i.e. performance) dips as a result.[xlvi]

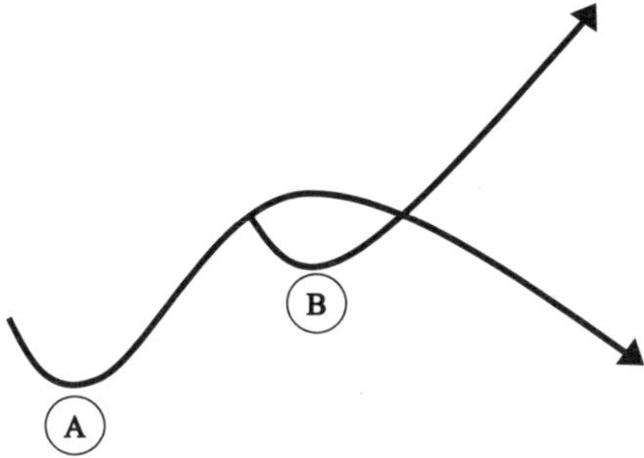

FIGURE 2.1 Ahead of or behind the curve? (Source: adapted from Handy, C. (2016). *The Second Curve: Thoughts on Reinventing Society*. Random House.)

Over time, the investment begins to pay off, and performance improves until eventually, because of changing external factors, such as market maturation, changing customer preferences or renewed competition, the company's strategy no longer creates the value it once did. In a dynamic environment, what worked in the past will not work in future and established business strategies (including products and services) and organizational capabilities have a natural shelf life and that *'oblivion'* is inevitable sooner or later.[ibid]

The solution is to embark upon a 'second curve' (point B in the diagram) by investing in new strategies, capabilities and resources, better suited to take advantage of external opportunities and defend against threats in future.[ibid] What is critical, as Handy notes, is the point at which the second curve is introduced. Ideally, it should be before the first curve peaks. Otherwise, the company runs the risk of going into decline and running out of resources. Revisiting the Shell example discussed earlier, point A in the diagram might be compared to its current state as a predominantly petrochemical energy company. By contrast, the second curve (point B) represents its stated low- and no-carbon realignment, and the dip in performance is a point of transition from one state of equilibrium to another.

When operating in a dynamic environment, any attempt to maintain an outmoded strategy will inevitably result in a decline in performance over time, or so the logic goes. The act of moving from the first curve to the second curve resonates closely with strategic realignment – the process of intentionally realigning an enterprise to overcome disruption and embark on a new pathway to sustained performance. And, of course, a realigned enterprise may be radically different from its previous incarnation. Enterprises failing to realign run the risk of falling behind the curve, from which they might not recover.

Considered in this way, strategic realignment to establish a new equilibrium is a critical factor in enterprise performance and competitiveness in dynamic and disrupted business environments. Good or poor leadership makes all the difference to the success of strategic realignment outcomes. So, how should leaders approach strategic realignment as a key responsibility? How should they approach it as both a challenge and an opportunity?

This chapter is intended to provide enterprise leaders with food for thought and a practical toolkit – a blueprint, as the title of the book suggests – for how to think about realigning their enterprise. Key considerations include:

- the multiple drivers of change to the business environment;
- a multi-level taxonomy of the impact of environmental change and disruption;
- a framework to identify different approaches to strategic realignment according to what is considered important and urgent to overcome disruption and improve performance;
- the introduction of an additional key framework – the *Strategic Alignment Framework* – to help leaders make sense of different strategic approaches that might be adopted in seeking to align and realign their business strategies, organizational capabilities and architectures;
- and, finally, the opportunity for enterprise leaders in creating a vision of the future-aligned enterprise, inspiring change and embedding the difference as the 'new normal'.

As noted in the introduction to this book, business environment change and disruption can represent an opportunity for far-sighted leaders to introduce fundamental organizational changes that might not be possible in so-called normal times. When reviewing the following sections, think boldly about how you might realign your enterprise for good. First things first, what might drive your realignment requirement?

Multiple drivers of strategic realignment

Chapter 1 touched upon how different industries have been affected by the Covid-19 global pandemic, with some suffering great hardship and others considerable opportunities for growth. It is important to note that the global pandemic is merely one disruptor, even if it is the most visible in recent times. More usefully, we can think of change and disruption to business and management practice as stemming from the political, economic, social, technological and legal environments, to use the well-established PESTL (political, economic, social, technological, legal and environmental) framework.[xlvii]

Political events such as Brexit or the US–China trade war of recent years can profoundly affect market confidence and trading conditions. *Economic* trends also dictate market conditions. These include the use of central controls such as interest rates by governments and shock events such as the 2008 global financial crisis, the fallout of which was still apparent over a decade later. *Social* factors ranging from demographic change, mass migration, social movements and public sentiment shape customer buying behaviour, employee expectations and the societal standards against which enterprises are judged. *Legal* factors in the form of new public policies, laws and regulations also define the rules in every public and private sphere where enterprises operate, nationally and internationally.

Consider the example of the agreement reached in 2021 by the G7 group of advanced economies to tax multinational companies. The deal is intended to prevent tax avoidance by requiring companies to pay more tax in the countries in which they do business. The agreement establishes a global minimum rate of corporation tax of 15 per cent to prevent individual countries from undercutting each other.[xlviii] Raising taxes on multinational company activity has been a long-standing challenge and highly controversial.

Still, the issue has become supercharged in recent years by the extraordinary growth of technology companies, many of which declare profits in countries with relatively low corporate tax rates even if revenue is derived from sales elsewhere in the world.[(ibid)] Taxation is a sovereign matter, which makes co-ordinated international efforts all the more difficult. However, the agreement sets a precedent for international co-ordination and a set of common policies and standards, which will influence how multinational companies do business in future.

Disruption to the business environment is not a monolithic phenomenon – it is context-specific most of the time. The different drivers of change identified above impact various industries and businesses in different ways. For example, the late and great Clay Christensen of Harvard Business School and colleagues distinguished between new technologies that *sustained* the status quo and those that *disrupted* it.[xlix] It helps to ask, therefore, what is the extent of the *impact* of these various drivers of change on the business environment and the enterprises operating within it?

Technological factors in the form of the introduction of new technologies have had an incredibly profound impact upon the business environment and all actors within it, whether they are governments, customers, investors, enterprises and their people. Notable disruptive technologies in the Industrial Age included the introduction of the double-action steam engine, the moving production line and materials technology. On a similar scale but much more recently, information technologies have driven an explosion in communications, connectivity and personal and mobile computing, creating new markets and profoundly disrupting existing ones.

Other new and potentially disruptive emerging technologies at the time of writing include: 5G technology; unsupervised machine learning; automation; augmented and virtual reality; spatial computing; additive manufacturing; quantum computing power; and the Internet of Things, to name but a few.[l] Undoubtedly, these new technologies offer solutions to many acknowledged problems but present their own challenges – anxiety over a loss of control and the ethics of integrating machine and human capability, for example. All of these new technologies will again create new markets and reshape existing ones.

Consider the case of 'cultured meat' as an example of highly disruptive technological innovation. Unlike 'faux-meat', which is based upon plant extract, cultured meat possesses the same chemical composition as animal-based meat. However, unlike animal-based meat, it is produced from cell cultures and is grown in a bioreactor (or vat).[li] There are a number of positives that make this technological innovation appealing for investors and consumers. First, cultured meat does not require the slaughter of animals. Second, unlike animal-based meat, which can take many months or years to grow, cultured meat takes only two to four weeks, and growth is limited to only the parts of an animal that are eaten. This cuts down significantly on what would otherwise be wasted (e.g. bones). Third, cultured meat production is estimated to reduce greenhouse gas emissions by more than 70 per cent when compared to its animal-based meat equivalent.[lii] This is significant when the global meat industry is considered to be responsible for 15 per cent of global greenhouse emissions, with demand for meat expected to double by 2050.[liii] Many start-ups are investing heavily in cultured meat, as are established companies, such as Cargill in the US and Mitsubishi in Japan.[liv] By some estimates, cultured meat will be price-comparable with animal meat by 2024.[10] If price parity is achieved, some predict that it will profoundly disrupt the global animal meat industry, which is worth over $2 trillion per year at the present time and employs more than 4.5 million people in the US alone.[lv]

Even the PESTL means of classification does not cover the whole gambit of what enterprise leaders should consider in their strategic realignment decision-making. Climate change is another source of disruption emanating from the physical *environment* (we can add another E to the original means of classification to form 'PESTLE'). This requires enterprises to plan for the short, medium and long term to mitigate their contribution to a potential crisis and respond to its consequences.

Returning to the example of the Covid-19 global pandemic, whether winners or losers in the face of universal disruption, all enterprises have been scrambling to manage under state-imposed restrictions, including enforced lockdown measures introduced to curb rates of infection. For example, working from home might once have been considered a perk or a rare treat. But it became an indefinite necessity for the vast majority of office workers during the pandemic. It was an abrupt learning curve for bosses and employees alike, with appreciable advantages and disadvantages.

[10]It used to be much more expensive. The first cultured beef burger produced in 2013 is said to have cost more than $250,000. In contrast, cultured chicken nuggets can be bought today (2021) in Singapore (the first country to approve the sale of cultured meat to the public) for $12 (source: Browne, A. (2021). 'Golden Nuggets: The Fake Meat Revolution Is on Its Way'. *The Spectator*, June 2021).

On the plus side, many workplaces (if such a term is still relevant; it probably is, but time will tell) experienced higher levels of engagement in the initial months of the pandemic as managers worked hard to communicate with their people as much as possible in the absence of in-person interaction. Many executives told me that long-standing barriers to close collaboration between geographies and time zones eroded significantly when 'Zooming' became the primary means of connecting and collaborating between previously separated teams. Nobody is 'separate' when everybody is, by default, separated.

Some also claimed that digital working platforms are great equalizers, reducing the distance between individuals, teams and levels in hierarchies. This is not just internally. Companies connected with their customers and partners more frequently and efficiently when using platforms such as Microsoft Teams. Alongside the enhanced connectivity, special attention was paid to mental health and employee well-being. All of these are positives that should be retained in future.

Hybrid working came to the fore during the pandemic, which translates into working policies organized along the lines of space and time – where we work and when we work.[lvi] In the future, many companies are likely to permit their employees much greater flexibility to divide their time between home, the coffee house or the office. Indeed, offices may themselves come to serve as social hubs, or 'club houses' as one of my clients put it, rather than a largely taken-for-granted physical manifestation of the organizational chart.

On the flip side, as the pandemic wore on, many employees expressed a longing for a return to the office in some form or other and the opportunity to interact with colleagues in person. Working remotely via collaboration platforms is arguably a poor substitute for quality in-person interaction. It is hard to build a distinctive corporate culture, for instance, in the absence of face-to-face working or the in-person role modelling of desirable behaviour.

The human relations movement tells us that human connection is a critical need to be met in securing work satisfaction, self-esteem and collective identity, all of which are necessary to fulfil individual potential and high performance.[lvii] Google, for instance, adopted a future *'Work from office policy'*, requiring its people to dedicate the majority of their time to working from one of its offices. It believes that its collaborative culture would be impossible to achieve otherwise.[lviii] What is clear is that different enterprises responded to the Covid-19 disruption in different ways.

These different sources of disruption – political, economic, social, technological, legal, ecological and health-related – are not standalone in their influence; they are all deeply interconnected. Change in the political environment has a knock-on effect on the economic and social environments and vice versa. New technologies test existing legislation and regulation, and vice versa. Our globally connected business environment has supercharged the reach and significance of a wide range of potential sources of disruption that executives need to consider in their strategic decision-making.

When advising or teaching executives, I have found that using a simple 'level of analysis' framework helps them to make sense of disruption to their business in terms of its source and the extent of its impact. Use the different levels listed below to analyze the impact of change and disruption in your environment:

- *Economy-wide*: Disruption that encompasses an entire economy, whether the global economy, the regional economy (e.g. Americas or Asia) or domestic (e.g. US or UK). Disruptions are often political and economic and are measurable in, for example, rates of unemployment or gross domestic product. Which economy-wide threats and opportunities are most likely to prove disruptive to your enterprise, and what are the implications for the markets in which you operate and compete?
- *Industry-wide*: Disruption that is of concern for all actors operating within a particular industry, such as new regulations or new technologies that may be global, regional or domestic in scope. The introduction of new rules in the banking industry following the 2008 global financial crisis is one example. What changes are underway in your industry, and how they might disrupt how you go about your business in future? Is disruption to your sector an opportunity to steal a march on competitors or a threat to be mitigated as much as possible? Are you leading industry disruption? If not, should you be?

And concerning the enterprise and all groups and individuals within it:

- *Enterprise-wide*: Disruption that affects an entire enterprise, its functions and operations, whether structured as lines of business or geographies or both. Disruption may stem from a variety of sources, such as targeted sanctions in the form of regulatory fines, or challenges from new or non-traditional competitors, which render the enterprise's status quo unsustainable.
- *Divisional or business unit*: Disruption of one or more parts of an enterprise, such as individual lines of business, departments, business units or country operations. Different sub-organizations within an enterprise are prone to external disruption in different ways and to different degrees. This is especially true in diversified and multi-divisional structures.
- *Group and team*: Disruption to how individual teams (or groups) work resulting from, say, a change in enterprise-level strategy or policy. Which factors in either the external or (more likely) internal environment requires your team to change its way of working? Does your team need to change its composition and membership to ensure it possesses the knowledge and skills needed to fulfil objectives? How are those objectives changing over time, given changes in the environment and enterprise direction?
- *Individual*: Disruption occurring and understood at the level of the individual. For example, what are the implications of disruption to job security stemming from the automation of work? While we measure the impact of rates of 'technological unemployment' at the level of the economy, it can, of course, be highly disruptive at the level of the individual. There are always winners and losers in change, as the old saying goes. How can we, as enterprises, maximize opportunities for positive change for our people? How can we lessen the negative impact of necessary realignment as much as possible for the individuals affected by it? How can individuals help themselves to mitigate the risks of, say, technological disruption?

All of these multiple levels of analysis are also deeply connected and interdependent. Indeed, each one is contingent upon the others, from both top down and bottom up. Understanding disruption requires a nuanced approach, therefore, as must any response to overcome it. Sophisticated leadership in today's business environment means being able to analyze the full range of influencing factors at all levels, the implications of those factors and the strategic choices to either mitigate them as risks or capitalize upon them as opportunities.

It might also be said that each of the levels described above represents a leadership horizon. Which level is the focus of your attention (and perhaps leadership ambition)? At which level can you exert positive influence as a leader? The individual level? Certainly. Your team? Most likely. But how about your division? Or perhaps your entire enterprise or even your industry? The further your horizon, the more factors you will need to consider in your thinking and decision-making. So how to make sense of it all?

Making sense of the business environment

You would be easily forgiven if this all seems a bit overwhelming. As noted in the previous chapter, the business environment has become more complex than it once was. Today, enterprise leaders are required to process unprecedented volumes of information to make sense of their environment and navigate it as best as possible. In the flood of information, it is often difficult to separate a clear signal from the background noise and form robust assumptions, forecasts and make evidence-based decisions.[lix] And yet, strategically realigning an enterprise requires leaders to take a long-term view and make choices based upon the best available information. Every choice is a gamble, of course. Still, an evidence-based approach to decision-making – or a more informed approach simply – can help to mitigate the degree of uncertainty under which decisions are made.

To make sense of all these factors and their impact at multiple levels, consider the following simple tabulation exercise. You can perform this alone or with your team. It can be fascinating when you involve various important stakeholders, such as partners and customers. It can be a quick and 'dirty' exercise or something more systematic and detailed. Either way, it should consider your business environment in the short term (defined as the immediate future), medium term (say the next three years) and, critically, the long term (say the next five to 10 years):

1. ***Factors***: First, compile a list of political drivers of change shaping your future business environment. Do the same for economic, social, technological, legal and other factors you consider important. You can use the PESTL framework of categorization or any other, or you may choose to adapt it by adding additional categories, such as the physical environment. Your focus should be on significant factors as best as you understand them. Critical, however, is to ask: are you aware of all of the factors affecting your enterprise that you should be? How can you broaden your horizons and develop a comprehensive and accurate portrait of your business environment and the trends, changes and disruptions occurring within it? What authoritative information do you require, and how can you reliably obtain it?
2. ***Levels***: Second, having compiled a list of significant environmental factors, consider their impact at the multiple levels of analysis. For example, what is the impact of artificial intelligence (AI) on the global economy? Closer to home, what is the potential impact of AI on your industry or enterprise specifically, either as an opportunity for enhanced capability or as a competitive threat? What might AI mean for individual lines of business or divisions within your enterprise? Will some lines of business be more affected than others? In what way? And what about your team? What about you personally? How do these developments shaping your business environment make you think differently about your role and leadership priorities?

   You can consider each level of analysis separately, or you can take a more linear top-down approach. For example, you could consider the nature of the impact of new regulation on your industry first, and subsequently on your enterprise, its lines of business/divisions, teams and individuals. Either way, the point is to consider changes in the business environment and their potential impact at multiple levels, which sets the context for prioritization.

3. ***Priorities***: Third, of all of the factors and their potential impact, which represent the greatest opportunities – either for growth or the opportunity to differentiate from competitors, for example? Equally, which pose the greatest potential threats? Which are likely to introduce new competitors into your marketplace? Which might erode your market position or render your existing strategy unviable? Which might pose additional costs of 'doing business'? We can seek to understand the impact of all environmental factors at these multiple levels to frame how we choose to respond, maximize opportunities or mitigate risks.

Your considerations can be plotted on a table like the one illustrated in Figure 2.2. To use a metaphor, the table represents a radar receiver, presenting the results (or 'returns', to risk beating the metaphor to death) from the scan of your business environment. How often are you scanning your environment? Once a year? More frequently? Again, there is no hard or fast rule, but the faster the change in the environment, the more frequently leaders should seek to scan for new developments. Equally, how powerful is your radar? How far can you see, and what is the accuracy of the radar return?

Having performed a scan of your environment and considering all of the potential drivers of change and their potential impacts, which are

2	1 Political Factors	Economic Factors	Social Factors	Technological Factors	Legal Factors	3 Impact Priorities
Industry-level Impact	e.g. what is the impact of political factors on your industry/industries?	?	?	?	?	?
Enterprise-level Impact	?	e.g. what is the impact of economic factors on your whole enterprise?	?	?	?	e.g. of all these factors, which have the greatest potential impact on the enterprise either as a threat or an opportunity?
Division-level Impact	?	?	e.g. what is the impact of social factors on your division / line of business?	?	?	?
Team-level Impact	?	?	?	e.g. what is the impact of technological factors on your team?	?	?
Individual-level Impact	?	?	?	?	e.g. what is the impact of legal factors on you and other individuals?	?

FIGURE 2.2 Making sense of business environment change and impact

sending back the strongest signals? Which demand a response in the form of strategic realignment? Furthermore, what form should your response take? In other words, how should you approach strategic realignment to maintain or improve alignment within your enterprise and its changing environment? The following section provides a helpful framework for how to think about the strategic realignment requirement.

The strategic realignment requirement

There is more than one way to go about the process of strategic realignment. As in all things contingency related, adopting a strategic approach requires leaders to choose between different options and select the most appropriate form of realignment according to requirements. Illustrated in Figure 2.3, a simple two-by-two framework can help us make sense of our options.

The first criterion of the framework is *importance,* and it is plotted on the y-axis. Importance forms a scale to estimate the difference between minor and major environmental disruption to the established status quo. Minor disruption is where any impact is modest in scale and scope. Major disruption is the opposite, rendering existing strategies, organizational capabilities or management practices, for example, unviable for the future. Consider the following:

1. *Importance*: How important is the impact of likely disruption to your business? In the context of your operating environment, as best as you understand it, consider the potential for each source of disruption to have a minor or major impact on how you go about your business. What does it add up to overall?

The second criterion of the framework is *urgency,* and it is plotted on the x-axis. Urgency forms a scale by which to estimate the difference between the short-term and longer-term impact of potential disruption. Short term is defined as disruption to the established status quo occurring immediately and up to one year in the future. Longer term refers to five to 10 years in future.

Consider the following:

2. *Urgency:* How urgent is the impact of likely disruption to your business? Again, having considered all of the potential sources of disruption you are facing, which require an immediate response and which are longer term in their impact? Short-term disruption poses an immediate challenge whereas longer-term threats (and opportunities, of course) permit planning and a more considered response.

According to these criteria, we are presented with four broad categories of disruption:

1. *Less important but urgent*: minor impact of disruption occurring in the short term.
2. *Less important and non-urgent*: minor and longer-term impact of disruption.
3. *More (most?) important and urgent*: major short-term impact of disruption.
4. *More important but non-urgent*: major long-term impact of disruption.

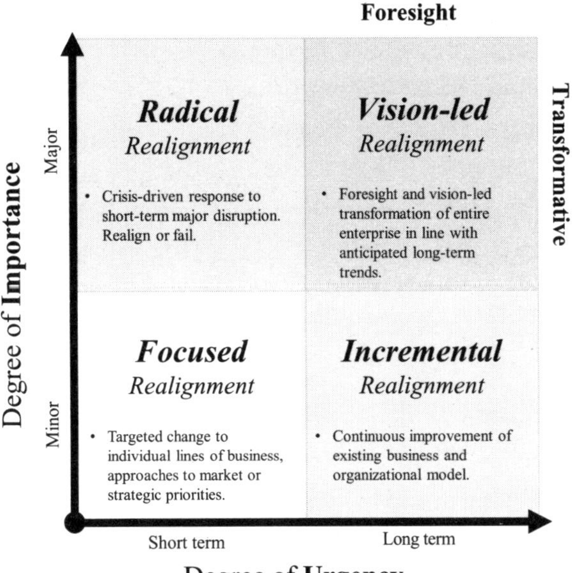

FIGURE 2.3 The strategic realignment requirement

Each of the four broad categories listed above corresponds to a different approach to strategic realignment:

1. *Focused realignment*: Disruption that is relatively minor in its impact, but urgent nonetheless, requires a *focused* approach to strategic realignment efforts. Focused realignment involves the targeted change of individual elements of an enterprise – such as lines of business or approaches to market or strategic priorities – and not enterprise-wide change. The focus of targeted change is to improve performance in the short term, perhaps correcting some form of misalignment or responding to a specific change in the business environment.[iii]

   Consider the example of mega-bank, HSBC.[11] Before the economic disruption posed by Covid-19, HSBC announced a headcount reduction of 35,000 employees (out of approximately 240,000 worldwide) as part of a deep overhaul in response to *'plunging profits'*.[lx] Like other major banks, it has undergone rapid expansion in the last two decades, especially in terms of its size (both headcount and assets), diversification of its lines of business and geographic reach. Its portfolio of financial products and services is considerably more complex than it once was – indeed, it is today one of the biggest and most complex banks in the world.

   Different elements of its portfolio are highly successful (its Asian business, which accounts for 90 per cent of its profitability); others much less so (investment banking in the Americas, for example).[(ibid)] Poor performance in one area can affect the strategic advantage of the entire group. Competing in these different markets requires HSBC, like any enterprise, to be organizationally capable of competing successfully at multiple different things. Such ambidexterity is hard to achieve in practice, especially at scale. HSBC is strong in Asia but has not had the opportunity to establish itself and

[11]This example expands on a short article: Trevor, J. (2020). 'How to align your organization in times of change'. *Oxford Answers*. Oxford Saïd Business School, University of Oxford.

develop the competencies for superior investment banking in the US, which is intensely competitive with multiple long-established market incumbents. Regardless of Covid-19, HSBC is committed to a reorganization that reflects a shift in strategic priority to double down on what it does best – banking in Asian markets. Covid-19 disruption has merely served to accelerate these changes.[iii]

2. *Incremental realignment*: Disruption that is relatively minor but longer term in its impact on an enterprise requires an *incremental* approach to strategic realignment. Incremental realignment is defined as continuous improvement of the existing business and organizational model in the short term and incremental adaptation over the long term to establish a new equilibrium.

   Consider the example of the microchip manufacturer, Intel. Simultaneously a rival (in chip design) and partner (in chip manufacturing) to ARM mentioned in the previous chapter, Intel has dominated the microchip business for decades. Its annual revenues in 2020 were more than $78 billion, and it had a 30 per cent operating margin.[lxi] Nevertheless, Intel faces stiff competition in the future from new sources, such as Nvidia, the company that offered to acquire ARM in 2020, and non-traditional competitors. Companies that were once customers, such as Apple, now have their own microchip aspirations and are fast becoming competitors, especially in the high-growth and lucrative mobile technology market.[lxii]

   The view from analysts is that Intel missed the smartphone and tablet revolution. It was too focused on its core personal computing market, which is in decline today by an average of 2.5 per cent globally. It has also been slower than competitors to push forwards new designs and is no longer considered cutting edge within the industry.[(ibid)] Combined with manufacturing difficulties, for which it has had to compensate key customers like Apple, it is blamed for a drop in market capitalization of more than 50 per cent in 20 years.[lxiii] In a long-term strategic realignment of core elements of its business, Intel may outsource its manufacturing activities to enable it to focus solely on microchip design. It may also shift its focus away from graphics processors (and direct competition with the likes of Nvidia) to target the growing market for powering artificial intelligence. A focus on chip design, specializing in AI and outsourcing manufacturing represent key elements of its long-term strategic realignment over a five-to-10-year horizon.(ibid)

3. *Radical realignment*: Disruption that is major and short term in its impact requires a *radical* approach to strategic realignment if the enterprise is to survive. Consider the example of British Airways (BA). As noted in the previous chapter, BA has, like many airlines, introduced drastic cuts to both its routes and its level of staffing during the Covid-19 global pandemic. Fully 12,000 of its 42,000-strong pre-pandemic workforce were made redundant from all sections and ranks, including ground crew, cabin crew and aircrew (pilots), in addition to administrative and managerial staff.[lxiv] It also cut back on routes, suspended flights, grounded aircraft and ruthlessly reduced operating costs to ensure its survival during the *'Worst crisis to ever hit the travel industry'*.[lxv] Moreover, like major employers in many key industries during the pandemic, BA had to take advantage of state financial support in the form of the staff furlough scheme. As an alternative to redundancy, it provided companies like BA with the financial flexibility to weather the consequences of the Covid-19 global pandemic hitting the bottom line. Redundancy, scaling back, reorganization and other such measures are a radical realignment of the company in the face of the immediate-term challenge of a collapse in passenger travel – a focus on survival.

At the same time, BA also adopted a strategic approach to overcoming pandemic-related disruption. Even in the depths of the passenger slump, it embarked upon a long-term strategic realignment of its product portfolio, modernization of its fleet, decommissioning of older flying stock (the venerable and much-loved Boeing 747, alas), optimization of its landing slots and change to its legacy employment policies, including working custom and practice that predated its privatization in 1987.[(ibid)] Arguably, the disruption of 2020 and 2021 provided the company with the opportunity to introduce far-reaching organizational changes that would have been difficult or politically unpalatable to implement in the pre-pandemic operating environment.

BA's international competitors were also spurred to action, and introduced a range of innovations. For example, United Airlines, the US carrier, announced at the height of the travel slump its plan to buy an initial order of 200 electric flying taxis to provide a convenient and environmentally friendly airport shuttle service by 2025.[lxvi] The new service required an investment of $1.1 billion in flying taxi firm, Archer, in combination with a regional US-based carrier, Mesa, to provide enhanced international and national route connectivity.[(ibid)] Investing for the long term during a crisis demonstrates a forward-looking leadership focus and willingness to radically realign the enterprise to overcome short-term disruption.

4. *Vision-led realignment*: Disruption that is major in scope but longer term in its impact requires a *vision-led* approach to strategic realignment. It is classified as major because it likely requires an enterprise-wide transformation along every linkage of the enterprise value chain. It is a long-term commitment to transition to a new state over several years – to establish a new and different equilibrium.

Consider the example of the car manufacturer, Jaguar Land Rover (JLR). JLR, like the story described in Section 1 of this chapter, has a storied past. Revolutionary early models of automobiles such as the XK or, most famous of all, the E-Type, have helped to propel Jaguar to become one of the most famous automotive brands in the world. Jaguar has undergone multiple realignments in its history, switching from private to public ownership and back again. It was bought by Ford Motor Company in 2002 and, most recently, by Tata in 2008. From having been a niche brand, JLR embarked in the 1990s and early 2000s on a strategy to extend its range of saloons and SUVs in the premium car market. In doing so, it went head to head with the likes of BMW, Mercedes and Audi, and exploited opportunities for growth in the massively expanding Chinese market. It has been a highly successful strategy.

Today, however, the sale of diesel vehicles – which dominate JLR sales across its on-road and off-road range – are in terminal decline, with governments committed to banning the sale of petrol and diesel cars by 2030 (in the case of the UK, with other governments poised to follow suit). Under intense consumer and legislative pressure, in 2020, JLR's CEO, Thierry Bolloré, announced a major pivot to offer only an all-electric range of vehicles by 2025.[lxvii] Additionally, JLR is also pivoting away from the premium car market to return to its roots as a luxury carmaker. The implication is that JLR will in future produce fewer cars, which are all-electric and targeted at the luxury end of the car market. It is a major shift in strategic focus, which will see it compete with brands such as Bentley and Rolls-Royce and target a lower volume of production, but increased profit per unit.[(ibid)]

Its realignment requires massive investment in new green technologies, such as high-mileage batteries and ultra-lightweight chassis. But it also requires significant organizational changes over time, including the consolidation of production locations, the closure of some sites and a significant reduction in the management population. The outcome of JLR's strategic realignment will be that it is more focused, leaner and smaller in future.

The framework described above rests on several immutable principles. First and foremost, strategic realignment is a requirement in every quadrant and doing nothing is not an option. However, realignment takes different forms according to the nature of the disruption facing the enterprise. A leadership team's approach to realigning their business is itself contingent upon the challenges it faces – there is no one-size-fits-all approach.

Second, different elements of an enterprise (such as different lines of business or different geographies) may each require an individual approach to realignment. Again, it depends upon the external forces facing the enterprise and the unequal impact on some elements of a business and not others. The choice of which approach to realignment to adopt dictates the comprehensiveness and speed of change within an enterprise.

Third, this framework views disruption mainly in external terms, and strategic realignment is the response. In other words, disruption is the 'independent variable', and realignment is the 'dependent variable', to use academic jargon. However, the internal environment of the enterprise can also be a major source of disruption. Employee resistance to change can prevent an enterprise from responding effectively to external pressures, for example.

To start an honest conversation about the realignment requirement where you work, think of your enterprise in its entirety or, as you may have done in the previous section, think of a sub-unit (e.g. a line of business) that is of particular importance, such as a growth area or a key source of income, and consider the following questions:

1. What are the key sources of disruption to your enterprise?
   a. What about your customers/clients? How does a better understanding of their context make you think differently about your own?
2. What is being disrupted? Is it your strategy? Or your organizational structure? Or people capability? What is no longer sustainable because of, say, competitive pressure? Equally, which risks might you need to mitigate? One link of the enterprise value chain may require special attention and reconfiguration. But remember, in an aligned enterprise, a change to one of the linkages of the enterprise value chain likely requires a change to all in some form or other.
3. What is the realignment requirement given the challenges and opportunities your enterprise faces in its environment?
   a. How important is the need to realign? Is it a minor or major concern? What is the consequence of failing to realign?

   b. How urgent is the requirement to realign your enterprise? How much time do you have before your existing strategies, organizational capabilities and systems become unfit for purpose?
   c. Does your team share the same view as you? Is there enough of a sense of urgency? Is there an adequate appreciation of the scale of realignment you might be facing?
4. Depending upon your answers to question 3, how should you approach the strategic realignment of your enterprise?
   a. Is it focused realignment?
   b. Or incremental?
   c. Or radical?
   d. Or perhaps vision-led?
5. Do the changes you identified and the importance and urgency attached to them apply to the whole enterprise (i.e. enterprise-wide change) or individual parts (e.g. individual lines of business)?
6. Finally, and critically, what form will strategic realignment take? What represents a better strategy to market, say, or organizational structure? Perhaps it is obvious what you might need to change, but is it equally obvious what you need to change to?

This last question is perhaps the biggest challenge of all: *what is the ideal outcome of strategic realignment for your enterprise?* The next section offers a core framework to help you navigate your strategic alignment and strategic realignment choices.

SECTION 2.3 STRATEGIC REALIGNMENT, THE LEADERSHIP CHALLENGE

If the previous section focused on *what to realign*, this section covers the equally thorny question: which form should strategic realignment take? In other words, *realign to what?* The challenge for enterprise leaders is that there is no one-size-fits-all prescription for a winning business strategy, or any other dynamic link of the enterprise value chain, that guarantees superior business performance in all circumstances.[lxviii] Nor is there one best response to disruption. A nuanced and context-specific set of solutions is required in all cases. From a wide range of potential options, enterprise leaders must choose which varieties of business strategy, organizational capability, organizational architecture and management systems will ideally support the fulfilment of their enterprise's enduring purpose.[ii] Choosing poorly or attempting to emulate the choices of others typically results in sub-par performance and a lack of competitiveness over time.[lxix]

Unhelpfully, mainstream business and management research offers enterprise leaders a stark choice between two contrary models of work organization: the Industrial Age 'bureaucracy' and the not very imaginatively entitled Information Age 'post-bureaucracy'. Many believe post-bureaucracy will eventually succeed the bureaucratic approach as the dominant logic of organizing work, just as bureaucracy superseded pre-Industrial work organization. However, it is wrong to see these two approaches as mere points in an evolutionary transition over time. When considered here, bureaucracy and post-bureaucracy sit at opposite ends of a continuum, which establishes an important principle from a strategic realignment perspective. Both approaches possess advantages and disadvantages, as does every point on the continuum between them.

Bureaucracy and post-bureaucracy and all things in between

Industrial Age approaches to strategy and organization emphasized growing fast and large efficiently. Businesses succeeded by maximizing economies of scale – selling as much product as possible at the least possible cost to the firm. Competitiveness was a function of firms' ability to match stable (and therefore predictable) demand and predictability of supply in terms of volume, quality and cost, as efficiently as possible. The best available vehicles for doing so were large, formally governed *bureaucracies*, built around hierarchies of authority, divisions of labour and elaborate controls enforced through impersonal rules.

While ideal for the efficient mass production of simple, stand-alone, standardized products and services, this approach has natural limitations. As the famous saying attributed to Henry Ford in 1909 goes: *'Any customer can have a car painted any color that he wants so long as it is black.'* But many tried-and-tested industrial strategies fail to meet the new realities of competing for custom in the 21st century global marketplace.[xiii]

Customers today are demanding more than low prices. They value greater choice (the offering of variety), smart bundling (the offering of valuable synergies between different offerings) and personalization (the offering of distinctiveness, meeting needs without compromise) of the goods and services they buy.[lxx] Consider the now ubiquitous smartphone as a metaphor. Its high value to users, reflected in its premium price tag, is because it bundles multiple highly complementary technologies, such as web browsing, photography, media and voice.

Even so, it remains a standardized (albeit high-functioning) multipurpose tool upon purchase. But application ecosystems, such as the Android platform or Apple's 'app store', enable the end user to continually personalize the functionality of their device to match their changing preferences post-sale. The smartphone is a valued departure from the 'dumb' phone because it harnesses *connectivity* between complementary technologies and enables *agility* around personal preference to offer end users uniquely different functionality in each case.

Critics have been calling time on the bureaucracy for decades – see the article 'The Coming Death of Bureaucracy', authored in 1966 by Warren Bennis, for an early example or the more recent 'The End of Bureaucracy', published in the *Harvard Business Review* in 2018.[lxxi] Unlike the bureaucracy, *post-bureaucratic organizations* (PBOs) – and the variety of other names they also go by[12] – emphasize a network and

[12]The post-bureaucratic organization shares many of the same principles as: *organic organization* (Aiken, M. & Hage, J. (1971). 'The organic organization and innovation'. *Sociology*, *5*(1), pp. 63–82.); *network organization* (Baker, W., Nohria, N. & Eccles, R. (1992). 'The network organization in theory and practice'. *Classics of Organization Theory*, *8*, p. 401.); *I-form organization* (Miles, R.E., Miles, G., Snow, C.C., Blomqvist, K. & Rocha, H. (2009). 'The I-form organization'. *California Management Review*, *51*(4), pp. 61–76.); and the *Enterprise Ecosystem* (Trevor, J. & Williamson, P. (2019). 'How to Design an Ambidextrous Organization'. *The European Business Review*, March – April, pp. 34–43) – all of which are the antithesis of the efficient machine-like bureaucracy described by Weber in the early 20th century (see Pugh, D.S. ed. (2007). *Organization Theory: Selected Classic Readings*. Penguin UK).

not a hierarchy-based organizational structure.[lxxii] This means they are characterized by:

- horizontal and not vertical integration across their network structure;
- personal and not impersonal treatment of staff and customers;
- distributed and not centralized knowledge;
- information sharing and transparency and not compartmentalization;
- staff empowerment and delegation and not control;
- engagement through shared values and not enforced rules;
- flexibility prized over efficiency;
- a focus on inputs and not outputs simply;
- externalization of resources and expertise.

The final point is one of the biggest differences between the bureaucratic and post-bureaucratic logics of organizing work.[xiii] By leveraging external networks (or ecosystems), so the thinking goes, enterprises can develop an abundance of strategically valuable capability that would otherwise be too costly to replicate if relying upon internal resources alone. Externalization or 'openness' can be thought of in two dimensions: upstream and downstream innovation.[lxxiii]

Upstream open innovation involves sourcing outside knowledge and insights early on in product and service development. Knowledge powers innovation capability, whether it is customer insights or partnering business expertise. Examples include Procter & Gamble's 'open innovation' initiatives'[lxxiv] or Coca-Cola's 'fan first' interactions.[lxxv] ARM mentioned in Chapter 1 is another excellent example of a partner ecosystem that powers the novel design of its ever-more powerful processors.

On the other hand, *downstream* open innovation is the reliance upon a network of external partners and suppliers to deliver services directly to the customer on behalf of a commissioning enterprise. Apple's iTunes is one example of developing a partner ecosystem for flexible delivery capability, but virtually every industry is exploring taking a similar approach.[xiii]

While it all sounds great in theory, there are notable disadvantages to the post-bureaucratic approach to organizing work. Informal structures and processes enable creativity and flexibility but often at the cost of efficiency. Post-bureaucratic organizations are also difficult to control and can easily become chaotic in the absence of rules. The flexibility that is prized by many knowledge-economy companies is often a barrier to growth because the absence of formal structures, processes and routines can limit the ability of an enterprise to scale up its operations safely.

For example, throughout its explosive growth from start-up, Facebook had a famous maxim of *'Move fast and break things'*, reflecting its disruptor mindset, relatively small size and nimble posture. The original spirit was one of 'creative destruction' using digital technology to reshape how people everywhere socialize in line with *'Our mission to make the world more open and connected'*.[lxxvi] But as Facebook grew, its hundreds of employees became tens of thousands, and its one line of business became a diversified platform portfolio.[xiii] Size and diversification increase enterprise complexity and an absence of control can easily become an impediment to operating at scale.[i] Facebook has a new maxim: *'Move fast with stable infrastructure'*. It speaks to the challenge of managing many thousands of employees in different lines of business all over the world and striking a balance between flexibility and efficiency.[(ibid)] Facebook is just one example of a PBO that has adopted elements of bureaucratic work design – adopting formal processes, prescribed work routines, standard policies and centrally enforced spans of control – to maintain organizational coherence throughout its rapid growth.[lxxvii]

So, despite calls for its *'death'* or its end, bureaucracy has proved remarkably durable. So much so that the Boston Consulting Group, a management consultancy, asked in 2020 if it is *'The End of the Bureaucracy, Again?'*[lxxviii] But the bureaucratic approach also has downsides, of course. Routine and standardized ways of work run counter to the highly discretionary and idiosyncratic working patterns required to deliver highly customized offerings or the development of cutting-edge innovations. Innovation requires inefficient experimentation to overcome the inevitable uncertainties encountered when creating something new. Efficiency requires enterprises to embrace precisely the opposite attributes when organizing work – efficient routines to maximize output and minimize costs when producing something known.

As organizational design options, both bureaucracy and post-bureaucracy offer managers advantages and disadvantages strategically and organizationally. One of the most challenging paradoxes of administration is balancing the apparent trade-off between bureaucratic efficiency and post-bureaucratic flexibility.[xx] Few firms then, if any, can be equally efficient *and* flexible. They are competing values. Developing superiority in one area requires sacrificing superiority in the other. This poses a major leadership dilemma – which approach is best? Bureaucracy or post-bureaucracy?

The only correct answer for a contingency theorist is, of course: *it depends!*

And that is the challenge for every dynamic link of the enterprise value chain. There are multiple options to choose from in each case, each with advantages and disadvantages. The challenge for enterprise leaders is: strategically, which do you prioritize between, say, efficiency and flexibility if you cannot be superior at both? Similarly, which business strategy is best? Cost competitiveness or innovation based? How do you decide which is the best way to organize your enterprise to gain a competitive edge? Should it take the form of a hierarchy or a network? Specifically, how can enterprise leaders know which variety of each dynamic link of the enterprise value chain might be the best fit for fulfilling their enterprise's purpose? What information do they require when attempting to decide? And by which decision-making process might they make the best choices possible?

SECTION 2.4 THE STRATEGIC ALIGNMENT FRAMEWORK

To help enterprise leaders address the challenge outlined in the previous section, a conceptual framework – the *Strategic Alignment Framework* (SAF) – is introduced here. Illustrated in Figure 2.4, the SAF is the golden thread running throughout all dynamic links of the enterprise value chain. It is how leaders can make sense of how to strategically align – or realign – their enterprise's *business strategy*, *organizational*

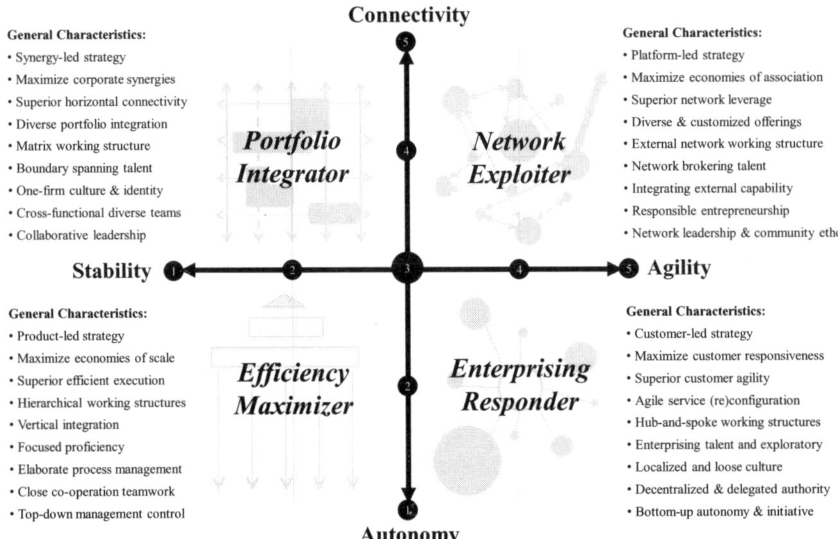

FIGURE 2.4 The Strategic Alignment Framework

capability, *organizational architecture* and *management systems* to fulfil their enterprise's long-term *purpose*.

Conceptually, the SAF builds upon many existing influential strategy and organization frameworks.[13] Its novel contribution is to integrate enterprise purpose, business strategy and organizational design considerations into one coherent conceptual framework. It does this by recognizing organizational capability as a critical integrative variable between the different links of the enterprise value chain. Second, it incorporates recent advances in network theory (e.g. ecosystem thinking), post-bureaucracy and complex adaptive systems research. It uses these to recognize the increasing importance of organizational *connectivity* and organizational *agility* as strategically valuable organizational capabilities in the current and future operating environment.[lxxix]

[13]See for example the Prospector, Defender and Analyser strategy typology developed by Miles, Snow et al (Miles, R.E., Snow, C.C., Meyer, A.D. & Coleman Jr, H.J. (1978). 'Organizational strategy, structure, and process'. *Academy of Management Review*, *3*(3), pp. 546–562.), or the *Competing Values Framework* by Cameron and Quinn (Cameron, K.S. & Quinn, R.E. (2011). *Diagnosing and Changing Organizational Culture: Based on the Competing Values Framework*. John Wiley & Sons).

What the SAF does

The SAF offers a range of useful, practical applications to help leaders in their decision-making. It enables leaders to:

1. *Map their current and future enterprise*: The SAF provides a canvas upon which an enterprise's current and future approach to strategy and organization can be charted. It can also be used to make sense of the nature of customer demand or competitors' capabilities. The first benefit for decision-makers is to understand the enterprise landscape in more objective terms than would otherwise be possible. The second is to assess the potential fit of different strategy and organization options.

   For example, the SAF has been utilized by boards to map their various business lines and identify potential synergies or conflicts between them. This format provides the means to envision a range of scenarios for how each business line might compete differently in the future, based upon robust assumptions about changing market conditions. In a similar vein, it has also been employed to map the products and services of competitors and evaluate their strengths and weaknesses to inform discussions about competitive differentiation.

   Likewise, it has been used to diagnose suppliers' and partners' organizational strengths and weaknesses to understand how closely they align (or not) to that of a commissioning entity. Perhaps most importantly, it has helped bring together leaders in various enterprises to engage in forward-looking and open-ended discussions about the function and form of their enterprise, given changing customer expectations and the threats posed by current and future competitors.
2. *Measure the strength of their enterprise's alignment*: The SAF can help decision-makers measure the degree of misalignment – or gap – between the current state of their enterprise and its ideal strategy and organization future state. Like a microscope, the SAF can be used to measure alignment at the level of the enterprise or for individual business lines, geographies and

functions – and even gaps in understanding or differences of opinion, between individual teams and team members.

For instance, do all team members, such as an executive board, view their enterprise in the same way? If joint decision-making and messaging are essential, they must do so, and the SAF is a powerful method of auditing team alignment. Such multi-level considerations identify opportunities for improved alignment ranging across the entire enterprise value chain (or 'from soup to nuts', as one executive described it in the vignette in Section 1 of this chapter).

The SAF has helped executive boards measure the strength of alignment of multiple different parts of their enterprise and identify areas for performance improvement through targeted change management initiatives. It has also been utilized to consider likely integration issues in mergers and acquisitions by assessing differences between acquiring and vendor enterprises in their approaches to strategizing and organizing.

3. *Prioritize interventions*: The SAF can help to inform, prioritize and articulate change management efforts. It can help identify specific change management opportunities to improve everyday performance and to make sense of broader transformational change to bridge the gap between an enterprise's current state and its ideal future state over the long term. This can be on a business line by business line basis or for the whole enterprise. The SAF can also support the development of a narrative for strategic realignment and help overcome resistance, whether from employees, partners, investors or customers.

The 'before and after' images of changing strategy and organization priorities have supported numerous strategic realignment initiatives. Specifically, the outputs of the SAF application as a decision-making tool have been used to convey the direction and urgency of change, helping leaders and their teams understand how their enterprise is changing, why and what it means for working differently in future. For example, it has been employed by corporate functions to develop a robust image of their internal (within enterprise) client base to provide the impetus to reinvent how they support front-line business units and how they organize as a function.

How the SAF works

The SAF is constructed from two dimensions of organizational capability. Each dimension is a continuum of opposing values with multiple points of variation in between. The first dimension opposes organizational *stability* with organizational *agility*. The second dimension opposes organizational *autonomy* with organizational *connectivity*. The two dimensions combine to form a matrix in which complementary values from each form distinctive – and aligned – approaches to business strategy, organizational capability, organizational architecture and management systems. These are referred to as *strategic approaches*, and they define how enterprises can strategize and organize to compete and win in an aligned way.

A fundamental assumption of the SAF is that an enterprise cannot develop two opposing organizational capabilities simultaneously within the one business line. For example, the development of organizational capabilities necessary for product and service consistency (i.e. stability) precludes the development of organizational capabilities necessary for product and service customizability (i.e. agility). Put more simply, an enterprise cannot excel at *both* product/service standardization *and* customization simultaneously in the same market. They must choose *either* one *or* the other according to strategic requirements, reflected in the capabilities they seek to develop organizationally. A senior executive I worked with recently described the trade-off as: '*Despite what the gurus say, you can't play basketball and tennis on the same court at the same time and expect to be good at either.*'

Each dimension of the SAF can be summarized as:

- *X-axis: Organizational stability or organizational agility?*
  Organizational *stability* is defined as the capability to limit variation or fluctuations of operation or prevent unwanted disruption to the organizational status quo. Stability implies a high

degree of consistency, system endurance and the ability to return quickly to a 'normal' state, or equilibrium, following a disruption.

- As the opposite, organizational *agility* is defined as the capability to adapt quickly and easily to better fit the changeable conditions of the environment to improve chances of survival.[lxxx] Highly agile firms can quickly change their offerings to market – whether innovative products or highly personalized services – to attract custom and counter competitive threats.[lxxxi]
- Organizational stability and agility support either mass standardization or customization of products and services, respectively.

And:

- *Y-axis: Organizational autonomy or organizational connectivity?* Organizational *autonomy* is defined as the capability to exercise managerial self-determination and act independently of others. Autonomous lines of business, for example, operate freely and rely upon their individual efforts and abilities to pursue a singular goal and avoid the complexity that arises from aligning to the interests of others.
- As the opposite, organizational *connectivity* is the linking of two or more organizational entities – such as different internal departments, teams, technologies or even external partner enterprises – to realize value greater than the sum of the individual contributions or capabilities of each. For example, superior connectivity allows diversified businesses to combine different varieties of people, geographies, functions and technologies into distinctive customer bundles. These may either better match market requirements or offer some form of synergistic strategic advantage over competitors.[lxxxii]
- The trade-off is that the higher the degree of connectivity between different departments, the less freedom each of those same departments enjoy to prioritize their individual interests or ways of working.

A variety of strategic approaches

As noted previously, from the combination of the two dimensions emerge a range of different *strategic approaches*, each representing a distinctive way an enterprise might strategize and organize to gain a competitive edge. These strategic approaches are referred to as the:

- *Efficiency Maximizer*
- *Enterprising Responder*
- *Portfolio Integrator*
- *Network Exploiter*

Each is a combination of complementary values from the two dimensions. For example, in its form and function, the *Efficiency Maximizer* combines organizational stability and organizational autonomy.

Simply put, each strategic approach is different from the others by virtue of its organizational capabilities and how it competes. The *Enterprising Responder* is a combination of organizational agility and organizational autonomy. The *Portfolio Integrator* is a combination of organizational connectivity and organizational stability. The *Network Exploiter* is a combination of organizational connectivity and organizational agility.

Each strategic approach is given a name consistent with how it seeks to secure a competitive edge. For example, the *Efficiency Maximizer* succeeds by maximizing opportunities for exploiting economies of scale as efficiently as possible. Each strategic approach is explored in detail in subsequent chapters corresponding to individual dynamic links of the enterprise value chain.

Most two-by-two matrices in business and management literature are referred to as 'maturity models'. They consist of an x-axis and a y-axis, representing conceptually important dimensions, and progression is measured linearly against each axis. A high score on both axes usually leads to the top right quadrant of the matrix – the most mature and, by implication, the best, i.e. high is better than low in every situation.

The SAF is not a maturity model (i.e. a high score on each axis is not necessarily best or most 'mature'). It provides the tools to make strategy and organization choices depending upon circumstances. Illustrated in Figure 2.5, when considering their own case, enterprise leaders should start from the middle of the SAF (and not the bottom left as is the case with standard maturity models) and work outwards along each of the two dimensions in whichever *one* direction is considered most strategically desirable.

Critically, no one quadrant – or strategic approach – of the SAF is better or worse than any other. All possess advantages and disadvantages. The least capable position within the SAF, and therefore least desirable strategically, is the centre. The goal for any enterprise is to push towards the edge of the framework in whichever direction is most strategically desirable, given customer demands and competitor threats. A showcase of the practical application of the SAF is shared in detail in Section 5 in Chapters 4, 5, 6 and an illustrative case study in Chapter 7. Do you need to change your strategic approach to give your enterprise the best chance of winning and fulfilling its enduring purpose? The next section outlines the leadership opportunity to realign your enterprise for good.

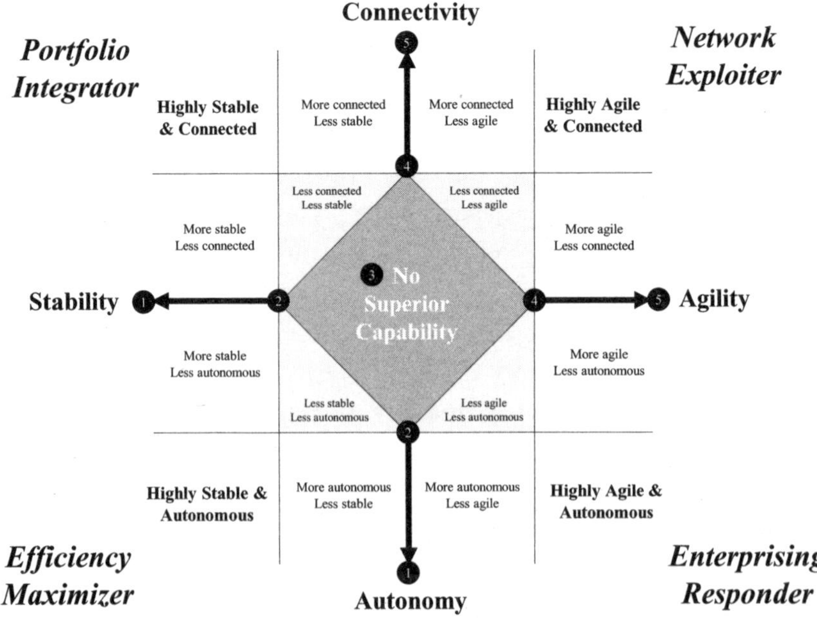

FIGURE 2.5 More or less capable of performing different strategic approaches

SECTION 2.5 STRATEGIC REALIGNMENT, THE LEADERSHIP OPPORTUNITY

The previous section explored the leadership challenge of choosing between opposing forms of business strategy, organizational capability and architecture. Good choices give enterprises the best chance of fulfilling their enduring purpose in the context of their business environment; poor choices produce harmful misalignment and lead to poor performance and decline. This decision-making process – selecting the appropriate form of each link of the enterprise value chain – is made doubly hard when the envisioned ideal state (i.e. what the enterprise should be) is different from the current state (i.e. how it is today).

To close the gap, enterprises need to *realign*, either to improve their performance or to maintain performance over time by adapting to the changing business environment and new opportunities and disruptive threats. Realignment is a matter of strategic concern, therefore, and it is the role of an enterprise's leadership to make these tough decisions in a joined-up and far-sighted way.

Frameworks like the SAF are intended to help enterprise leaders navigate these trade-offs and tricky choices and be positive agents of change. Throughout the following chapters, you can use the SAF to diagnose different approaches to business strategy (Chapter 4), organizational capability (Chapter 5) and organizational culture, structure, processes and people (Chapter 6). The SAF can be used further to create a vision of the ideal future state of your enterprise. Each chapter also provides illustrations – in the form of vignettes, examples and case studies – of how other leaders have sought to realign their enterprise and close the gap between its envisioned ideal state and its current state. In a strategically aligned enterprise, there should be no difference between the two.

As much as it is challenging, strategic realignment represents a personal opportunity for an enterprise's leadership team to influence positive change and leave a long-lasting legacy. Whether to 'do better' (i.e. improve alignment) or 'build back better' (i.e. overcome disruption), influencing positive change is core to the leadership role. The classical distinction between managers and leaders is that managers execute (i.e. deliver results) and leaders change (i.e. change the direction of travel). It is a simplistic distinction, and in today's complex enterprises, the line between the two roles is blurred more and more. However, leading positive change remains the cornerstone of effective leadership. Linking to strategic realignment, the influential work of Max Landsberg provides us with a helpful way of framing this leadership opportunity, with three components to the leadership role broadly: *vision*, *inspiration* and *momentum*:[lxxxiii]

Consider the following questions within the context of your personal leadership opportunity:

- *Vision*: The visioning role is where leaders create a positive image of what the enterprise could be in future. Consider for your case, and in the context of your changing business environment, what should your enterprise look like in future? Which form of business strategy – an efficiency-based approach (the *Efficiency Maximizer* described in the previous section) versus a synergy-based approach (the *Portfolio Integrator*), for example – will best support the fulfilment of your enterprise purpose? Which distinctive organizational capabilities are essential to deliver your differentiated business strategy? Is it a focus on efficient execution, or is it the ability to leverage networks for superior innovation? Which form of organizational structure will support ideally the development of your strategically valuable capability – should your enterprise be organized as a hierarchy or a matrix, for example? Which values and behaviours should be the most highly prized? The answers to these questions and other strategic considerations provide the foundational principles needed to build your vision. Your vision is a coherent and meaningful image of what your enterprise should aspire to be in future. It also sets the scene for what you might need to realign about your enterprise to make it a reality.
- *Inspiration*: The inspiring role means to motivate others, whether employees or external stakeholders, to depart from what they might otherwise choose to do and make your vision a reality instead. Having developed your vision of your highly aligned and fit-for-purpose future enterprise, the opportunity

is to inspire and influence others to implement the chosen vision through compelling communication, education and engagement. Which groups are most important to you in your strategic realignment journey? What are you asking them to do differently in future? What is in it for them (idealistically and not just financially)? What is your message, and how can you deliver it in the most meaningful way possible? What are the barriers to implementing positive realignment, and how might you overcome them? If you haven't succeeded in realigning your enterprise in five years, say, what is the most likely reason(s) why? What are the toughest choices you might need to make in the process of realigning your enterprise for good?

- *Momentum*: The sustaining role is successfully embedding the change to become the 'new normal'. In other words, to move successfully from one state of equilibrium to another that is a better fit for the environment in which you are trying to succeed and fulfil your enterprise's enduring purpose. What does good look like in the future enterprise? How can you engage your line managers to make realignment real for their people? How do you make the change stick?

This book equips you as an enterprise leader (or an aspiring one) with a leadership blueprint to take advantage of this opportunity via the process of strategic realignment. The opportunity is to ask good questions, have better conversations and make the best possible choices to align your enterprise for the first time (in a start-up environment, for example) or, more likely, to realign it to overcome disruption and improve performance. The following chapters are packed with concepts, frameworks and illustrations to help you on this journey. You can cherry-pick from each chapter as you wish, but our journey starts with the next chapter's subject and the first link in the enterprise value chain. Let us proceed with purpose!

3

ENTERPRISE PURPOSE

SECTION 3.1 WHY SHOULD WE CARE?

'Outsource Co.' was a phenomenon. Its growth was nothing short of extraordinary. From years in the doldrums of operating at below £100 million in annual revenues, it was now set to exceed £1 billion. This had been achieved in less than 10 years. It had established itself as a major player in the tough margin-squeezed market of staff outsourcing because it was supremely well managed. 'Smart and disciplined' was how investors and City analysts described Outsource Co. The face of the company was 'Jocelyn', its CEO, and 'Clive', her deputy.

Jocelyn had not founded the business, but her appointment as CEO had transformed it. Right from the get-go, she had driven the company to be as efficient as possible. She had recruited the most loyal of lieutenants in the form of Clive. Together, they concerned themselves in the minutiae of all aspects of the business under their command. In the early days, everybody working for Outsource Co., either in the extremely lean HQ function or at the front line, knew precisely what the company was about and what was considered important. Interpersonal relationships dominated management co-ordination – if you wanted something done, you picked up the phone.

It seemed that Jocelyn and Clive were everywhere at once, supporting or pushing their people. The culture was one of 'just do it'. Action was prized above all else. Indeed, Jocelyn was allergic to what she referred to as 'fluff' – anything that wasn't practical and directly results oriented. Open-ended discussions about Outsource Co.'s purpose, or its direction or culture, were soon closed down by an impatient Jocelyn. Jocelyn was the decision-maker-in-chief, and Clive was the fixer. His job was to get things done. It was a partnership that had worked supremely well when Outsource Co. was relatively small and simple.

Today, considerably larger, it was an approach that was producing obvious tensions. Outsource Co. had grown both organically and by making acquisitions. And it had diversified. Where once it had only needed to focus on one business (running administrative operations for corporate clients) in the UK, it now operated many businesses and in different countries. Jocelyn and Clive could no longer be everywhere all at once. Staff complained about a lack of senior management visibility. Business unit managers and their staff felt less aligned to the company overall as time went by. This manifested itself in a tendency for some business units to 'go rogue', necessitating a tough conversation first with Clive and, if that wasn't enough, the big gun in the form of Jocelyn.

In my meetings with the two of them, they gave the impression the company's managers couldn't be wholly trusted to operate free from supervision. Clive was spread thin trying to maintain control. At the same time, Jocelyn and Clive were also increasingly frustrated by the inaction and lack of initiative within the business. Their managers had at one time been entrepreneurial and buccaneering, seeking forgiveness and not permission from Jocelyn and Clive personally. Now, if not rogue, they seemed struck by inertia, waiting to be told what to do and, in the absence of instructions, not doing anything except for maintaining the status quo.

Outsource Co.'s staff population had grown significantly and was now over 50,000. The bigger Outsource Co.'s headcount, the lower its staff engagement scores seemed to fall. Interestingly, research into the problem indicated that staff identified with their immediate superiors far more than they did with the company itself. There was little in the way of a shared sense of corporate purpose or identity. Staff concerned themselves with their own area of the business and viewed other areas with distrust or ambivalence. When a manager left, it could have a devastating knock-on effect within the immediate business, as staff demonstrated little loyalty to the company and followed their boss to the exit.

Customers and investors were also asking difficult questions, especially about Outsource Co.'s long-term prospects. In the early days, the company had been known for being small, lean, nimble and aggressive at cutting costs. This was in sharp contrast to its competitors. Today, Outsource Co.

increasingly resembled the giants it had once taken on as David to their Goliath. What was its purpose? What was its narrative? What were its guiding principles and values? The lack of clarity around its long-term strategy, or why it had made the choices it had (over acquisitions, for example), was frustrating to staff, customers and investors alike.

Jocelyn's aversion to 'fluff' had meant that the intangible aspects of building a scaled business had been neglected, especially its sense of a meaningful common purpose. Its people didn't understand why they were being asked to do the things they were, and, beyond receiving a pay cheque, why they should care. Its managers were unclear about the overall logic of the business they were supposed to be leading and responded by avoiding any risk to the status quo. Fundamentally, Jocelyn and Clive had failed to make Outsource Co.'s purpose meaningful to all those who mattered to the business, including their people. Nor had they helped to translate its purpose into a coherent strategy or design of an organization that was fit for the future. And they hadn't answered whether it even had a future beyond a billion pounds, and why.

SECTION 3.2 ENTERPRISE PURPOSE

Whether commercial, governmental or social, every enterprise is created with a purpose in mind. *Enterprise purpose* is the first link in the enterprise value chain and the enduring *end* to which all other links, as the *means*, should be devoted. The importance of an enterprise's purpose is never brought more into focus than in times of crisis. Consider the example of the global logistics company, DHL. DHL was responsible for distributing 90 per cent of medical supplies to hospitals in Northern Italy, which was one of the worst-affected Covid-19 'hot spots' in Europe in the early stages of the global pandemic. DHL battled to keep essential medical supply lines open despite the disruption. Its *raison d'être* as a company took on life and death importance for its customers (hospitals and their customers in the form of patients).

An enterprise's enduring purpose is how we make sense of what it does over the long term, why it does it and why it should matter, especially to those outside of the enterprise itself. It is the foundation upon which all aspects of an enterprise are built. As noted in Chapter 1, the best-aligned enterprises are the best-performing ones because their business strategies, organizational capabilities, organizational architecture and management systems are arranged ideally to support the fulfilment of the enterprise's purpose.[ii] The implication is that to be highly aligned and high performing, all enterprises should be led by their purpose.

Purpose is a fashionable concept in business at present. A search on Amazon.com for 'company purpose' yields more than 7,000 book results alone. A search on YouTube will throw up thousands of video clips, ranging from high production value TED Talks to 'gurus' recording at home, all of whom offer guidance about how to 'lead with purpose' or 'live a more purposeful life'. For them, being purposeful can mean simply that, as individuals, we should be more 'present' and deliberate in our attempts to find a balance between work and life.[lxxxiv]

For many others in a business context, purpose is now synonymous with corporate social responsibility. It can be interpreted as an obligation to 'do the right thing' and achieve some form of positive social and environmental impact set apart from, or even instead of, profit-making.[lxxxv] For others still, the essential purpose of any business is, and will remain, to make money. These viewpoints are valid, but from a strategic alignment perspective, purpose means something different.

What is enterprise purpose?

Its purpose is the *raison d'être* of an enterprise. It is the reason for which it was created, why it is maintained and the idealistic motivation for performing its work in future.[lxxxvi] The maxim of 'you are what you do' applies to an enterprise setting. Fundamentally, an enterprise's purpose articulates *what it does* as a business or a government agency, for example, and *why it matters* for those important to the enterprise, be they employees, investors, policymakers or customers. An enterprise's purpose defines its identity and provides the basis for the subsequent determination of its strategic and organizational priorities.

Consider a well-known example of a purpose-led company. Famously, Disney's purpose was '*To make people happy*'.[(ibid)] This has expanded recently to become '*Create happiness by providing the finest in entertainment for people of all ages, everywhere*', but the premise remains the same, as does the strength of its alignment.[lxxxvii] Disney's *enterprise purpose* translates directly into deliberate strategy and organization choices. For example, Disney chooses to fulfil its purpose – in the form of its stated *business strategy* – through three primary categories of product and service aimed at most major customer segments: (1) products (e.g. merchandizing); (2) entertainment (e.g. television, movies and more recently, its proprietary streaming service, Disney+); and (3) integrated physical and digital experiences (e.g. resorts, theme parks and complementary 'apps').[ii]

Disney gains a competitive edge by pursuing excellence within each vertical line of business *and* by managing them horizontally as a portfolio to exploit valuable synergies, i.e. movies support merchandizing and vice versa.[(ibid)] Portfolio integration is a critical *organizational capability* at Disney, which requires the development of collaborative cultures and structures (think *organizational architecture*) across the group company and affiliates to support the sharing of resources and the connecting of creative talent.[lxxxviii]

Enterprise purpose should not be confused with simple measures of success, such as profit.[ii] Profit is just one measure of a business performing its purpose well. Equally, enterprise purpose should not be confused with vision statements, which are simply high-level expressions of an enterprise's business strategy and are not intended to be enduring. Nor is enterprise purpose to be confused with company values. A company's values are a guide to behaviour for the enterprise and those acting on its behalf. Values cannot be ends in themselves.

Enterprise purpose is the only *enduring end* towards which all such goals, vision statements, strategic objectives, values and measures should be aligned. To change an enterprise's purpose is to embark fundamentally upon a new enterprise, regardless of whether the trappings of the old enterprise (logos and brands, for instance) are retained or not.

SECTION 3.3 ENTERPRISE PURPOSE, THE LEADERSHIP CHALLENGE

Suppose you will permit me to indulge my love of science fiction for a moment. In that case, the following quote from the legendary sci-fi author, Frank Herbert, spells out admirably the biggest challenge relating to enterprise purpose for many companies, government agencies and charities. Whether describing an inter-galactic empire led by a messianic figurehead in the year 10,203 or a humble and very much Earth-bound enterprise in 2021, it is the case that, in the Words of Muad'dib by Princess Irulan:[14]

> *Empires do not suffer emptiness of purpose at the time of their creation. It is when they have become established that aims are lost and replaced by vague ritual.*[lxxxix]

All enterprises are created for a purpose. Whether it is for a good purpose or not, it takes considerable time, effort and treasure to bring an enterprise into existence. Too much is sacrificed in the act of creation for it to be accidental. And yet, as an enterprise matures over time, it becomes all too easy to lose sight of the original purpose – the reason for which it was created. The significant risk for any established enterprise is that its culture, rituals, structures, procedures and practices supplant its enduring purpose to become ends in themselves. Ideally, they should only ever be the means.

Many enterprises like Outsource Co., described in Section 3.1, lose sight of their purpose or fail to articulate it in a meaningful way to those who matter. In these cases, poor performance occurs because they lack the guiding point on the compass behind which to align the critical links of their value chain, including the best efforts of their people. In the interests of securing high alignment, and especially when seeking to realign their enterprise, leaders have a twofold responsibility.

Their first responsibility is to preserve the integrity and meaningfulness of their enterprise's purpose despite changes in the external business environment (assuming it continues to be a purpose worth performing, of course). Consider the example of the multinational natural food grocery chain, Whole Foods Market Inc. (Whole Foods). The first Whole Foods Market was founded in 1980 with ambitions to be 'America's Healthiest Grocery Store™'. Its purpose was *'To nourish people and the planet'*.[xc] Its purpose and its values around organic produce, sustainable sourcing and health and nutrition were core to differentiating it from other supermarkets, including market leaders such as Walmart and Target. Its differentiation and appeal to the developing wholesome foods market

[14]The quote is from Herbert's second novel in the excellent *Dune* series, *Dune Messiah* (Herbert, F. (2019). *Dune Messiah*, p. 57. Hodder, London.)

are responsible for its rapid expansion throughout the 1980s, 1990s and 2000s to become an international chain of leading grocery stores.

However, more recently, Whole Foods' annual revenues have declined due to competition from larger retailers introducing healthier options into their stores. Amazon Inc. acquired the Whole Foods Company in 2017 for $13.7 billion, and brought new capabilities to the Whole Foods proposition, including improved data management, customer intelligence and channels, revamped stores and a far superior national and international delivery infrastructure.[xci] Importantly, the essential and enduring purpose of Whole Foods remained the same. The new capabilities made possible by the acquisition give it the best chance of winning in its market when aligned to its enduring enterprise purpose.

The second responsibility for leaders is to ensure a well-arranged value chain supports the fulfilment of their enterprise's purpose.[ii] No matter how noble, well understood or valued, its purpose is merely an aspiration unless an enterprise can implement it. As noted in Chapter 2, the leadership challenge is first to formulate (and reformulate as required) the enterprise's *business strategy* to support the fulfilment of its enduring purpose over the short, medium and long term. Second, to decide which *organizational capabilities* are required to implement the chosen strategy successfully. Third, to determine which configuration of organizational structure, culture, processes and people – the *organizational architecture* – will best support required organizational capability development. Fourth, and finally, to select which functional *management systems* will achieve and maintain desired performance levels.[(ibid)] And, of course, how all the linkages of the enterprise value chain should be realigned to overcome disruption and improve (or maintain) enterprise performance in the changing business environment.

The remainder of the book is devoted to this second responsibility, but let's return to the first before we proceed – ensuring the enterprise purpose is as meaningful as possible.

SECTION 3.4 LEADING ON PURPOSE

What is your enterprise's purpose, and how meaningful is it for those who matter to your enterprise the most? How well does it articulate what you do as an enterprise, and why does it matters that you do it? How can you best use your enterprise purpose to inform business strategy, organizational capability, architecture and management system choices? This section helps enterprise leaders to consider the meaningfulness of their enterprise's purpose according to two key factors: (1) how well it is understood and (2) how much it is valued.

How well understood is your purpose?
An enterprise's purpose cannot be meaningful unless it is well understood by those who are important to the enterprise. Repeatedly encountering questions like *'What do we do?'*, *'Why does it matter?'* and *'Who would care if we ceased to do it?'* is indicative of a lack of understanding over the enduring purpose of an enterprise. Ideally, the answers to these questions are more than common knowledge. They are the core premise behind everything the enterprise does and every conversation about its future.

In our Industrial Age past, a company's purpose was often not – and did not need to be – common knowledge. For example, employees did not need to know the why or wherewithal of the organization they worked for. Frederick Winslow Taylor (1856–1915), the father of scientific management, envisaged work purely as a transaction and workers as mere cogs in a hierarchically managed and impersonal machine. Their job was not to think but to perform to required standards by following the orders of their superiors unquestioningly. The fundamental principles of a business, and why it exists, what it does and why it matters, was a concern for those solely at the top.

The *'Ours not to question why, ours but to do and die'* mentality is a poor fit for our Information Age future. It is increasingly important that an enterprise's people – which means anybody upon whom the enterprise relies to perform its work – are united behind a common sense of purpose. This is for two primary reasons. First, purpose-driven work has been linked directly to enhanced employee engagement, commitment and performance.[xcii] The premise is that the more employees identify with the purpose of their employer, the more likely they are to work hard and demonstrate commitment and loyalty.

A recent study found that employees who perceive meaning in their work are twice as likely to be satisfied with their job and three times more likely to remain with their employer when compared to their peer group average.[xciii] This is important when you consider that up to 71 per cent of employees classified in the millennial age range (i.e. those born between 1981 and 1996) are reportedly *'Not engaged or are actively disengaged in their work'*.[xciv] Additionally, research indicates that customers also demonstrate greater loyalty to brands they perceive as purposeful.[xcv] The inclusion of employees and consumers in the purpose of an enterprise produces positive returns for the enterprise itself, both economically and socially.

There is a second, more practical reason why putting purpose at the forefront of the work proposition is not just desirable but necessary. The traditional assumption behind hierarchical work design was that an employee's superior would know more about her, his or their work than the employee themselves. However, many knowledge economy roles rely upon employees to self-direct and exhibit discretionary effort to perform their work successfully. Attributes such as initiative, creativity and collaboration are critical to developing firms' innovation capabilities.[xcvi] To compete in the knowledge economy, firms should encourage their talented people, or innovators, to be as capable as possible, developing knowledge that surpasses that of their hierarchical superior in all likelihood.

Therein lies the management challenge of 'information asymmetry' (as economists refer to it). How can you supervise someone who knows more about their work than you do? The simple answer is, you cannot. In such circumstances, firms should create a positive work environment in which their core people are *empowered* to perform their work at their own discretion (to varying degrees, according to requirements). If they are aligned to the overall purpose of the enterprise, they can be trusted to work free from supervision. If they are not aligned, because the purpose is not well understood, or their personal interests run contrary to it, they cannot be trusted to act at their own discretion. Discretionary effort is a critical element of a firm's innovation capability, but it relies upon trust between employer and employee. That trust is based upon unity of purpose.

Consider your own enterprise: who matters to you the most? Who would care if your enterprise ceased to be, and why? Given their importance to you, how well do they understand your enterprise purpose? Is it truly a shared understanding?

If an enterprise's purpose is not well understood, no amount of investment in elaborate strategies or organizational designs will act as a substitute for the power that comes from people sharing the same idealistic motivation for performing the enterprise's work.

How valued is your purpose?

The *unitarist* logic of work organization described in Chapter 1 (i.e. an enterprise is a group of people acting together to achieve a common aim) makes an explicit link between enterprise purpose and performance.[xcvii] The more aligned an enterprise's people are behind its purpose (i.e. unified), the higher performing the enterprise will be, all other things being equal. But to align with it, they first need to *understand* it, as noted already. However, even if they understand it, it does not necessarily follow that it will be meaningful as a source of motivation and direction. An enterprise's people also have to *value* its purpose to be motivated by it. It has to be seen as a positive force for good economically or socially (or both) for them and others outside of the enterprise itself, be they customers or society.

Simply put, an enterprise that is solely self-regarding is not a viable business. It is incumbent upon an enterprise's leadership to make its purpose as relevant as possible to all stakeholders by constantly revisiting why the enterprise does what it does and why it matters. As my Oxford colleague Dr Andrew White describes it:

> *The outcome of this process is not a polished statement of purpose – but significant decisions grounded in a deep understanding of purpose characterized by a quiet sense of service to something greater than the immediate needs of customers and short-term demands of investors.*[xcviii]

Consider the anonymized example of a recent public sector client of mine, 'GovOrg'.[15] GovOrg's executive board recently undertook an exercise to reflect on its enterprise purpose as part of a wider strategic realignment initiative. It wanted to rearticulate it in the most meaningful way for its 9,000-strong workforce, its delivery partners (i.e. other organizations delivering public services on its behalf, including private

[15]We will be revisiting GovOrg. in more detail in Chapter 5: *Organizational Capability.*

sector firms) and, especially, the consumers of its services – its citizens. After much deliberation, the following was agreed upon: *'To help all people in our region to lead the best lives they can.'*

To the uninitiated, GovOrg's statement of purpose does not seem especially meaningful. However, it implies several key assumptions that define the philosophical underpinnings of its *raison d'être* as an enterprise. It provides guiding considerations for downstream strategy (how it intends to fulfil its purpose) and organization (how it organizes to implement its strategy) decision-making.

Broken down, these assumptions are:

> [**To help** = *our chosen role as an enterprise*] [**all** = *our chosen scope*] [**people** = *our chosen customers*] [**in our region** = *our chosen 'market' / geography*] [**lead the best lives they can** = *our desired customer outcomes*].

The assumptions behinds its purpose statement tell us a lot about GovOrg and what it values.

1. Its chosen role is an operative one – that of enabling or helping through the provision of public services.
2. Its scope is to help all people, and not simply a select few or a specific segment of the marketplace. This is not a trivial commitment when you consider that more than 1.4 million people with hugely diverse and complex social and economic interests and needs reside in GovOrg's region.
3. GovOrg's customers include individual citizens, communities, businesses and institutions.
4. GovOrg's chosen market is that of its specific region, and no further.
5. Lastly, and perhaps most importantly, the statement conveys its desired outcome and definition of success – '*to help its citizens to help themselves to lead the best lives they can*'.

This is a marked departure from the traditional supply-side logic of the provision of public services. Previously, the state sought to dispense public services regardless of the individual preferences of citizens.

The only opportunity for citizen input was via the political process every four to five years (i.e. elections).

In one statement, GovOrg has defined the first principles of its role, its range and volume of customers (citizens, in other words), its market (geographically limited in this case to its region) and its definition of success as an organ of the state. The challenge for its executive board is to make the purpose meaningful for GovOrg's own people, who are tasked with performing the purpose, and its customers for whom the purpose represents a contract. It is what they expect in return for their payment of local taxes and their participation in civil society.

The additional challenge is to choose *how* to fulfil GovOrg's enterprise purpose strategically and organizationally:

- Which public services should GovOrg offer to help its citizens to lead the best lives they can?
- Which public services should it discontinue, given constraints on resources?
- What are citizens demanding of the services they consume, and how are their preferences changing over time?
- How should GovOrg organize itself to be ideally capable of implementing its strategy and fulfilling its purpose?

Consider your own enterprise. What does your purpose say about you and why your enterprise is important? How much is your enterprise's purpose valued by people you consider important, whether they be internal stakeholders (e.g. employees) or external stakeholders (e.g. investors, customers or communities)? If your enterprise's purpose is not valued, how can you rearticulate it in such a way as to convey its importance, relevance and value in future?

Furthermore, how well does your enterprise purpose define not only the idealistic motivation for performing the enterprise's work but also the guiding principles for downstream strategy and organizational decision-making, including realignment to overcome disruption and improve enterprise performance? The next link in the enterprise value chain – business strategy – articulates *how* you intend to fulfil your well-understood and highly valued enterprise purpose.

4

BUSINESS STRATEGY

SECTION 4.1 STRATEGY, WHAT STRATEGY?

'Tyler' was the CEO of 'Professional Service Firm' (PSF), a Limited Liability Partnership accountancy firm. He was a rarity. Standard practice within the industry was to appoint a managing partner from within a firm's ranks. Not only had Tyler been a lateral hire (brought in from the outside and not brought up through the professional hierarchy), he wasn't even an accountant. His background was general management in big company telecommunications. However, there was no doubt that his appointment had supercharged the firm's growth. In just five years, the firm had gone from 10 partners and 100 associates to more than 90 partners and 1,000 associates. PSF was considered 'one to watch' in the industry.

Tyler had built a strong sense of common purpose among the firm's partners and staff. His message advocated PSF being a disruptor in a sclerotic professional market that was ripe for change. True to his word, where other firms had failed (even gone out of business), PSF had been a recession-busting success. It had become highly adept at identifying competitors in distress and acquiring them on good terms. As a result, PSF had grown inorganically by a factor of 10 in just five years. It resembled a patchwork of independent practices of varying shapes and sizes operating across multiple domains of accountancy expertise. Each offered different accountancy services, sometimes in competition with each other.

Despite its stellar growth, opportunism and not strategic deliberation determined which accountancy services PSF offered to the market. While revenues had grown with every addition to the balance sheet, there were few attempts at meaningful integration. It was difficult to make sense of the whole of the firm's offerings to the market or how it was different from competitors. As successful as it had been, there was also a growing recognition within the firm that client demand was shifting in several important respects. PSF faced customer and competitor challenges that required a *business strategy*.

The firm faced competition from new and unexpected quarters. Existing and new clients were demanding far greater transparency over the fees they were being charged. 'Value for money' was now a common term and featured prominently in buying behaviour. At the 'basic accountancy' end, there were many new entrants to the market. Accountancy service 'warehouses' located in emerging markets with significantly lower operating costs were vacuuming up significant volumes of the firm's low-end client work. The introduction of digital accountancy platforms was especially disruptive. Online platforms were springing up more and more frequently, providing increasingly sophisticated 'self-service' accountancy services for individual users and, most disruptive of all, enterprise users. PSF had no answer to these digital competitors who offered the same services at less cost and more convenience. Longer term, there was talk about the use of 'robo-accountants' – automation of the same services that were the firm's primary source of revenue. The firm was at risk of becoming uncompetitive in its cash cow markets for commoditized accounting services.

At the other end of the scale, the firm couldn't easily compete with the 'wizard' accountants of the so-called 'big four' firms in London and internationally. Although it had very talented partners and associates, the firm simply didn't have a reputation for handling novel, complex or complicated accounting and audit work. The consensus was that the ideal market would be to compete for customized accountancy services work for corporate clients. The idea of the firm as a 'one-stop shop' for mid-size companies was particularly attractive. Its scale and range of accountancy expertise would put it in a naturally differentiated position compared to smaller firms, but not have it going toe to toe with larger firms.

It sounded great in theory, but Tyler seemed reluctant to commit to it as a formal plan. Where others saw an opportunity, he saw only obstacles. Standardized cookie-cutter accountancy services were the comfort zone for many of the firm's partners, and he didn't have faith they could manage much more. It would also be difficult to encourage a more connected approach across the firm's different accountancy practices and offices. Turf wars between partners were common. Partners guarded 'their' client relationships jealously, often refusing to share information or opportunities unless it was of direct personal benefit. Pinning the firm's hopes on its partners collaborating seemed like a tall order.

Consequently, PSF had no coherent plan for which services it should offer. Key questions went unanswered. How should it respond to the changing needs and preferences of its clients? How should it attempt to differentiate from its competitors? Nature abhors a vacuum, and the absence of a coherent business strategy meant that there was little rhyme or reason to the work being bid for or performed by the firm's partners. They found themselves caught in the middle between competing strategic priorities – cost and efficiency on the one hand and delivery of high-value bespoke services on the other. Partners regularly complained of being pulled in too many directions. When asked to describe the firm's strategy, more than one answered: *'Strategy, what strategy?'* They were aligned on that at least.

Very quickly, PSF became less and less differentiated in the market. What did it stand for? Clients didn't perceive the firm as being distinctively good at anything. It wasn't the cheapest, nor was it the most capable of bespoke services. Too often, it was an 'also ran' in competitive client tendering. Tyler responded by corralling his people to win any work going to maintain revenues in the short term while suffering the costs of being a complex and fragmented enterprise.

To give itself the best chance of succeeding, PSF urgently needed to realign its strategy to the changing realities of the accountancy marketplace. First, it had to revisit its choice of accountancy products and services, as well as the individual markets and customers it was targeting. Second, it needed to develop a differentiated position that also aligned with its target clients' changing demands. Its current dual-aspect approach of trying to compete on scale and niche specialization was not working. A lack of clear alignment behind both business models meant that the firm was good at neither – it was confused and unfocused.

A new strategy would also mean revisiting its organizational capability requirements. Still, for now, simply having more of a strategic focus, clarity of direction and established priorities was the essential first step to improved performance.

SECTION 4.2 BUSINESS STRATEGY

Enterprise purpose – the enduring *raison d'être* of an enterprise – is simultaneously everything and *nothing* unless there is an effective plan in place to accomplish it. This chapter reviews the second link in the enterprise value chain, *business strategy*. It considers how leaders might go about planning to fulfil their enterprise's purpose in the constantly changing business environment in which they are trying to succeed.

The business press, management journals and blogosphere are replete with checklists, 'hacks' and 'top five must-dos'. All prescribe how businesses and their leaders can secure a competitive advantage. If only formulating a business strategy were as easy as watching a 10-minute TED Talk. Alas, there is no shortcut or one-size-fits-all recipe for how to succeed in the dynamic operating environment facing most enterprises. But that should also be cause for hope. If it is difficult for you, it is very likely equally difficult for your competitors. Making good business strategy choices is an important opportunity for competitive differentiation, just as it is for every link in the enterprise value chain. And, as a reminder, the '*Enterprise value chain is only as strong as its weakest link.*'[ii]

As noted in Chapter 1, the process of formulating a new business strategy or reformulating an existing one is a critical leadership responsibility. Whether commercial, governmental or social, an enterprise's business strategy should articulate clearly and coherently the following:[16]

1. *What you (as an enterprise) offer to the market in line with your stated purpose.*
   – i.e. your chosen <u>product(s) and service(s)</u>.
2. *To whom you offer it.*
   – i.e. your chosen <u>customer segment(s)</u>.

[16]An honourable mention in dispatches for one of my Oxford executive students, Nash Billimoria, for rearticulating this list in a very user-friendly way based upon his reading of the first edition of this book.

3. *Where you offer it.*
   – i.e. your chosen market(s) and geography(ies).

And:

4. *How you respond to the preferences and needs of your customers.*
   – i.e. how you choose to deliver your products and services aligned to current or future customer demand.
5. *How you differentiate from the best efforts of competitors.*
   – i.e. how you choose to be distinctive in the delivery of your products and services now and in the future.

Unlike enterprise purpose, which is enduring, an enterprise's business strategy is dynamic.[(ibid)] It *should* be adapted to encompass changing opportunities (e.g. new customers, new markets) and threats (e.g. new competitors, disruptive technologies). Therefore, the answers to the questions above cannot be set in stone. They should be regularly revisited by leaders to ensure the enterprise is fit for purpose and capable of maintaining peak performance in its dynamic environment.

To this end, strategic realignment has never been more important. As reviewed in Chapter 2, all enterprises in all sectors face a perfect storm of challenging business conditions. Tried-and-tested industrial strategies are failing to meet the competitive pressures of today's markets. Customers are demanding more than low prices of the goods and services they buy. They desire more variety, smarter bundling and enhanced personalization. They demonstrate little loyalty to long-standing established brands.

Entire industries are being turned upside down by new and non-traditional threats. Abundant information, disruptive connectivity and emergent buying behaviour are changing the rules of the game. Competitors no longer fit into neat industry verticals and geographic boundaries. The rise of platform businesses (think of Uber, or the world's largest retailer, Alibaba) is incredibly disruptive. For example, the new disruptor bank, Revolut, is now Britain's *'Most valuable fintech firm'*.[xcix] Recent fundraising gave it a market price estimated at £24 billion, making it more valuable than many established and formerly market-leading players, such as NatWest. Fintech, and other digital disruptors, may herald a bleak and commoditized future for industrially organized firms if they are unwilling or unable to match their information-rich, agile and intelligent supply chains.

For the business strategy link in the enterprise value chain, the strategic realignment challenge for enterprise leaders is twofold. First, to choose which product(s)/service(s) to offer to the market in line with their enterprise's purpose (corresponding to questions 1, 2 and 3 in the list on pages 113–14).[ii] Second, to choose which *strategic approach* – how the enterprise means to compete – aligns best to customers' preferences and outmanoeuvres rival firms to give the enterprise a competitive edge (corresponding to questions 4 and 5).[(ibid)] Before diving in, let us first define our terms.

What is business strategy?

From a strategic realignment perspective, business strategy is a critical link in the enterprise value chain. Unless an enterprise has a plan for implementing its enduring purpose, it will very likely go unfulfilled. PSF is one such real-life example. Formulating an enterprise's business strategy involves making tough choices about *what* it should offer to the market to fulfil its purpose and *how* it should try to compete in the markets in which it is seeking to win over customers and outmanoeuvre competitors. These considerations and choices are summarized here as *market offerings* – what an enterprise offers to market; and *strategic approach* – how it gains a competitive edge in those markets.

Market offerings

An enterprise's market offerings should never be random choices or opportunistic. Still, the allure of the promise of high returns can lead businesses into markets for which they are ill-equipped or do not align in obvious ways to their *raison d'être*. To be strategically aligned, each of an enterprise's market offerings (i.e. products and services) should support the type of positive impact it is trying to make. It needs to be consistent with the spirit of its purpose – *why* the enterprise exists in the first place. A good example is Disney, reviewed in the previous chapter. Its core market offerings include theme parks, film and media content, and merchandizing. The choice of these market offerings makes sense in the context of Disney's enduring enterprise purpose – '*Creating happiness through entertainment* [abbreviated]'.[lxxxvii] Thus, the first criterion for a strategically aligned business strategy should be the extent to which product and service offerings support the enterprise's purpose.[i]

Choosing what to offer to market requires the placing of bets on individual products and services or a portfolio overall. Placing bets often involves significant investment in product development, whether organically through internal research and development or inorganically, such as acquiring a firm with an existing and valuable customer proposition. Facebook's acquisition of the virtual reality company Oculus Rift in 2014 for more than $2.3 billion is a good example of a major corporation plugging a hole in its portfolio through acquisition. There is an obvious and potentially transformative synergy between the combined technologies of Facebook's social media platform and the immersive attributes of virtual reality.[c] Virtual reality would permit Facebook users to interact with each other in real time and under more lifelike conditions – a boon for remote and virtual working.

Or consider the competing market bet placed by a Facebook rival, Microsoft. Microsoft is investing heavily in integrating augmented reality into its products and services. Unlike virtual reality, which is a wholly digitally created world experienced through a headset, augmented reality involves 'mixed reality'. It is also experienced through a headset but combines the user's view of the real world with computer-created imagery and sound according to whichever programme is selected.[ci] Facebook and Microsoft are each placing bets on two competing technologies in a race to see which technology becomes mainstream in consumer markets. The jury is still out, but the winner will likely take all in the form of capitalizing upon the market potential of the most valued technology, with the loser counting the cost in terms of development and missed market opportunities.

Choosing not to offer or to discontinue a product or service range is also a business strategy choice. Consider the example of one of the world's largest food companies, Kraft Heinz. Following worse-than-expected sales and a loss of £10.2 billion in 2018, the total stock market value of the US food giant dropped by 27 per cent. It had to write down the value of two of its biggest brands – Kraft and Oscar Mayer – to the tune of $15.4 billion.[cii] Higher-than-expected manufacturing and logistics costs are blamed in part for the losses, but consumer behaviour is also a major factor. People are simply consuming less ketchup.[ciii]

Increasing awareness and concerns over health and nutrition are driving consumers away from established processed food brands towards organic and fresh produce. To reconfigure its poorly performing product portfolio and wipe the debt off its balance sheet, Kraft Heinz is looking at several potential divestitures. These include the sale of its Maxwell House coffee business, worth $400 million in earnings before tax and potentially $3 billion in a sale.[(ibid)]

An enterprise's market offerings should change over time in step with changes in the market and customer demand. Whether it is the choice to continue, start or stop offering a product or service involves risk. So too does the choice of which market(s) to compete in. Enterprise leaders need to consider *where* to offer their enterprise's products and services (e.g. different geographical markets or different sectors) and to *whom*, in the form of different customer segments (e.g. different demographic groups determined by age, or lifestyle or purchasing power). A single standardized product may be sold in multiple geographic markets with only minor customization to marketing and advertising being required (the tax and regulatory environment notwithstanding). Service offerings, on the other hand, may require substantial customization in each market according to local customer preferences and market conditions.

Choosing what to offer to the market is just the first element of formulating a business strategy. The second is choosing a strategic approach – *how* the enterprise intends to compete for customer loyalty and outmanoeuvre competitors.

Strategic approach

The principle of *equifinality* applies to market strategizing (and organizing too, for that matter). In an open system (such as a competitive marketplace for products and services), an end state or goal (such as achieving a large percentage of the market share or acquiring resources) can be achieved through many different means potentially. Put simply, there is more than one way to choose to compete for an advantage in any given market. This principle forms the basis for competitive strategy.[civ]

How an enterprise chooses to develop a competitive edge is encapsulated in its strategic approach and defines its competitive posture relative to its rivals. For instance, firms can compete based on cost leadership and beat competitors by being cheaper (or the cheapest) in the market. If based on innovation, they can offer new and highly sought-after products and services for which they can charge a premium.[cv] Two firms competing in the same market may choose radically different strategic approaches to differentiate their offerings from each other to secure customer loyalty. Like the choice of *what* to offer to the market, the choice of *how* to offer it is akin to placing a bet. Winners capture market share and perform well. Losers perform poorly and must review their choices and change tack if they are to do better in future.

Consider the various strategic approaches adopted by International Business Machines (IBM) as it changed its offerings to the market due to shifting demands and competitor challenges. The adage was *'Nobody ever got fired for buying IBM'*. From the 1950s to the 1970s, it was the gold standard in computing, selling mainframes in the burgeoning field of information technology. The now-famous story of its decline and subsequent turnaround at the hands of CEO Lou Gerstner is the stuff of legend. Gerstner realigned IBM from predominantly a hardware company selling servers to a software services vendor selling technology solutions and applications. This was to better align to the changing preferences of a marketplace in which new entrants, such as Microsoft, were disrupting markets previously dominated by the much larger IBM.

In its newer iteration, IBM resembled more of a professional service firm than a product manufacturer. Its strategic approach emphasized agility around client needs and the offering of joined-up solutions. IBM has undergone another corporate transformation to add cloud computing to its strategic focus. In doing so, it has again changed the domain in which it competes, and against whom it competes, and what is strategically important. Its enterprise purpose and 'IBMer' values remain largely the same, but over successive decades, and driven by shifts in the marketplace, its strategic approach for how to win has changed dramatically, as have the products and services it seeks to monetize.[cvi]

There is no definitive rule for how often a business strategy should be reviewed and renewed. It depends upon the pace and breadth of change in the operating environment. Of course, any substantial realignment of the enterprise's business strategy requires a realignment of the organization that supports it if the enterprise is to remain strategically aligned and fit to fulfil its purpose.

SECTION 4.3 ALIGNING BUSINESS STRATEGY, THE LEADERSHIP CHALLENGE

An effective business strategy is the result of purposeful and systematic decision-making by enterprise leaders about *how* they intend to fulfil their enterprise's enduring purpose in each moment of time.[i] The leadership challenge is to formulate a business strategy that aligns to customer preferences while also differentiating the enterprise's offerings from those of competitors.[ii] It needs to articulate coherent, forward-looking planning, priorities, actions and measures in respect of what to offer to the market (i.e. market offerings) and how to offer it (i.e. strategic approach). The leadership challenge is, of course, to decide how the business strategy should change over time given emerging (or disruptive, even) external opportunities and threats.

What to offer to the market?

In the first instance, enterprise leaders should consider their offerings to market. Consider for your own enterprise:

- *Your offerings:*
  - Which products and services do you offer to the market?[ii]
  - How are they consistent with your enterprise purpose?
  - How many products and services do you offer?
  - And to which markets, whether markets are defined geographically (e.g. domestic or international) or by specific segments (e.g. appealing to specific groups of customers, such as age groups)?
  - What is the revenue and profit potential (or public value outcome in the case of governmental enterprises) for each of

your market offerings, as best as you can understand changes in market demand over the short, medium and long term?
- Which market offerings are core to your business in the future, and which are ancillary?

For each product and service over the short term and long term (defined as the next five to 10 years), consider further which you should:

- *Continue offering*: because it remains core to your *raison d'être*, regardless of any form of disruption?
- *Stop offering*: perhaps because market demand does not justify the expense of production or marketing or because it offers limited scope for growth?
- *Start offering*: new or reconfigured products or services that you aren't currently because they represent an opportunity for market innovation and growth?

Additionally, *where* (i.e. which markets) and *when* should you choose to offer your refreshed products and services? As noted, domestic, regional and international markets may each require a different approach to ensure competitiveness. The obvious goal is to match demand as closely as possible. However, the primary criterion for all decision-making should be how well your chosen offerings to the market support the fulfilment of your enduring enterprise purpose.[i]

Each product or service is an expression of your enterprise's purpose and its desired impact on the world. What you choose as market offerings, whether in fast food or financial services, also defines the industries in which you compete, the customers you seek to attract and retain, and the competitors you must beat if you are to succeed.

How to offer it to market?

Having considered your offering(s) to market, reflect further on the nature of demand from customers and the capabilities and positioning of competitors. These considerations influence your choice of strategic approach – *how* you should seek to differentiate your offerings to the marketplace according to:

- *Your customers:*
  - What are your customers' preferences for the products and services you offer to the market, both now and in the future?[ii]
    - For instance, are your customers' preferences for value for money?
    - Or is it for customization or personalization of the products and services they purchase?
    - Or do they value choice and bundling of complementary products and services, for which they are prepared to pay a premium?
  - How should you realign how you offer your products and services to better respond to their changing preferences?
  - What would this reformulated customer proposition look like?
  - How would you market, advertise and brand it effectively?

Any type of customer, whether they are consumers (in the case of business-to-consumer transactions) or clients (in the case of business-to-business engagements) reward vendors who satisfy their preferences with loyalty and quickly discard those vendors who do not.

Consider further: what are competitor capabilities in each of the markets in which you choose to compete?

- *Your competitors:*
  - Who are they, and what are they capable of offering that you are not currently?
  - Are you exposed to new and non-traditional competitors that go about succeeding in the marketplace in a very different way?
  - New or established, how are your competitors changing their positioning in response to market forces, and what might they be capable of presently or in future that threatens your own market position?

The next section reviews the Strategic Alignment Framework applied to the business strategy link of the enterprise value chain. This is to help enterprise leaders to evaluate different strategic approaches and choose one (or more, if competing in more than one market) that might give them a competitive edge.

SECTION 4.4 THE STRATEGIC ALIGNMENT FRAMEWORK, BUSINESS STRATEGY

A critical challenge for enterprise leaders when formulating their enterprise's business strategy is to choose their *strategic approach* – how they are seeking to align their offerings to the preferences of customers and how they are seeking to differentiate them from the manoeuvrings of competitors. The Strategic Alignment Framework (SAF) introduced in Chapter 2 helps enterprise leaders to conceptualize the full range of strategic approaches at their disposal and choose the one which best fits their purposes.

Illustrated in Figure 4.1, the following section outlines the attributes and priorities of four primary strategic approaches, referred to as the *Efficiency Maximizer*, *Enterprising Responder*, *Portfolio Integrator* and *Network Exploiter* (different dimensions of the SAF). Each represents a unique

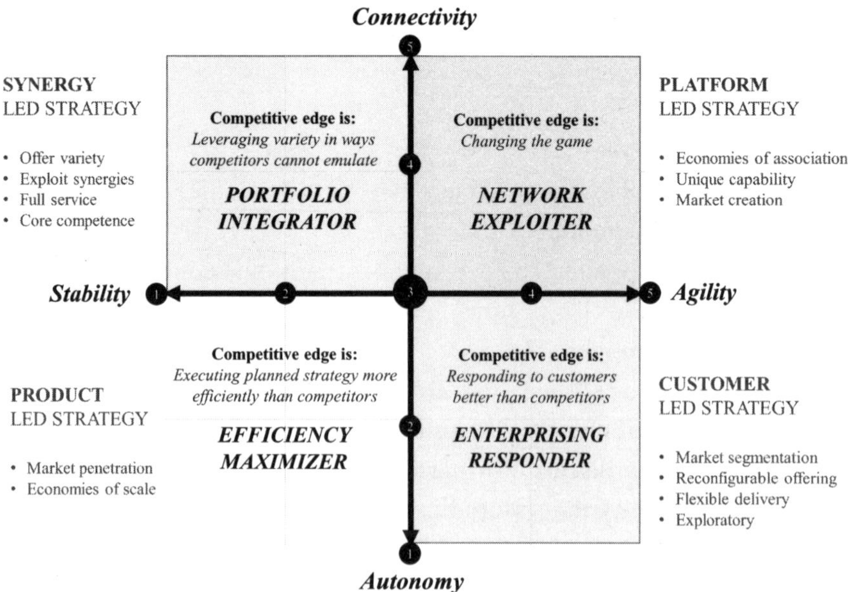

FIGURE 4.1 The Strategic Alignment Framework; business strategy

combination of the dimensions of the SAF and is characterized by maximization of product, customer, synergy or platform leadership, respectively. While the SAF highlights four strategic approaches, in reality, there are many more variations ranging across the SAF's two dimensions. As you might expect, each possesses advantages and disadvantages.

The Efficiency Maximizer

The first, the *Efficiency Maximizer*, is perhaps the most familiar in management theory and practice. The *Efficiency Maximizer* relies upon organizational *stability* and *autonomy* to efficiently exploit known market opportunities and create surplus value by maximizing economies of scale. Organizational stability and autonomy permit efficient reproduction of standardized and stand-alone (i.e. can be sold separately) products and basic services sold at scale and in multiple different consumer markets. An *Efficiency Maximizer*'s business strategy might be characterized as product-led but can also include standardized and stand-alone services. Succeeding for *Efficiency Maximizers* means executing the planned strategy more efficiently than competitors.

The relative stability of demand and supply enables *Efficiency Maximizers* to optimize their rational planning and machine-like production capability to exploit known market opportunities. That is not to say that *Efficiency Maximizer* market offerings cannot be of high value or innovative, but they are standardized and typically need to be sold in high volume. As the name suggests, *Efficiency Maximizers* succeed by maximizing economies of scale, selling as many units of production as efficiently as possible. This requires a high degree of repetition to perform tasks as well as possible according to established standards of performance. Simplicity is also vital; the simpler the offering to market, the more likely it is to be reproduced with the fewest possible errors and as quickly and cheaply as possible.

McDonald's as discussed in Chapter 1, is a classic example of this approach. Its ability to serve millions of customers daily is possible due to its disciplined focus on efficiently maximizing sales of a limited range of products within one industry – fast food. It faces myriad competitors for its custom, and not simply other fast-food vendors. Starbucks, for example, is a direct competitor. However, by sticking to its main offering and not diversifying beyond its core competence, McDonald's can focus on what it does best and maintain its market-leading position: *'We serve 3.8 million customers a day, and 90 per cent of the population [in the UK] come to us at least once a year. Other people will undercut you or disrupt the market that you're in ... You will be able to spot those brands that have listened to their customers and disrupted their own markets'*, according to the UK CEO of McDonald's.[cvii]

Innovation in *Efficiency Maximizers* often takes the form of scalable product and process development, either creating new products or refreshing existing product lines. Product development remains primarily focused on producing innovative but still standardized offerings that can be produced within an acceptable margin of cost and benefit. In some cases, product ranges can remain essentially static for decades, assuming stable demand from customers. The focus for successful *Efficiency Maximizers* is how to do the same better and find improvements incrementally.

The Enterprising Responder

A second approach, the *Enterprising Responder*, relies upon organizational *agility* and *autonomy* to respond flexibly and in innovative ways to market and customer needs. One way to secure a competitive advantage is to offer non-standard products and services to avoid becoming trapped in commoditizing and potentially contracting (for which read 'squeezed margins') marketplaces. An *Enterprising Responder* business strategy might be described as customer-led (as opposed to product-led in the case of the *Efficiency Maximizer*). Succeeding means responding better than competitors to changing needs of individual market segments or customers.

Unlike the large stable bureaucracies of the Industrial era, organizational agility enables *Enterprising Responders* to rapidly reconfigure their market offerings, whether in the form of innovative products or highly personalized services. Organizational autonomy permits a singular focus on exploring new opportunities. Autonomous and agile enterprises are self-reliant, versatile and creative. *Enterprising Responders* all share the same traits of seeking to engage the best talent and affording high levels of freedom to respond quickly to the changing requirements of markets and customers.

Consider the long-established and highly successful private client bank Coutts & Co (Coutts). Its clients include the British royal family, and its strength is offering the highest standard of personalized financial service. The success of Coutts is predicated on its ability to distinctively configure its services to the needs of individual clients and reconfigure them continuously as clients' needs change over time. Client relationships are described as close 'partnerships' because that enables the firm to develop in step with its clients for the long term.[cviii]

Succeeding for agile service innovators like Coutts means being more responsive to client needs than competitors. Bespoke and personalized financial services are valued more highly than off-the-shelf financial services, and clients are prepared to pay a premium over standardized and impersonal alternatives. Personalized client and customer relationships like these are sticky. Hard-to-win customers are more likely to remain as the relative costs of transferring to another service provider become higher the more embedded the relationship.

Harnessing the enterprising abilities of their talent, *Enterprising Responders* set themselves apart by their ability to offer new products and services to market. This is in contrast to *Efficiency Maximizers*, who seek to exploit known and existing customer opportunities more and more efficiently. While supply-led *Efficiency Maximizers* require customers to align to their standardized offerings, customer-centric *Enterprising Responders* do precisely the opposite.

The Portfolio Integrator

A third strategic approach, the *Portfolio Integrator*, relies upon organizational *connectivity* and *stability* to maximize the synergies between different lines of business, geographies, teams and technologies. Unlike the vertically separated and 'siloed' *Efficiency Maximizer,* or agile but autonomously operating *Enterprising Responder*, *Portfolio Integrators* win by exploiting valuable connections *between* their different business lines, functions and geographies. Superior horizontal connectivity allows diversified businesses to combine different varieties of people, functions and technologies in novel and distinctive configurations.

These either better match market requirements or offer some form of synergistic strategic advantage over competitors. *Portfolio Integrators*' connectivity makes them distinctively capable in several strategically advantageous ways.

Most basically, connecting across what would otherwise be separated and independent business lines permits exploitation of efficiencies, knowledge sharing and exchange of good practice. Shared services are the most obvious example of attempts to rationalize and simplify administrative and mid-office services infrastructure (centralized payroll or facilities management, for example). More importantly, by connecting the different offerings of its entire organization and even those of external partners, *Portfolio Integrators* can offer a large variety of complementary goods and services. These can be organized into a coherent and convenient product or service bundle.[cix] Connected 'one-stop-shop' businesses are better able to share customer insight between different business lines and develop new business by cross-selling complementary goods and services to variety-hungry customers.

Horizontal connectivity is also a pathway to innovation and growth.[cx] Cross-functional collaboration allows *Portfolio Integrators* to innovate beyond what an individual business line could manage on its own. The Chinese conglomerate BYD (Build Your Dreams), for example, invested heavily in connecting the resources of its three subsidiary companies specializing in automotive, semiconductor and battery manufacturing. Combining technologies, personnel and capability has enabled BYD to launch rapidly into the growing hybrid and electric car market. By connecting existing resources in novel ways, it has created a new avenue for growth beyond its traditional commoditized core markets, where it faces stiff cost competition.[cxi] The approach illustrates their ambition to compete distinctively in a fiercely competitive global market.[cxii]

Integrating diverse resources – whether talent or technology – fuels innovation and offers a powerful means of differentiating corporately from rivals who lack either the same diversity of resources or the ability to form close collaborations to create opportunities for product and service innovation.[cxiii] By establishing valuable connections between the full and varied range of resources within their portfolio, *Portfolio*

Integrators are capable of projecting power into the marketplace beyond the range of capability of any one of their business lines individually or those of their competitors.

The Network Exploiter

A fourth and final strategic approach is the *Network Exploiter.* This approach relies upon organizational *connectivity* and *agility* to exploit the capabilities of its extended internal and external networks. This creates the potential to offer customers enhanced choice (more variety), smart bundling (valuable synergies between different offerings), immediacy (value of timeliness) and personalization.

Recent developments in information technology have dramatically reduced transaction costs, making possible real-time interaction and co-ordination between many different business partners. Where the *Efficiency Maximizer* succeeds by maximizing economies of scale, the *Network Exploiter* succeeds by maximizing economies of association. Network thinking embraces enterprises as networks of partnering actors, in which complementary capabilities are flexibly harnessed.[cxiv] As well as technology, this is made possible at scale by sophisticated monitoring and governance. This can bring together a diverse group of network actors and align them behind a common purpose and distinctive offering(s) to market.[cxv]

Network Exploiter business strategy might be described as platform-led (as opposed to synergy-led in the case of the *Portfolio Integrator*, or customer-led in the case of the *Enterprising Responder*). Success for *Network Exploiters* means changing the game (i.e. disrupting established business models) by leveraging their network to satisfy known or nascent customer outcomes. *Network Exploiter* offerings can be configured to customer requirements and rapidly reconfigured as requirements change. They are demand- and not supply-led and rely upon external partners (or actors) to maximize economies of association to offer the greatest possible variety of products and services. When bundled together, they form a truly differentiated offering aligned to customer requirements and beyond the easy reach of rivals.[cxvi]

Platform businesses such as Uber and Airbnb are powerful examples of this approach. However, network thinking also applies to established complex businesses. Rolls-Royce is a blue-chip brand in aerospace, producing some of the most technologically innovative jet engines for commercial, military and energy customers. In a game-changing departure from the former industry standard business model of cost-plus (cost of the equipment plus after-sales maintenance and parts), Rolls-Royce introduced Power-by-the-Hour (PBTH).[cxvii]

Under PBTH engagements, customers literally purchase hot air – the units of thrust necessary to keep their fleets moving. PBTH is a customer outcomes-based approach. A Rolls-Royce executive described the difference between the old cost-plus model and PBTH as the figurative difference between selling a drill and selling a hole. Customers don't want a drill; they only want a hole – but in the past, they had little choice but to purchase the hardware to drill the hole themselves.[cxviii]

Customers today don't want to purchase complex and expensive-to-maintain engines (i.e. the hardware). They want power, simply. Rolls-Royce provides these power solutions under a full-service one-stop-shop engagement (i.e. the requirement for connectivity) contracted for a fixed period and fully customized to individual customer requirements (i.e. the requirement for agility). A senior Rolls-Royce executive described the network approach to delivering customer outcomes as follows:

> *So it's line of sight, driven by the customer demand … with a very clear vision of what we're trying to do, where we can push new product introduction through these facilities much more quickly than we've ever done and essentially that we get the whole organization engaged in these objectives, rather than it being hitherto what had been a management problem to solve, we get the minds and intellect of the whole organization* [including partners] *into solving our problems.*[(ibid)]

PBTH was introduced as a business model 50 years ago, but in an industry with notoriously long lead times on commercial relationships and research and development, it is only over the past two decades that it has redefined the rules for competitiveness in the military and civil aerospace industries. Competitors have been forced to follow suit to remain competitive.[cxix]

Sticking with the aerospace sector, another example of this type of thinking is the MQ-Next requirement of the United States Air Force

(USAF). MQ-Next is a call to aerospace manufacturers to develop a new generation of autonomous uncrewed combat air vehicles (UCAV) to fight and win future aerial conflicts. Its goal is to replace the ubiquitous and highly successful MQ-9 Reaper drone currently in service around the world. Unlike the MQ-9, which is a single uncrewed drone capable of reconnaissance or attack and controlled from the ground, the bold vision for the future is *swarms* of co-operative crewed (i.e. piloted) *and* artificially intelligent uncrewed autonomous aircraft.[cxx]

Each aircraft, or 'system' as the USAF refers to them, possesses a different but highly complementary capability (integrating reconnaissance seamlessly with attack, for example). Possessing more capability than any one system (i.e. aircraft) ever could, the swarming 'system of systems' can also autonomously reconfigure itself to respond rapidly to the dynamic external environment in which it operates and offer any mission commander *'A continuum of platforms most effective to [any] given problem'*.[(ibid)] The system of systems is a shapeshifting network of diverse capabilities; in other words, capable of responding in real time to emerging threats and opportunities in ways competitors cannot easily match.

Network Exploiters tap into the potential for product and service variety within their extended network. Using their superior connectivity, they harness it in ways that can be configured to customer requirements and rapidly reconfigured as requirements change.[cxxi]

SECTION 4.5 REALIGNING BUSINESS STRATEGY, THE LEADERSHIP OPPORTUNITY

It is tempting to ask which of the four broad strategic approaches described in the previous section is the best. Perhaps you have guessed the answer already. It is, of course (again): *it depends*.

The best strategic approach, or any of the myriad variations that range across the two dimensions of the SAF, is the one that best supports the fulfilment of an enterprise's purpose in a distinctive way aligned to customer and market requirements. For example, the *Efficiency Maximizer* is the best strategic approach for enterprises competing in markets that reward economies of scale, but it is a poor fit in different contexts. No one strategic approach outlined within the SAF is better than another because each possesses unique advantages and disadvantages. The key consideration is: which is best for you in the market environment in which you are – or wish – to succeed? And importantly, multiple lines of business within one enterprise may each require a different strategic approach.

Instead of asking which approach is universally the best (a fool's errand for a contingency theorist, as I hope you are by now), the infinitely better question to ask is: which is best for your enterprise specifically? When thinking about realigning your enterprise to improve performance or overcome disruption, this fundamental question about strategic approach combined with market offerings forms the bedrock of your business strategy considerations.

To apply this thinking in practice, gather your team for an open-ended and intentionally high-level conversation about your enterprise's business strategy. Ideally, you will each need to come prepared with up-to-date market information, customer insights and competitor intelligence about the short term (within the next year), medium term (within the next three years) and long term (the next five to 10 years, say). Structure the conversation along the lines of the following questions and make sure to use the SAF to capture your thinking diagrammatically.

The first consideration is your *offerings* to the market in line with your enterprise purpose:

- Which existing products and services should you *stop* offering to the market, because they are easily commoditized perhaps, or provide the limited potential for future growth?
- Which should you *continue* offering because they remain core to your *raison d'être*, regardless of any form of disruption?
- Which new products and services should you *start* offering because they represent an opportunity for market innovation and growth?
- Additionally, *where* (i.e. which markets) and *when* should you choose to offer your refreshed products and services. Domestic, regional and international markets may each require a different approach to competitiveness.

Your choices should form a list, perhaps categorized by the short, medium and long term, or perhaps by priority according to customer demand or growth potential. Try to capture your thinking in a way that others could easily make sense of it. *Telling* your important stakeholders (or anybody) what to think tends not to work because it forces them to make a leap of faith. *Show* the quality of your thinking using evidence (e.g. market data, customer insight) and logic. Give them the opportunity to make up their own minds about which products and services are critical to your enterprise's success based upon the quality of your argument and evidence. It is a much better way of securing support to lead realignment.

The second consideration is which is the ideal *strategic approach* to secure a competitive edge. To test drive how the SAF can work, try this simple exercise. Select one (or more) strategically important business line or market offering from the list above, either because it is a mainstay of your balance sheet or a potentially high growth area, and plot it on the SAF. Use the SAF to critically evaluate what customers and markets are demanding by answering the following questions:

a. *X-axis*: Using a scale of 1–5, what is the customer requirement for *either* organizational stability *or* organizational agility for your selected line of business or market offering(s) (with organizational stability being 1 and organizational agility being 5, and varying degrees in between)? For instance, are your customers more interested in low prices and something off the shelf, or a bespoke offering for which they are willing to pay a premium?
b. *Y-axis*: Using the same scale, what is the customer requirement for *either* organizational autonomy *or* organizational connectivity (with organizational autonomy being 1 and organizational connectivity being 5, and varying degrees in between)? For instance, do your customers value a specific product or service, or do they value a connected bundle of products and services?

As noted in the previous section, combinations of these two dimensions offer four different potential avenues to competitive advantage: (1) economies of scale (i.e. standardized offerings produced efficiently); (2) customer centricity (i.e. customization and even personalization of offering); (3) corporate synergies (i.e. a portfolio of offerings and smart bundling); and (4) economies of association (i.e. exploiting networks to disrupt the playbook of established markets).

Using Figure 4.1, plot your answers to question (a) on the x-axis of the SAF (the requirement for either organizational stability or organizational agility) and your answers to question (b) on the y-axis of the SAF (the requirement for either organizational autonomy or organizational connectivity). The results indicate your understanding of the customer landscape and the strategic approach that is most aligned to customer expectations. Is your team aligned in its views of what your customers value? Are the results surprising? Are you aligned currently to what your customers are demanding? Is there a gap?

A similar exercise can be performed to analyze competitor capability. Consider further: how can you differentiate your current and future offerings from the best efforts of competitors? Where would you place your competitors on the SAF? How are they trying to succeed in the marketplace? For example, is it scale play (*Efficiency Maximizer*) or a synergy play (*Portfolio Integrator*)? How much does their position overlap with your own? What are they capable of that you are not?

Finally, what do you observe from your reflections and discussions? What do the results imply about your enterprise's realignment requirement? What is the degree of gap between your current state and your ideal future state? Any gap illustrates your strategic realignment requirement: *what you need to realign to* if you are to succeed in future.

As you develop your vision of your ideal business strategy, there are some important things to think about – and killer trade-offs to manage.

Choose a strategic approach and align behind it

Each of the four (or more, ranging across each of the two dimensions) strategic approaches described in the previous section are a distinctive way in which to align strategically to the demands of customers and stand apart from competitors. By the terms of the SAF, enterprises can pursue only *one* strategic approach at any one time within any one market in which they are competing for an advantage. A number of important points should be noted.

First, enterprise leaders must choose the strategic approach they think is best. While it may seem obvious, many leaders fail to actually commit to any course of meaningful action. Even if they do, often they fail to communicate their choices in such a way that it guides effort and implementation of the enterprise's business strategy. The case of PSF described in Section 4.1 is one such example. It is incumbent upon enterprise leaders to select a strategic approach, having considered all salient factors and based upon the best evidence available to them, and align their enterprise behind it. Once selected, it should be the primary focus of management attention and effort and form the direction of travel to which all other aspects of the enterprise are aligned and realigned as necessary.

Second, committing to a strategic approach means sacrificing any potential advantage offered by any other strategic approach. The choice is not to be taken lightly. For example, enterprises cannot differentiate themselves based on superior organizational stability and organizational agility at the same time. A key challenge is to manage the complex trade-offs inherent in choosing the one strategic approach that may give you an edge in the market(s) in which you are competing.

Third, two enterprises competing in the same market may choose very different strategic approaches to outmanoeuvre their competitors. This has implications for what they prioritize strategically and organizationally. No one strategic approach is enduringly fit for purpose, especially in highly changeable market environments.[cxxii] As noted in Section 4.2, enterprise leaders must realign their strategic approach to match the pace of change in their operating environment if they are to maintain a state of high alignment over time.

Figure 4.2 illustrates the results of a research exercise performed with the executive board of a leading bank. The firm competed in one of the most overbanked sectors in the world (by the number of banks per head of population) and faced stiff competition from both domestic and international rivals. The bank offered a full range of financial services, from retail banking to investment banking. It was considered an innovator in terms of its ability to bring new products to market quickly.

Three of its key market offerings are plotted on to the SAF: (1) its retail banking business; (2) its private client banking business; and (3) its corporate banking business. The executive board were asked to form a consensus about the current strategic approach of each of these and their ideal strategic approach in future based upon their knowledge of

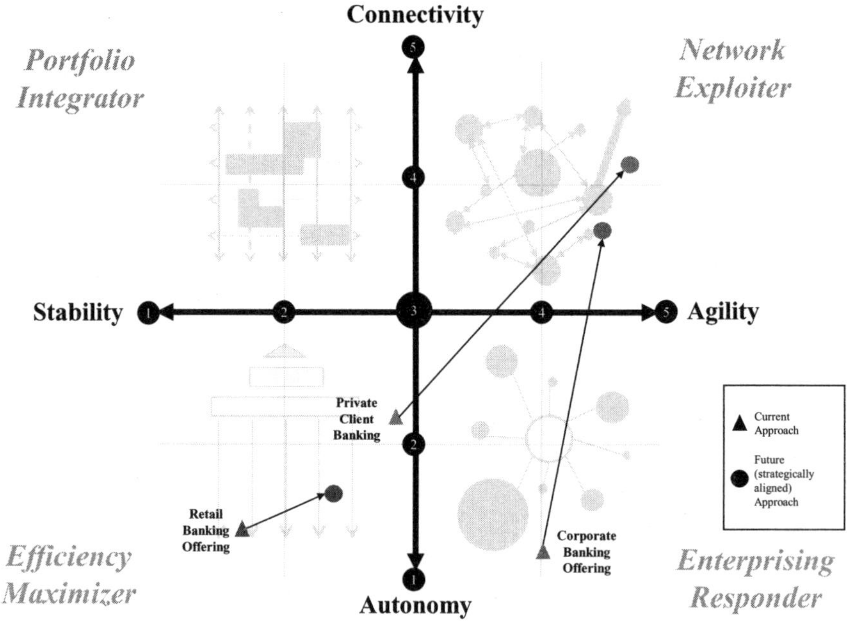

FIGURE 4.2 A gap between current and ideal future strategic approaches

the changing marketplace. The triangles indicate current positioning, and the circles indicate the executive board's five-to-10-year forecast for each line of business.

The results of the research exercise were revealing and a cause for dismay for the executive board. In every line of business except branch retail banking, the executive board perceived the bank would need to drastically realign its strategic approach to respond to changing customer preferences for enhanced variety, smarter bundling and personalization of the financial products and services they buy. The results indicate that competing based on superior agility and connectivity is at the heart of the bank's future success as a *Network Exploiter* in private client and corporate banking. Both lines of business are not aligned currently to this most sophisticated, but also most challenging to manage, of strategic approaches.

As the bank's enterprise leadership, the executive board's challenge was twofold. First, to incrementally realign its private client and corporate banking businesses over the next five to 10 years to remain competitive in both markets. Second, to manage the co-existence of two very different strategic approaches for value (the *Efficiency Maximizer* strategic approach for its retail banking business and the *Network Exploiter* strategic approach for its private client and corporate banking businesses). Failure to realign their enterprise, or to manage each line of business for value, creates the risk of misalignment and, with it, poor performance and declining competitiveness over time.

Embracing more than one strategic approach requires very careful management
Managing multiple lines of business, each requiring a different strategic approach, significantly increases the complexity and challenge of achieving superior strategic alignment corporately. How enterprise leaders respond to the challenge depends upon the requirement for organizational autonomy or organizational connectivity. In diversified enterprises with largely autonomous lines of business (i.e. conglomerate structures), the focus of strategic realignment occurs at the level of the individual business unit. The role of 'corporate' often takes the form of simple financial control and the enforcement of minimum standards. Corporately, the enterprise is, to all intents and purposes, a grouping of profit and loss statements on a financial balance sheet.

In cases where there is a strategic requirement for high levels of organizational connectivity between different lines of business, the focus of strategic alignment must be both at the business-unit level *and* the enterprise level and takes the form of *strategic control*.[cxxiii] Unilever's famous mantra of being a *'multi-local multinational'* in the fast-moving consumer goods sector speaks of an ambition for the integrated whole (the corporation) to be more valuable than the sum of its individual parts (for which read 'brands and local markets'). This style of strategic alignment requires highly sophisticated management capability at all levels to offset the risk of operating the enterprise as a complex adaptive system.[cxxiv]

As per the questions at the beginning of this section, how many lines of business are you trying to succeed in, and what are the strategic requirements of each? Of course, more than one line of business may share the same strategic approach, as in the case of McDonald's. However, if more than one strategic approach is required, the urgent strategic realignment priority is to develop the capability to be ambidextrous.[cxxv] Adopting a one-size-fits-all approach to competing for advantage for different lines of business with diverse requirements leads inevitably to misalignment and poor performance in each domain and corporately overall.

Even worse, future core activities can easily become infected at their infancy by the dominant logic of an established strategic approach when, to be strategically aligned, they should be designed and managed much differently from the outset. Critically, how different is each line of business in your enterprise (assuming there is more than one) in terms of the organizational capabilities required to win? The priority for leadership teams is to understand potentially competing strategic and organizational requirements of their different lines of business and design and manage each appropriately – perhaps very differently – for value. Therefore, a key challenge for enterprise leaders is:

> *To foster performance without cannibalizing its different activities, a firm implementing two business models simultaneously needs to balance the benefits of keeping the two business models separate while at the same time integrating them enough so as to allow them to exploit synergies with each other.*[cxxvi]

And at what level does integration occur in your enterprise – corporately at board level or lower at the operational management level? Where should it occur ideally?

Be ambitious but do not overreach your grasp

'Ah, but a man's reach should exceed his grasp, Or what's a heaven for?' Robert Browning's poem 'Andrea del Sarto' encourages us to reach to seize opportunities beyond what we might be capable of grasping. However, it is a reckless management team that commits to a strategy they know they are incapable of delivering or, even worse, in the mistaken belief they can. Put simply, enterprise leaders must be wary to ensure their reach does not exceed their grasp.

If enterprise leaders cannot strike a balance between organizational complexity and manageability to maintain strategic alignment on a sustainable basis, extreme corrective action is often required. Barclays bank, reviewed in Chapter 1, is an example. Another is General Electric (GE). In its heyday, GE's market valuation was close to $400 billion. Today, it is closer to $150 billion, and many analysts consider it to be in trouble, with its share price falling by almost two-fifths in the past five years alone.[cxxvii]

GE famously invested heavily in diversifying its portfolio of businesses, moving beyond its traditional asset-heavy emphasis on engineering (e.g. electrical goods, power generation, industrial plastics, aviation) to health care, technology and financial services. The strategy of diversification seemed a strength of GE, famed for its distinctive approach to management that appeared to produce superior results in every industry to which it was applied. Ultimately, however, the demands of operating a highly diverse and complicated portfolio business served to divert attention from structural problems in both its established and newer business.

Over the course of the past decade, GE has successively withdrawn from many of its businesses, with its financial services business, GE Capital, being the latest, highest-profile casualty. Under CEO John Flannery (CEO 2017–2018), and continuing today, GE initiated an aggressive strategy of cost control, culture change and cuts. The expected disposal of assets over the two-year period to 2020 totalled $20 billion, all as part of a corporate turnaround equal in scale to its legendary growth in the 1980s and 1990s. For two decades, it was the best-regarded company in the world. The future for GE is to be smaller and simpler, or perhaps even split apart. It is reducing its ambition in order to realign itself to be fit for purpose for the future.

Enterprise leaders need to consider several factors carefully when designing the shape and size of their enterprise to be as simple as possible. How many different lines of business should you pursue? Which lines of business are a core priority for growth and sustainability in future? Which are ancillary because they offer little future market potential even if they are important today? Non-core activities can be unduly distracting for leadership teams and put future development at risk.

Embrace the potential for innovation in every approach

There is potential for innovation in all four strategic approaches and their myriad variations, but it takes different forms and needs to be aligned to support the chosen approach to the market.

The value of innovation for *Efficiency Maximizers* is to enable them to become even more efficient at scaling up new products and services. This can be initial product development, or continuous operational improvement, or the adoption of a new technology that enables the better monitoring of performance. For *Enterprising Responders*, the value of innovation is the novel adaptation of core products and services in the form of market customization and customer personalization.

For *Portfolio Integrators*, innovation may take the form of collaborative leadership and the pooling of intellectual resources across different business lines. This is to facilitate the offering of unique combinations of products and services or the development of a shared customer interface and infrastructure. For *Network Exploiters*, innovation can take the form of novel – perhaps even radical – ways in which partnering firms create, capture and deliver value through network leverage, i.e. business model innovation. The rise of platform business models is one such example.

What is the value of innovation for your strategic approach to the market, and what form should it take to give you the best chance of succeeding? For example, how can you leverage the potential advantages of new technologies (e.g. automation, big data or augmented human performance) in such a way as to align to your chosen strategic approach, whether it be efficiency, customer, synergy or network related?

Don't flip-flop between different strategic approaches

Extending the strategic alignment logic further, firms should seek to push as far to the edge of the SAF for their chosen strategic approach to be as distinctively capable as possible. The challenge is that excelling at one approach to secure competitive advantage likely requires sacrificing superiority in other areas.[cxxviii] As noted, highly efficient firms sacrifice the ability to easily customize or integrate their products and services in the interests of consistency, simplicity and repeatability. Conversely, highly agile firms sacrifice efficiency to explore and experiment creatively with novel offerings to markets and customers.

Navigating the trade-offs between different strategic approaches and committing to one deemed best in a given moment of time poses a dilemma. To be competitive, enterprise leaders should seek to develop strategically valuable organizational capability in ways superior to rivals.

However, core competencies can also form 'core rigidities', creating limitations to enterprises diversifying in future beyond what they are good at currently.[cxxix] The example of Xerox reviewed in Chapter 1 illustrates this point. The more an enterprise commits to any one strategic approach, the more the risk of becoming trapped by it over time increases. However, failing to commit poses the risk of not being competitive in the short term. Many enterprise leaders attempt to hedge their bets by switching between different strategic approaches. The risk is for firms to flip-flop between different approaches in successive rounds of disruptive strategizing and reorganization.

Consider the case of 3M. When James McNerney, formerly of General Electric, joined 3M as its CEO in 2001, he immediately introduced a raft of changes designed to make it more efficient. The culling of 11 per cent of the workforce, cuts to research and development (R&D) spending, and the introduction of Six Sigma succeeded in increasing 3M's profits and pushed up its stock price.[cxxx] However, the emphasis on efficiency ran counter to the original creative ethos that had previously been the hallmark of 3M and its culture. McNerney's successor, George Buckley, when taking over the CEO reins in 2005, sought to roll back his predecessor's initiatives, channelling additional spend on R&D and shifting the emphasis from 'profitability and processes discipline to growth and innovation'.[(ibid)]

Flip-flopping between radically different strategic approaches runs the risk of failing to develop valuable (which is to say, strategically aligned) organizational capabilities.

Avoid becoming a jack of all trades and master of none

In seeking to hedge their bets about which is the best strategic approach to commit to, especially if uncertain, the risk for many enterprise leaders is to try to be good at everything – to try to be equally stable, autonomous, agile and connected at the same time.

Illustrated in Figure 4.3, enterprises such as PSF (the subject of Section 4.1) find themselves falling into the centre of the SAF – responding to market pressures by becoming a *jack of all trades and master of none*. Firms occupying the centre ground are not superior at anything. As noted previously, enterprises can only meaningfully differentiate

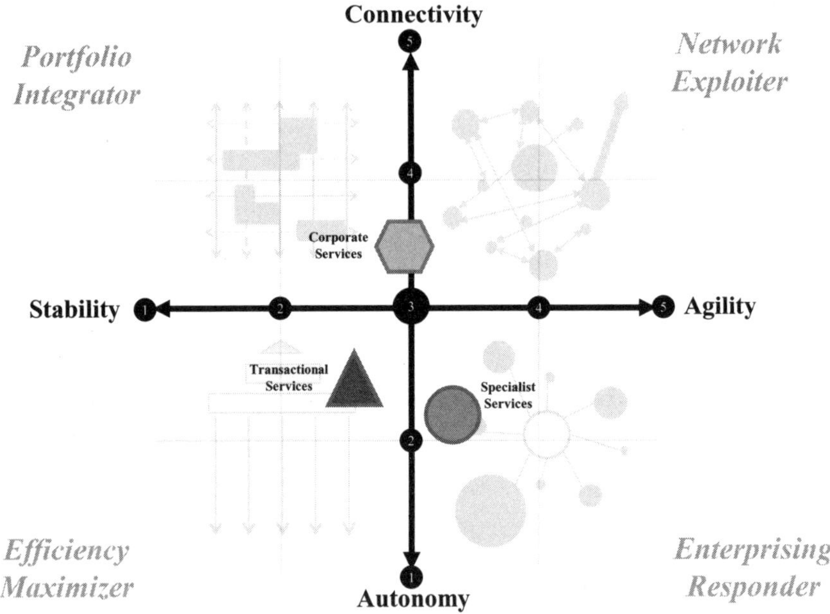

FIGURE 4.3 Jack of all trades and master of none

themselves from their rivals if they pursue excellence at one approach to the exclusion of excellence in others.

Practically, the centre ground is beset with energy-sapping conflicts and compromises because of competing priorities and a lack of strategic focus behind which to align the organization's culture, structure, work processes and people.[cxxxi]

Business strategy is a vital link in the enterprise value chain. However, even the best business strategy in the world is worthless unless an enterprise is capable of implementing it. *Organizational capability* is the next link in the enterprise value chain and the subject of the next chapter. It is easily overlooked but is where an enterprise's true value resides.

5

ORGANIZATIONAL CAPABILITY

SECTION 5.1 GOOD INTENTIONS POORLY IMPLEMENTED

'Prod Div.' (or the division) was a North American division of a larger multinational conglomerate, 'Plexi Plc'. Plexi Plc's management of Prod Div. was hands-off, except for financial governance and performance monitoring for both its business-to-consumer (B2C) and its newer business-to-business (B2B) operations. 'Helen', the division's general manager (GM), had held the reins for almost five years. In that time, there had been an astonishing fourfold increase in staff with no appreciable improvement in performance.

A former management consultant, Helen had impressed many in her first hundred days. She quickly introduced an ambitious new business strategy to combat the division's squeezed margins in its contracting cash-cow B2C business. There was muted grumbling that she hadn't consulted widely enough when drawing up her plans. Indeed, one of Helen's first acts was to bring in an external (and expensive, rumour had it) management consultancy. For more than two months, the division's main office had been home to a small army of 'young suits', beavering away over spreadsheets and PowerPoint presentations.

Grumbling aside, there had been at least a clear sense of strategic direction. Helen's business strategy (as it later became known) called for, first, expansion of the division's B2C business and a refresh of its products to be 'new and improved'. Second, and more ambitiously, to launch a new and high-potential B2B business alongside, in order to provide additional avenues for growth. With the blessing of Plexi Plc, Prod Div. bought in the B2B capability it lacked by acquiring an innovative start-up.

Less clear was how the two-pronged strategy would be implemented. Both at the board level and on the shop floor (so to speak), there was no clear sense of the capabilities required to make it a success. Almost immediately, implementation had run into unforeseen problems. The hoped-for revenue growth didn't materialize in the B2C business, and the division was left with a profit-killing cost base of new staff hired to support the planned expansion. Like so many others, the B2C business was disrupted by new and low-cost international competitors. Helen and her team recognized they were increasingly outpriced in a contracting market. She had inherited an already labour-intensive organization, which made the expansion of staff numbers doubly hard to justify in hindsight. There was good reason to think it wasn't going to get better any time soon. The B2C business required scalability and cost-competitiveness to succeed. Operational excellence and efficiency – maximizing outputs and minimizing inputs (including the cost of its people) – was vital to its success. Prod Div. had struggled to be good at *efficient execution* long before Helen arrived. Still, the influx of new staff had diluted its existing operational culture and made it even less capable.

Much hope had been pinned on the fledgling B2B offering. However, it continued to be a minor interest on the division's balance sheet despite investment and extensive support. Where the B2C business needed to be good at efficient execution, the B2B business was a whole different ball game. Its success depended upon offering its clients highly customized services integrated with those of external partners to form a coherent 'one-stop-shop' suite. It was a complex business to manage – relatively low volume, but very high margin if you got it right. To succeed, the B2B business needed to be highly capable of *network leverage*. This was an unprecedented set of organizational capabilities for the previously purely product-centric and hierarchically organized division.

But the B2B business was falling well short of expectations. Helen's response was to double down on trying to make it work. Integrating the acquired B2B business into the divisional fold had not gone well from the start. With the best of intentions, every effort had been made to be inclusive and make everyone feel part of the same team. However, every interaction seemed to produce the opposite of what was intended. Managers in the B2B team complained bitterly about 'interference from division'. Attempts at integration were resisted, passively at first and more actively over time.

Complaints were raised that the division's established routines, procedures and processes were infecting the smaller B2B business and crushing the life out of it. Despite generous packages, many of B2B business's best people had left within two years of the acquisition. The B2C business seemed in terminal decline, and the B2B business was failing to launch. The reason for both was a misalignment between Helen's strategy and the different organizational capabilities that each business required to succeed.

The Plexi Plc executive tasked with picking up the pieces following Helen's eventual and somewhat hasty departure conceded grudgingly that her business strategy had been well intentioned. However, looking back, the strategic realignment of Prod Div. could be summed up in one phrase: '*good intentions poorly implemented*'.

SECTION 5.2 ORGANIZATIONAL CAPABILITY

For decades, business strategy has occupied the lion's share of management literature and executive attention. It is the subject of the bestselling management books of all time, including *Competitive Strategy* by Michael Porter and *In Search of Excellence* by Tom Peters and Robert Waterman.[17] What has received much less attention is the subject of *organizational capability*. This refers to the organizational competencies, abilities and powers required by an enterprise to succeed in its business environment. Beyond the basics merely needed to function, organizational capabilities are a source of competitive advantage when they support the implementation of an enterprise's chosen business strategy.[i]

From a strategic alignment perspective, the startling disparity between the treatment of these two essential components of the enterprise value chain – business strategy and organizational capability – is nonsensical. As illustrated by the real-life inspired case of Prod Div., an enterprise's

[17]See for reference: Porter, M.E. (2008). *Competitive Strategy: Techniques for Analyzing Industries and Competitors*. Simon & Schuster; and Waterman, R.H. & Peters, T.J. (1982). *In Search of Excellence: Lessons from America's Best-Run Companies*, p. 360. New York: Harper & Row.

business strategy is merely a set of good intentions if it does not possess the appropriate organizational capabilities to support implementation. Despite its importance, I frequently observe that responsibility for the development of strategically valuable organizational capability does not fall within the domain of any one leadership group. Despite an explosion in the past two decades of ever-more specialized chief-level (C-level) senior roles, organizational capability is an area neglected entirely.

In addition to the well-established CEO, CFO (finance) and COO (operations) roles, we can now add the following: chief marketing officer (CMO), chief human resources officer (CHRO), chief technology officer (CTO), chief diversity officer (CDO), chief innovation officer (CIO), to name but a few. Google has appointed a chief happiness officer (CHO) recently, and the titles of chief trust officer (CTRO) and chief experience officer (CXO) are also gaining traction. The rise of digital technology has fuelled the growth in C-suite roles even further, including, for example, chief data officer (CDO – not to be confused with diversity), chief digital officer (CDO – not to be confused with diversity or data which, of course, it often is), chief digital transformation officer (CDTO).[cxxxii] The list is growing all the time.[18]

There is a chief strategy officer (CSO) job title, of course. And yet, there is no chief capability officer (CCO anyone? No?). Nor is there likely to be, despite organizational capability being the vital connection between strategic intent and operational implementation. Organizational capability makes or breaks an enterprise in terms of performance and competitiveness because, as noted, the best business strategy in the world is just a set of good intentions without it.

Strategically valuable organizational capability is the product of the quality of people, culture, structure, process and system (and other resources, including technology) choices at the organizational architecture link of the enterprise value chain.[ii] Arguably, it is the most challenging component of any enterprise to realign. It is where

[18]For an excellent review of the C-level job title explosion, I encourage you to visit the following blog post: https://blog.ongig.com/job-titles/c-level-titles/. It is as funny as it is comprehensive. My favourite job title is *chief visionary officer* (CVO). Imagine that on your business card!

the rubber hits the road, and the point at which the consequences of realignment become 'real' for an enterprise's people, whether employees, contractors, partners or customers. It is so important, but why is it so neglected?

I do not have a good answer. Two reasons spring to mind. First, organizational capability is tricky to define. It is also tricky to manage. It is a more significant enterprise-wide concern than the affairs of any one corporate function or management group. It requires joined-up enterprise leadership to be effective. Second, it is the only link in the enterprise value chain without a corporate home. When it is considered at all, organizational capability is often split between general managers or different corporate functions (operations, HR, finance or information technology, or any of the other job titles listed previously). These groups are often disunited in their functional interests, assumptions and decision-making. A failure to develop the required organizational capability is the inevitable consequence.

Regardless, the leadership challenge is that many enterprises need to develop new organizational capabilities to maintain their edge in the face of intense and non-traditional competition. The leadership opportunity is to realign to the new realities of competing for value in the changing business environment. This chapter sets out a process in the form of questions to ask, conversations to have and choices to make regarding strategically valuable organizational capability. It reviews the Strategic Alignment Framework to frame those choices and identify critical organizational design priorities. But first, let us grapple with trying to define our terms of reference.

What is organizational capability?

Organizational capability is defined here as the possession of organizational competencies, abilities and powers that support the implementation of an enterprise's business strategy. Along with the enterprise's *organizational architecture* (the subject of Chapter 6) and *management systems* (the subject of Chapter 7), organizational capability forms part of a broader concern about how enterprises are organized to be fit (for which read 'capable') to perform their enduring purpose in line with their chosen business strategy.[(ibid)] For example, suppose an enterprise's business strategy is based on price competitiveness (i.e. the cheaper its offerings to the market, the more competitive it is). In that case, its chances of succeeding in the marketplace depend primarily on efficient execution – its ability to produce its offerings efficiently to required standards and at a low cost.

However, organizational capability is a tricky concept to define and can mean different things to different people. For some, organizational capability refers to 'know-how'. Simply, the functional knowledge required to run a business day to day, e.g. fiscal discipline and budgeting. Know-how can be extended to include industry-specific capabilities – specialist knowledge needed to ensure enterprises are proficient in their domain of focus, e.g. financial services skill-sets in banking, or the latest coding skills or programming knowledge in software businesses.[cxxxiii] Neither functional know-how nor industry-specific capabilities provide the basis for competitive differentiation. They are factors of hygiene organizationally in so much as enterprise performance and competitiveness suffer in their absence but are not enhanced by their presence.

For others, organizational capability is linked to competitive differentiation and refers to the possession of universally valuable capabilities and resources that are superior in all contexts, e.g. access to cutting-edge technologies. Put simply, an enterprise in possession of the best capabilities and resources available (e.g. 'we have the best people in the industry') will outperform its competitors every time, or so the 'universalistic' theory goes.[cxxxiv] What is considered valuable changes over time, of course.[cxxxv]

Strategically valuable organizational capability

A strategic alignment perspective rejects the idea of generic organizational capabilities being of strategic value in all situations. Basic know-how and industry-specific capabilities are table stakes to get and keep an enterprise in the game. An enterprise's organizational capabilities in the form of its competencies, abilities and powers, all of which can be mobilized to fulfil a specific strategic end, are only of strategic value when they support directly the implementation of the enterprise's chosen business strategy in ways superior to competitors.

Different organizational capabilities support the implementation of different strategic approaches. Importantly, only those which support directly how the enterprise is trying to gain a competitive edge should be a top priority for development. An enterprise may need to develop multiple different sets of organizational capabilities, depending upon the business strategy requirements of its various markets. Misalignment occurs when enterprise leaders fail to match the development of their enterprise's organizational capability (or capabilities) with the requirements of their chosen business strategy. The consequence of misalignment is the poor implementation of their business strategy and, in the long term, an increasingly insurmountable barrier to enterprise performance and competitiveness.[i]

The idea of strategically valuable organizational capability is closely related to the concept of the 'core competency'. This is defined as the *'Harmonized combination of multiple resources and skills that distinguish a firm in the marketplace.'*[cxxxvi] Generally, core competencies enable firm competitiveness when they:

a) provide access to a wider range of markets;
b) enhance the value of products and services for customers;
c) they are difficult for competitors to emulate.[cxxxvii]

Enterprise-wide organizational capabilities (or competencies) can, for example, support a range of strategically similar offerings to the market.[cxxxviii] The very same organizational capabilities required to sell burgers at scale enabled McDonald's to quickly introduce coffee products to its menu at multiple locations globally. From a product leadership perspective, coffee and burgers share the same attributes of being simple, separable (from other products) and highly standardized. Therefore, as products they conform to the same strategic approach – that of the *Efficiency Maximizer* described previously. The introduction of the 'McCafé' and McDonald's range of coffee products is credited with a 15 per cent rise in revenues in participating restaurants.[cxxxix]

However, there is a careful trade-off to be managed when seeking to become distinctively capable as an enterprise. Enterprise leaders should seek to develop *superior* organizational capability in line with their business strategy – that is, to be more capable than competitors pursuing the same strategic approach in the same market. However, in doing so, they incur an opportunity cost because the more capable an enterprise is at certain things, the less capable it can be at other opposing things.

For example, enterprises cannot be equally stable and agile. One must give way to the other. The implication is that the capabilities required to be highly efficient are sacrificed to develop the capabilities required to be highly flexible and vice versa. If enterprises cannot be equally capable at everything, which organizational capabilities should enterprise leaders seek to develop as a matter of strategic importance?

SECTION 5.3 ALIGNING ORGANIZATIONAL CAPABILITY, THE LEADERSHIP CHALLENGE

The answer to the question posed at the end of the previous section is, as I am sure you have already guessed: *it depends!* What enterprises need to be distinctively capable of organizationally depends upon their business strategy and how they intend to compete in their market(s).[ii] The leadership challenge is that there is no one organizational capability or set of capabilities that is superior in all contexts. Individual enterprises need to be capable of different things organizationally, according to what they offer to a market and how they are attempting to respond to customers' preferences and outmanoeuvre competitors.[(ibid)]

Chapter 2 introduced a range of strategic approaches outlined in the Strategic Alignment Framework by which enterprises might best respond to their customers' preferences and stand apart from competitors. To be implemented effectively, each strategic approach requires the support of a distinct set of organizational capabilities. Consider for your enterprise:

- Which organizational capabilities should you seek to develop as a priority to implement your enterprise's chosen business strategy (whether it competes for market share or resources)?
- If competing in more than one market (either geographically or because of multiple lines of business), do you need to be 'multi-capable' to establish and maintain a competitive edge? If so, how different are the capabilities you need to develop to succeed in your various markets? Are they complementary or competing values?

- And how might your organizational capability requirements change in future (say over the next five to 10 years) in line with changing strategic priorities and an increasingly complex, changeable and uncertain external operating environment?

By referencing the Strategic Alignment Framework (in the next section of this chapter), enterprise leaders can make sense of different varieties of organizational capability and how each might best support strategy implementation (described in Chapter 4).

SECTION 5.4 THE STRATEGIC ALIGNMENT FRAMEWORK, ORGANIZATIONAL CAPABILITY

This section refers again to the Strategic Alignment Framework (SAF). Illustrated in Figure 5.1, the SAF uses the combination of two dimensions of opposing organizational capability introduced in Chapter 2 to help enterprise leaders to identify the capabilities required to implement their chosen business strategy.

Which strategic approach did you select in the previous chapter to give your enterprise a competitive edge in the market(s) in which it competes? Your choice of strategic approach determines your requirements for

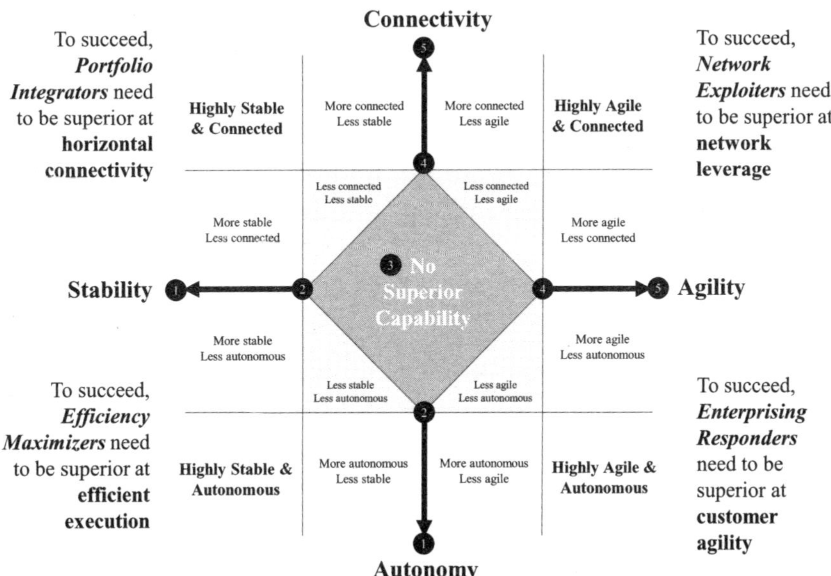

FIGURE 5.1 The Strategic Alignment Framework; organizational capability

either organizational stability or organizational agility; and, further, your requirements for either organizational autonomy or organizational connectivity. These two dimensions combine to form four distinctive organizational capability configurations, each of which has the potential to support the implementation of your chosen business strategy.

The Efficiency Maximizer

As a reminder, *Efficiency Maximizers* succeed by exploiting a known market opportunity to maximize economies of scale. This requires them to sell as much of their product or service as they can at the least possible production cost. Market offerings typically take the form of highly standardized, separated (i.e. not bundled with other products) and relatively simple products and services, all of which lend themselves to product-centric market strategies and scalable opportunities. The efficient reproduction of existing market offerings and the introduction of potentially innovative but still standardized new market offerings provide the necessary capacity for market growth.

What the Efficiency Maximizer needs to be capable of:

What *Efficiency Maximizers* need to be distinctively capable of is *efficient execution*. This requires the development of superior organizational *stability* and superior organizational *autonomy* as complementary organizational capabilities. Organizational stability supports the consistent reproduction of the enterprise's standardized offerings. Organizational autonomy supports a singular focus on producing the enterprise's offerings as simply and as efficiently as possible.

Superior execution is measured by the relationship between gains from outputs of a business operation, such as revenue and profit, and the inputs, such as people, capital costs and time. The lesser the value of the inputs and the greater the value of the outputs, the greater the degree to which a business can be considered efficient. This ratio applies to all varieties of enterprise, regardless of strategic approach, but it is the lifeblood of the *Efficiency Maximizer*. Illustrated in Figure 5.1, the *Efficiency Maximizer* occupies the bottom left corner of the SAF.

Efficient execution requires project teams, for example, to perform their tasks with the least possible investment of effort, time and expense.

In manufacturing operations, operational efficiency equates to reduced costs of production, minimization of wastage, improved product quality and maximum intensity of work performed (e.g. the elimination of manufacturing downtime).

Features of efficient execution (or 'operational excellence' or 'execution excellence', as it is also referred to) often include management practices such as continuous improvement. This is the incremental improvement of efficiency over time (such as Lean Thinking, Six Sigma) and culture management techniques designed to enforce positive behaviour in the form of discipline, timeliness, work intensity, problem solving and operational focus.

Consider the most famous example of the *Efficiency Maximizer* logic at work – the automobile manufacturer Toyota Motor Corporation (Toyota). Considerable volumes have been written about the Toyota Way and the Toyota Production System (TPS) introduced in the mid-1970s. Both these facets of operational excellence have propelled Toyota into a pre-eminent position in the global automotive industry and have been the subject of emulation across multiple different industries by firms in search of efficient execution.

Toyota's core organizational capability around efficient execution has enabled it to deliver automotive products at a predictably high level of quality and at competitive prices. It is perhaps one of the most famous examples of innovative approaches to production and operations management. It has the capability to minimize errors and manage cost while also maximizing speed, production intensity and quality against specified standards. Toyota's products may in themselves be innovative, albeit standardized, but its critical competitive differentiator is its operational excellence and efficient execution.

The efficient execution capability trade-off:

While ideal for the efficient mass production of relatively straightforward, stand-alone and standardized products and services, there are natural limitations to the *Efficiency Maximizer* approach.[cxl] The organizational stability that enables *Efficiency Maximizers* to efficiently reproduce standardized products and services at scale inhibits customization and agility around idiosyncratic market segments or individual customer preferences.

Equally, *Efficiency Maximizers* can move quickly to realign the focus of their production efforts, but only if a replacement product, for example, is similarly straightforward, standardized and stand-alone. In addition, *Efficiency Maximizers* are not highly connected horizontally across their operations. The vertical arrangement of their specialized business divisions prevents the easy formation of novel product and service combinations and the exploitation of synergies.

The Enterprising Responder

Enterprising Responders succeed by responding flexibly and innovatively to the changing preferences of markets and customers. Market offerings often take the form of either highly customized services or being first to market with novel products and services that align closely to nascent and emerging demand.

What the Enterprising Responder needs to be capable of:

Enterprising Responders need to be distinctively capable of *customer agility.* This requires the development of superior organizational *agility* and superior organizational *autonomy* as complementary organizational capabilities. Organizational agility enables the configuration and reconfiguration (for which read 'flexible adaptation') of an enterprise's offerings to align closely with the idiosyncratic preferences of individual markets and customers. Sharing parallels with the *Efficiency Maximizer*, organizational autonomy enables *Enterprising Responders* to have the freedom to pursue a singular focus on the external market and customers. Superior customer agility is measured by the degree to which the enterprise can adapt its offerings to the changing demands of the markets in which it competes. Illustrated in Figure 5.1, the *Enterprising Responder* occupies the bottom right corner of the SAF.

Characteristic attributes of *Enterprising Responders* include high levels of experimenting with new offerings to the market or the redevelopment of existing offerings in line with changing market conditions. They are characterized by the flexible deployment of staff around specific customer or client opportunities, albeit within a domain of specialism, and an expectation of comfort with the ambiguity that is inevitable when attempting something new. Organizational self-sufficiency and entrepreneurship are needed to take on risks and with few resources in order to create a market offering deemed valuable by the external market. Superior relationship management and insight into the unique preferences of an individual customer or market segment is vital. Finally, flexibility and creativity are required to respond in innovative ways to new and novel opportunities and threats.

Consider the example of academic departments in research-intensive universities. Researchers are supported by a functionally organized administration but left mainly to their individual devices to perform their research work – both regarding what they do (the subject of their research, for instance) and how they do it (their methodology or style of enquiry, for example). A prized feature of academic work is the freedom provided to researchers to pursue opportunities to create novel insights at their discretion and according to their judgement as experts in their field. Autonomy is considered key to being capable of research excellence. Collaboration and co-authorship exist for sure, but often with field-related peers at other universities (which, interestingly, are competitors in published rankings as well as collaborators – 'frenemies', as you might say). Loyalty to a professional field can be stronger in some cases than to one's enterprise, whether commercial, governmental or social.

Similarly, agility around exploring new opportunities for knowledge generation and dissemination is also a critical component of being an excellent research institution (and an excellent researcher). Knowledge of developments in the external professional field is arguably more important than internal administrative matters, which, rightly or wrongly, are often perceived as distractions from academic work. For instance, unoriginal ideas are not accepted for publication in highly regarded scholarly journals (but they are essential for teaching, of course). Therefore, researchers are incentivized primarily to pursue original research if they are to have any hope of receiving external recognition for the novelty and value of their innovativeness.

The customer agility capability trade-off:

There are natural limitations to the *Enterprising Responder* strategic approach. The organizational capabilities that enable firms to be agile prevent them from being easily scalable or extremely efficient.

Routine and standardized ways of work run counter to the highly discretionary and idiosyncratic working patterns required to deliver customized offerings to markets and individual customers. Innovation often involves exploration and experimentation to overcome the inevitable uncertainties encountered when creating something new. Creative variation and not repetition or standardization is the bread and butter of successful *Enterprising Responders*.

Enterprising Responders are also not highly integrated typically (horizontally at least). This is because individual and team freedom is prized above all else. Synergies are sacrificed in the interests of autonomy. High-performing individuals and localized teams often operate independently of each other. They are focused on their specialist tasks, or wholly aligned to their individual business lines or geographies.

Customers dealing with two different parts of the same firm may experience quite different ways of working or differing levels of quality. In extreme cases, highly agile but loosely coupled firms resemble associations of 'friendly pirates', capable of high degrees of versatility on their local turf, and socially collegial, but ultimately motivated by their own parochial interests and not those of the enterprise overall.

The Portfolio Integrator

Portfolio Integrators succeed by maximizing the value of synergies across different lines of business, geographies, teams and technologies. When highly horizontally connected, the enterprise forms a whole that is worth more than the sum of its parts. *Portfolio Integrators* find innovations in novel combinations of different products and services and offer customers enhanced choice and convenience by bundling offerings. *Portfolio Integrators* succeed by leveraging their diverse portfolio of products and services in novel and distinctive ways that competitors cannot easily match.

What the Portfolio Integrator needs to be capable of:

Portfolio Integrators need to be distinctively capable of *horizontal connectivity*. This requires the development of superior organizational *connectivity* and superior organizational *stability* as complementary organizational capabilities.

Horizontal connectivity supports the bringing together of unique combinations of product and service in line with market demand and the integration of teams and technologies for realizing nascent innovations or offering an enhanced menu of goods. Organizational stability provides the durable superstructure across which teams and talent connect and enables the selling of novel market offerings at scale. Superior horizontal connectivity is measured by the degree to which the whole of a connected portfolio of products and services, or different lines of business, functions or teams, is worth more than the sum of the individual parts. Illustrated in Figure 5.1, the *Portfolio Integrator* occupies the top left corner of the SAF.

For example, horizontal connectivity supports a range of activities through which 'cross-value' might be found. This can include the sharing of commercially valuable customer insight across different lines of business. Or the cross-fertilization of new business opportunities and innovative practice between different but complementary teams. Or the forming of collaborations enabling the creation of shared business opportunities that might not be possible otherwise.

One famous example is Morgan Stanley. Under the leadership of its CEO, John Mack, in the 1990s, it sought to become more horizontally connected by overlaying its formal functional structure with cross-cutting teams in its investment banking, equity, fixed income, merchant banking and other business lines. It was recognized that significant commercial opportunities lay *'at the intersection of different divisions'*. Furthermore, cross-divisional job rotation offered significant career development benefits for up-and-coming staff.[cxli] It was necessary to break down the functional and divisional silos and overcome the partisan interests of many of its directors, which was preventing a sense of a wider team; flexibility around global opportunities for client development; and simply better management of an increasingly large, diversified and complex international business.

In a series of firsts for Morgan Stanley, Mack instigated gatherings of the firm's leaders from across the world. The forum provided a collective voice on firm affairs. Performance management and employee development were also repurposed to emphasize group co-ordination and promote collaboration and the sharing of individual divisional business plans to create greater transparency.[(ibid)] Fiefdoms were out, and collaboration was in. John Mack's legacy of creating a 'one-firm firm' continues today. This is in the form of Morgan Stanley's streamlined divisional structure and the emphasis on common platforms (in wealth management, for example). Programme teams operate across departments to scan and monitor the external environment and quickly form the necessary bundle of functions to meet client expectations.

These capabilities helped propel Morgan Stanley forwards through the global financial crisis in 2008. More recently (and pre-pandemic), it generated more than $40 billion in revenues (and more than $11 billion in pre-tax profit) in the fourth quarter of 2018, a 4.85 per cent increase over the previous year and considerably ahead of its rivals, who experienced a contraction of -9.14 per cent in revenues in the same reporting period.[cxlii]

The horizontal connectivity capability trade-off:
Portfolio Integrators are ill-equipped to be agile around individual customer preferences because they typically operate at scale, for which standardized offerings are most efficient. They can offer an enhanced menu of goods and services and even package them in such a way as to align to mass-market segments, but personalization is counter-productive to maximizing economies of scale. The best they can hope for is often described as 'mass customization'.

Moreover, building relationships across different business lines is a slow process. It requires a significant investment of time and energy to overcome dissimilar incentives, cultures and ways of working that are the natural by-product of efficient divisions of labour and task specialization. Personnel within *Portfolio Integrators* often find themselves serving two or more masters and face a tricky political balancing act of reconciling vertical and horizontal accountabilities.[cxliii]

The Network Exploiter
Network Exploiters succeed by leveraging their diverse networks of distinctively capable internal teams and external partners and suppliers. This is to offer enhanced choice and personalization of products and services. Like *Portfolio Integrators*, *Network Exploiters* connect different

parts of their business to form a whole – a platform – that is worth more than the sum of its parts. Unlike most *Portfolio Integrators*, *Network Exploiter* connections extend much further to include (indeed depend upon) external partners. *Network Exploiters* use sophisticated data insights and customer intelligence to align their offerings to the preferences of narrow market segments and the unique needs of individual customers. *Network Exploiters* succeed by leveraging their extended and capability-rich networks in ways that competitors cannot match.

What the Network Exploiter needs to be capable of:
What *Network Exploiters* need to be distinctively capable of is *network leverage*, which requires the development of superior organizational *connectivity* and superior organizational *agility* as complementary organizational capabilities.

Organizational connectivity supports the *Network Exploiter* to establish functional relationships across a wide variety of independently capable internal and external partners. Through this, they are able to share insights, explore novel combinations of market offerings and engage in seamless joint delivery of a customer proposition in line with a shared task or purpose. Organizational agility supports the *Network Exploiter* to reconfigure the capabilities of its network to be able to customize its proposition and offerings to the varied or changing preferences of individual markets and customers. Superior network leverage is measured by the degree to which it supports the enterprise to form unique and flexible combinations of product and service. Illustrated in Figure 5.1, the *Network Exploiter* occupies the top right corner of the SAF.

Network Exploiters succeed by leveraging their extended and capability-rich networks in ways that competitors cannot match. They differentiate themselves through the reach and diversity of their networks of partners and the quality of their customer insight, and their ability to mine customer and market data. Knowledge sharing across the network for mutual enrichment is crucial. The convening and mobilizing power of the commissioning core of the network (the hub behind which the partners, as network nodes, align) is critical.

At the heart of every successful *Network Exploiter* is a primary enterprise, which determines the composition of the network by sourcing valuable capability and functionality from different internal and external sub-organizations (think partner-enterprises, teams and even individuals). The primary commissioning enterprise is responsible for selecting network actors but also critically for establishing and nourishing the connections between the different elements of the network for superior connectivity. Connections may be permanent or temporary.

Consider the example of one of the world's most valuable companies, Amazon. Amazon's original '*big hairy audacious goal*' was to provide '*every book, ever printed, in any language, all available in less than 60 seconds*'.[cxliv] Today, that goal has expanded to include virtually every conceivable type of consumer product available via its platform. Its platform is only one portion of its business, however, and its current mission statement is to be '*Earth's most customer-centric company*'.[cxlv] Its customers also include major corporations who use its servers to manage the computing needs of their businesses, as well as third-party sellers that rely upon Amazon to manage sales and transaction fulfilment.[cxlvi] Increasingly, as a network hub, Amazon generates income by acting as a middleman in financial transactions between vendors and consumers operating in its ever-expanding network.

Within its ecosystem, the sale of books and media content directs consumers to its Prime Service, which puts it into direct competition with Netflix and other streaming services. Unlike Netflix, however, Amazon can leverage through its connectivity a wide variety of complementary products – including everything from merchandizing to clothing and food (as noted in Chapter 3, Amazon purchased Whole Foods Market Inc. in 2017) – to target specific segments of the consumer market. Its home assistant, Amazon Echo, connects us to a variety of partnering businesses to be able to offer enhanced functionality through one smart but standardized platform. Representing only a few examples, through Amazon's Echo, one can play music, order groceries, interact with home security or manage temperature controls.

Amazon also dominates the market in web services, in competition with the likes of Microsoft and IBM. The cloud computing capability it uses to run its own business is available to others for a fee, including competitors such as Netflix (Amazon Web Services supports Netflix streaming). Within its portfolio, Amazon's services are all highly complementary and designed to provide sufficient variety to align to all the diverse needs of customers, whether individuals, companies or governments. All this is made possible by exploiting information technology to develop superior organizational connectivity and organizational agility.

The network leverage capability trade-off:
There are downsides to the *Network Exploiter* approach. It is a highly complex organizational form to manage in practice. There are few examples of established organizations that have transformed to do it well, despite it being very de rigueur in the business press and on the conference circuit. Practically, it requires the commissioning core organization to devolve responsibility and control for performing work to individual components, including external partners, while retaining accountability for performance.[cxlvii]

Strong organizational governance is a must to avoid chaos, dysfunction and suboptimal performance. Yet, the organic shapeshifting nature of the *Network Exploiter* makes this an inherently difficult task to perform. Finally, the further an enterprise seeks to push from the bottom left of the SAF, the greater the inherent uncertainty in its planning and control of outcomes. The *Network Exploiter* organizational form is the most sophisticated (i.e. most capable) of all strategic approaches but also the hardest to manage and get right.

SECTION 5.5 REALIGNING ORGANIZATIONAL CAPABILITY, THE LEADERSHIP OPPORTUNITY

When applied practically, the SAF can help enterprise leaders to make sense of which organizational capabilities might be of greatest strategic value. It can also diagnose which organizational capabilities you possess in the enterprise currently, and all its sub-organizations, and which capabilities might be needed for the future (and associated organizational design priorities). These are essential considerations for effective strategic realignment.

Building on your thinking from the previous chapter, consider further for your enterprise:

1. Which organizational capability does your chosen business strategy require you to develop to align to customers' preferences and stand apart from competitors ideally?
   a. Is your requirement for efficient execution?
   b. Or customer agility?
   c. Or horizontal connectivity?
   d. Or network leverage?

For instance, to implement a synergy-based business strategy effectively, an enterprise needs to be distinctively capable of horizontal connectivity. Horizontal connectivity supports collaboration and the realization of 'cross-value' between complementary lines of business, such as the sharing of valuable customer insights, cross-fertilization of innovative practice, pooling of resources and the co-creation of new market offerings.

A blue-chip multinational telecommunications company I worked with recently is an excellent example of this. Like other telecoms companies, it experienced an explosion in bandwidth demand at the beginning of the Covid-19 global pandemic. The strategic requirement for organizational connectivity – to pool the combined technological and human resources of the company operating across all its geographies and markets – was vital to it being able to respond to a tenfold increase in capacity for its digital services.

Alternatively, if customer-centricity is the basis for competitive differentiation, an enterprise needs to be distinctively capable of customer agility, the configuring and reconfiguring of its offerings to match its customers' preferences as closely as possible.

Consider further:

2. As an enterprise, do you need to be distinctively capable at one thing only (i.e. one signature organizational capability that forms a core competence?) or multiple things simultaneously (i.e. do you need to develop multiple co-existing organizational capabilities within your enterprise?)?

3. What are you distinctively capable of organizationally at the current time (according to the SAF), and what might you need to realign organizationally?
   a. How can you become more stable if that is what is required?
   b. Or more agile?
   c. Or more autonomous?
   d. Or more connected?
4. Using the SAF, what is the gap between what your enterprise should be distinctively capable of ideally and what it is capable of currently? Are you set up for efficiency maximization when customer agility is a better fit for purpose? Or the opposite, perhaps?

Each of these questions represents a strategic choice, and enterprise leaders are responsible for the consequences. As noted previously, critical trade-offs need to be considered carefully when choosing which organizational capability to develop. For instance, organizations cannot be highly stable (for efficient execution) and agile (for customizability), or highly autonomous (for independence, simplicity, speed and focus) and connected (for synergies) at the same time. Leaders are forced to choose between these competing values because no organization can be equally capable of everything.

5. When realigning your organizational capability, how closely can you push to the edge of the SAF in whichever direction is most appropriate to be as far away as possible from a 3 score? Your chosen organizational capability becomes the definition of what 'good' looks like for your people and your customers. What would this look like in practice?
   a. What would good (or great) efficient execution look like in practice?
   b. Or customer agility?
   c. Or horizontal connectivity?
   d. Or network leverage?

Moreover, unless realigned on a regular basis, organizational capability can become a 'core rigidity' over time and frustrate future realignment efforts. The implication is that enterprise leaders must choose wisely which organizational capability (or capabilities in diversified businesses) to develop for the long term in line with the requirements of their business strategy.

6. Related to the next chapter – Organizational Architecture – what might you need to change about your enterprise's organizational culture, structure, processes and people to become organizationally capable in strategically advantageous ways? More on this later.

Your answers to these questions add to your developing vision of your future enterprise in practical terms. To illustrate the SAF in action to support a strategic realignment initiative, the next section describes a case study of an ambitious government sector enterprise, 'GovOrg'.

Realigning GovOrg

'We are winning every battle but losing the war,' the CEO of GovOrg, 'Graham', said flatly in our first meeting. Energetic and articulate, Graham came to GovOrg via a route of other public-sector organizations, where he had effected a dramatic performance improvement. He also had private sector experience, where he had worked for prestigious household-name technology firms. Graham elaborated:

> *Times have never been tougher for our citizens. Businesses are struggling. Infrastructure is lacking. As a public value organization, we hit every target set for us by policymakers and politicians, despite aggressive budget cuts imposed on us. However, our services are not making the difference needed to the lives of our people. To make a difference, we need to be different.*

Public value enterprise purpose

Founded in the late 19th century, GovOrg is a local government organization serving one of the most diverse regions of the UK in terms of wealth, ethnicity and educational attainment. Life expectancy within the region varies between different socio-economic groups by up to 18 per cent. It employs directly almost 10,000 people and has an annual budget of nearly £2 billion. It has a statutory responsibility to deliver a diverse range of public services to 1.5 million citizens and is accountable for its performance to central government and locally elected politicians.

It is considered one of the best-performing enterprises of its kind when benchmarked against peers elsewhere in the UK and internationally.

Its areas of public service responsibility range from environment, waste management and transportation to social care for vulnerable adults and children in the community. It is the front line for tackling some of the most acute social and economic cases of hardship within society while simultaneously maintaining the necessary material and social infrastructure for the overall public good of all its citizens.

It was in the context of its indispensable but increasingly complex public service role that Graham's new leadership team sought to rearticulate GovOrg's enterprise purpose. Ambitiously, they envisaged that GovOrg's *raison d'être* should be '*To help every citizen in the region to lead the best life they can*' (as reviewed in Chapter 3).

A Network Exploiter future?

To fulfil its renewed sense of enterprise purpose, GovOrg also sought to reformulate its business strategy to embrace 'place-based' principles. The new strategy called for a dual focus: the provision of (1) a portfolio of customizable public services aimed at the entire citizenry and (2) highly targeted interventions tacking economic and social hardship at the community level, such as inadequate housing and social isolation.

Beyond complying with statutory requirements simply (the sole stated goal for many other public sector enterprises), the new strategy reflected GovOrg's 'Open Government'[19] ambitions to deliver demand-led services to its key communities and to do so in innovative ways, despite the challenges of an austere funding environment.[cxlviii] In response to the expressed preferences of its citizen customers following extensive consultation and testing, the new strategy committed to offering an enhanced bundle of public services customizable at the point of delivery to the preferences and needs of individual communities and even individual citizens. More choice of public services, better value and customized (even personalized) – Graham was committing GovOrg to a radical realignment of its customer proposition and style of delivery.

[19]The Organisation for Economic Co-operation and Development (OECD) defines 'Open Government' as '*Strategies and initiatives … based on the principles of transparency, integrity, accountability and stakeholder participation*': www.oecd.org/gov/open-government/

The new business strategy called for a holistic, organizationally connected and agile approach to providing GovOrg's public service offerings. GovOrg's enterprise leaders envisaged that they would need to adopt a *Network Exploiter* strategic approach to implement the new strategy – one that emphasized connectivity between multiple different public service offerings and agility around individual customer needs. It was a far cry from the standardized, one-size-fits-all approach to public service provision of the past.

Network Exploiter organizational capability

Illustrated in Figure 5.2, every member of GovOrg's leadership team (its 15 most senior executives) and their direct reports participated in an enterprise-level mapping exercise using the SAF. The purpose was to analyze and prescribe the organizational capabilities required to implement their new business strategy. The consensus was that in the future, ideally, the majority of GovOrg's service lines (illustrated by the dark grey circles) would require relatively high levels of organizational agility and organizational connectivity to be capable of implementing the place-based strategy.

GovOrg's most senior leaders envisaged a highly networked future enterprise, with individual departments, divisions and functions collaborating to customize their services according to the needs of individual communities and 'citizen customers', as they are called. They envisaged further the extensive leveraging of the capabilities of a diverse network of partnering institutions (other public service bodies, e.g. police, health) and external enterprises to source innovation and deliver services. As one senior leader described it to me:

> *We used to be the professional and exclusive deliverer of public services directly to the public. In the future, we will be the professional commissioner of other professionals from the public, private and not for profit sectors delivering our services on our behalf better than we ever could by relying purely on our own resources.*

The GovOrg vision for the future was to continue to deliver services directly to the public (especially where required by statute, or in the case of critical social work, for example), but also to serve as a platform for offering a suite of customizable public services delivered via an ecosystem of external partnering enterprises from different sectors. Digital technology would feature large in enabling the new service proposition, as would collaborative and entrepreneurial core people competencies. Still, the success of GovOrg would be determined by how well it could connect its entire ecosystem and how agile it could be around the changing needs of its citizens.

GovOrg's business strategy, then, required a radical shift in thinking: from delivering supply-led services on an in-house basis to becoming capable of superior *network leverage* to implement a demand-led platform strategy exploiting the capabilities of hundreds of partners potentially.

The Efficiency Maximizer current state

Ambitions aside, Figure 5.2 also illustrates the state of GovOrg's organizational capability prior to initiating strategic realignment. The shared view of its executives was that GovOrg's service lines were characterized principally by high levels of organizational stability and organizational autonomy – the opposite of what was required by the new strategy.

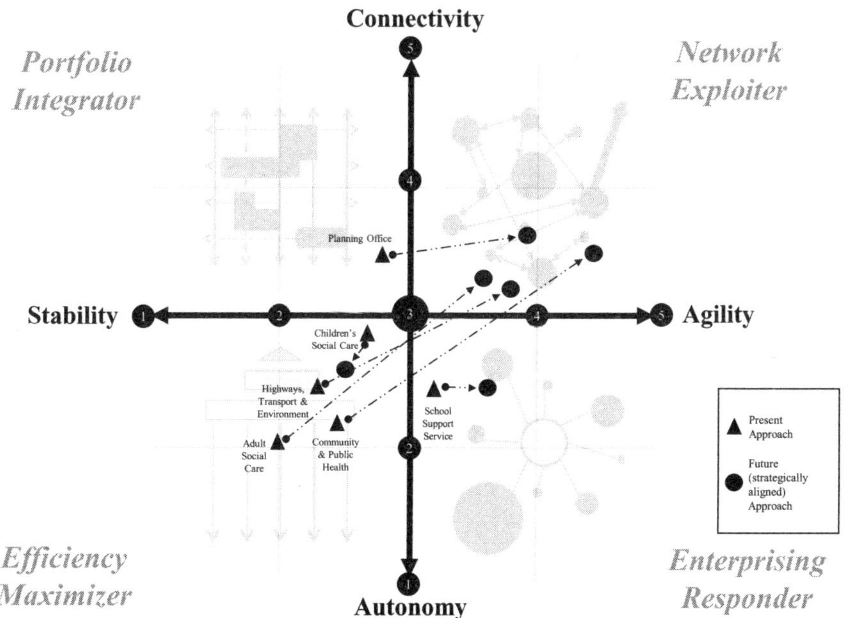

FIGURE 5.2 GovOrg's Network Exploiter future and Efficiency Maximizer present

Historically, GovOrg's strategic priority was to deliver standardized public services as efficiently and economically as possible to comply with public policy requirements and to operate within tight public funding constraints. In practice, this meant organizing to be highly internally focused, hierarchical, formally governed and vertically integrated. Individual services' lines operate autonomously of each other as their own separate sub-enterprises.

One widely accepted implication of how GovOrg was organized in the past was that it closed down creative, risk-taking and enterprising behaviour. *'We want our people to ask for forgiveness, not permission – but they are too afraid. Why?'* was a common sentiment from senior management. The reality was that GovOrg had simply not been organized for bottom-up initiative in the past. Its prevailing culture, structure, working processes and people were organized primarily to execute planned strategy, and not take risks or lead innovation. While an excellent employer, the day-to-day role of GovOrg's people was not to question why but to do and perform in line with the long-standing formal rules, procedures and customs.

Mind the gap

The results of the diagnostic exercise indicated that GovOrg was simply not capable organizationally of implementing its *Network Exploiter* place-based business strategy unless a change was made. In other words, its business strategy and organizational capability were misaligned. The longer it was unable to implement its chosen business strategy, the greater the chance was that it would fail to deliver value to the public in ways aligned to their needs and preferences as communities and individuals.

To be fit and capable of performing its purpose in the changing business environment (the business of government in this case), GovOrg needed to invest in developing capabilities around enhanced organizational connectivity and enhanced organizational agility for all of its service lines. Superior *network leverage* was an obvious prerequisite to implementing its chosen *Network Exploiter* strategic approach.

Realigning GovOrg to be future fit

The obvious follow-on question was *how* to develop the required organizational capabilities and implement its new and ambitious business strategy? The answer was to realign GovOrg's organizational architecture from an *Efficiency Maximizer* to a *Network Exploiter* and implement a raft of accompanying organizational changes.

First, the need was for its top talent to be better capable of leveraging a network of service innovators, including external delivery partners and suppliers to act on GovOrg's behalf. To do this, GovOrg invested in transforming its core people and their skills, behaviours and competencies via a dedicated Leadership Academy. Almost 500 of its senior and high-potential leaders embarked an in-depth educational programme to acquire the knowledge and skills to act as boundary-spanning network leaders.

Second, it embarked on a major culture-change programme to promote the behaviours required for enhanced collaboration (including externally), responsible entrepreneurship and the breaking down of service silos. Cross-functional collaboration had to become the 'new normal'.

Third, perhaps one of the most significant changes was to realign the GovOrg organizational structure from a formal hierarchy to an organic network design (at least for substantial parts of the enterprise). The restructure was intended to better support flexible and collaborative working internally between different business lines and externally between multiple partners.

Fourth and finally, it also sought to realign its core work processes to drive alignment against long-term and emergent objectives, not short-term efficiency-based measures focused on cost savings. These new measures attempted to reinforce exploratory ways of working, service innovation and collaboration.

All these changes represented a radical departure from the traditional model of the public sector bureaucratic hierarchy. Still, strategic realignment was essential at GovOrg if it was to stand a chance of fulfilling its enduring purpose in its increasingly dynamic and complex customer environment of the 21st-century state.

Organizational capability is vital to implement an enterprise's intended business strategy. But how do enterprise leaders develop strategically valuable organizational capability? This is the subject of the next chapter – Organizational Architecture.

6

ORGANIZATIONAL ARCHITECTURE

SECTION 6.1 NEITHER FISH NOR FOWL

'Jackson' was the CEO of 'Soft Co.'. He founded the company to be a disruptive influence in a software industry dominated by corporate giants. Soft Co. was small – a team of 60. It had been kept that way intentionally. *'Small is beautiful,'* Jackson told me, *'Especially if you want to maximize your people's creative output.'* The company was highly informal, with little to no hierarchy, processes or formal structure. Everything was a conversation, and developing relationships was the key to doing well.

There was a noticeable buzz around the trendy exposed-brick workspace in Amsterdam. It resembled a coffee shop more than an office. Creativity was the cornerstone of all hiring decisions, regardless of role. If someone had potential, they could rapidly progress to big responsibility. Attrition was high, as was absence. Stress was cited as the most significant reason, but team members were extremely hard-working and committed. The freedom the job offered was regularly cited as the best thing about working there.

Soft Co. had carved a niche for itself at the creative end of the software development market. It was capable of crafting bespoke and highly innovative solutions for corporate clients. It won many industry awards in the process. And yet, beyond a spurt in its first five years, the firm hadn't grown much. Every day was a scramble for new business. Profitability was down and falling. New business wins were becoming bigger but less frequent. It was hit or miss, with not much in between. It was unsustainable.

It was the hand-to-mouth grind that led Jackson to consider an offer from a large and established industry player, 'Digi Corp.'. Jackson had hoped that the parent company's support, networks and investment would supercharge growth. Naively perhaps, he assumed he would continue to enjoy the same autonomy as before – preserving *his* company's sacred freedom to operate on its own terms. From the start, Digi Corp. had a particular way of working that was completely different.

Where Soft Co. was flat, Digi Corp. was formally defined around elaborate hierarchies of supervision. It had a high division of labour and rigid structures for its essential functions (e.g. developers, sales). Where Soft Co. was input-driven, measuring the value of client work by the quality of resources assigned to it, Digi Corp. emphasized measurable performance outputs. It focused on cost management and efficiency with clear consequences for poor performance. Soft Co.'s culture was high-energy and built around adaptable and greatly empowered individuals. In comparison, Digi Corp.'s big company culture emphasized top-down decision accountability, rule following and enforcement of impersonal corporate standards. More and more, the two worlds collided. Inevitably perhaps, Digi Corp. demanded expanded oversight over Soft Co.'s management, especially as Soft Co.'s performance continued to decline.

Fast-forward a couple of years, and Soft Co. resembled a thick soup of conflicting cultures, structures, processes and people priorities. It was neither *'fish nor fowl'* – neither one thing nor the other. It was neither the best of Soft Co. nor the best of Digi Corp. Structurally, it wasn't an efficient hierarchy, and it wasn't flat and agile. Its organizational culture was less empowering than before – there were strict processes to follow, but it wasn't any more efficient. Things that had been overly informal were now excessively formal, and vice versa.

Contrary to Jackson's hopes, the decision to sell to Digi Corp. had made his life even harder. It had introduced unwelcome disequilibrium into Soft Co.'s organizational system. It was no longer obvious what differentiated it from its traditional competitors. There were also new and non-traditional competitors constantly emerging from unexpected quarters. Increasingly, Digi Corp. executives talked about the acquisition as *'One to chalk up to experience'* and *'Do better next time'*. For Jackson, of course, it was far more personal. The zing had gone. His people's entrepreneurial spirit, the source of Soft Co.'s strength, was flattened. It was cancelled out by the increasingly formal and rule-bound structure and culture imposed by Digi Corp. At least, that's how he saw it.

Truth be told, and way before Digi Corp., Jackson's long-term challenge was that he had failed to think strategically about how to organize Soft Co. as it transitioned from a start-up to a growing company. There was little clarity or forethought about critical skills or the ideal organizational structure to enable his people's best work. There was no real thought about what might be considered strategically desirable behaviour to be embodied in the organizational culture. Or which work processes would create alignment behind what was essential to the performance of the business.

Soft Co. was in genuine danger of losing sight of what differentiated it from its competitors (its organizational capability) and the source of its distinctive capability – its *organizational architecture*. Jackson's opportunity was to lead realignment and be the architect of how Soft Co. should organize in future – to define what 'good' should look like and guide his people towards it. The first step was to envision the ideal form of Soft Co.'s core organizational culture, structure, processes and people. The second was to have the courage to commit to the vision and make it a reality.

SECTION 6.2 ORGANIZATIONAL ARCHITECTURE

'Culture eats strategy for breakfast' is the business mantra attributed popularly to the 'father of modern management', Peter Drucker. Among its many interpretations, one standout message resonates strongly with a strategic alignment perspective. This is that the implementation of the best strategy in the world can be derailed by the absence of a supportive (for which read 'aligned') organizational culture.

To secure a competitive edge, enterprises must ensure their organizational culture aligns with what is important strategically. Otherwise, they risk operating within the constraints of the values, beliefs and behaviours their misaligned organizational culture imposes. This is one of the critical challenges facing Soft Co. It is a story that perhaps resonates with many serving senior executives, people managers and employees alike. Organizational culture is one of the hardest aspects of an enterprise to realign.

The noted management author Edgar Schein differentiated between three levels of organizational culture: (1) artefacts (think logos, office layout); (2) espoused values (think values statements); (3) more deeply, basic underlying assumptions (implicit beliefs and assumptions that exert unconscious influence on our behaviour and actions).[cxlix] The last category is the most resistant to change.[(ibid)] They are persistent, and any attempt to change them might simply reproduce them unconsciously.

The implication is that how leaders envision their enterprise's realignment is, perhaps, itself contingent upon the prevailing culture. That strategy is an extension of culture and not subordinate to it is another important interpretation of the Peter Drucker quote. Crisis events, such as the Covid-19 global pandemic, have the potential to jolt us to a new level of awareness and provoke us to choose to do something different from what we might have chosen otherwise. When describing this phenomenon to my students, I use the example of the blue pill and the red pill scene in the blockbuster movie, *The Matrix*.[20]

Like the movie's protagonist, Neo, it is often the case that we can only exercise conscious choice when the illusion of our taken-for-granted status quo is shattered by external disruption; in other words, a reality check. The choice then is either to maintain the status quo or to realign it to some new form. Disruption is simultaneously a leadership challenge and an opportunity, therefore. In adversity, there resides the potential for advantage if we make good choices when prompted. This has been a key theme of the book, and none more so than at this point in our strategic realignment blueprint – *organizational architecture*. It is where the rubber hits the proverbial road, and realignment takes on real-world consequences for an enterprise and its people.

Organizational culture is just one component of what makes an enterprise capable of implementing its chosen strategy. All enterprises are made up organizationally of the same common components – human capital (people), physical capital (property), organizational capital (structures and processes) and a variety of other basic features.[cl] What really gives an enterprise a competitive edge is the special attention paid to the selection, development and mobilization of its *core organizational components* – complementary varieties of people, organizational structure,

[20] Wikipedia helpfully summarizes the scene as the *'Choice between the willingness to learn a potentially unsettling or life-changing truth, by taking the red pill, or remaining in contented ignorance with the blue pill. The terms refer to a scene in the 1999 film* The Matrix.' (www.wikipedia.org/wiki/Red_pill_and_blue_pill)

organizational culture and work processes.[ii] Together, these support the development of strategically valuable organizational capability.[cli]

Otherwise well-run companies struggle to compete, for example, because they don't have the depth of talent to differentiate themselves from their competitors. Or perhaps because they lack the organizational culture necessary to elicit strategically desirable behaviours, such as entrepreneurial initiative, from their people. Or maybe because those same people find their initiative stifled by their enterprise's rigid organizational structure. What matters for performance is how well an enterprise's core organizational components complement each other and support how it is trying to differentiate itself from its competitors in customers' eyes.[clii]

The requirements placed upon an enterprise's organizational architecture (you might also say design) vary from enterprise to enterprise, depending upon its strategic approach. For instance, the people characteristics associated with efficient execution differ considerably from those associated with superior customer agility. The strategic alignment challenge for enterprise leaders is to select, develop and mobilize the appropriate variety of each of the four core organizational components and to combine them in complementary ways to develop strategically valuable organizational capabilities.[ii]

Such considerations and design choices are extremely challenging – both conceptually and practically. Conceptually, realigning an enterprise's organizational architecture is very complex, and the consequences of choosing poorly are grave. Practically, leaders can encounter huge resistance when seeking to implement organizational change. As noted in Chapter 2, most change programmes fail to deliver for these very reasons.[cliii] However, it is also an opportunity for leaders to leave a long-lasting and meaningful footprint on the enterprises they lead. Perhaps the opportunity is best described by revered architect and polymath Buckminster Fuller:

> *You never change things by fighting the existing reality. To change something, build a new model that makes the existing model obsolete.*

Yours is the opportunity to be the architect of your enterprise's future success and build a new model of how it should be organized. The process for realigning the organizational architecture is the fourth and penultimate link in the enterprise value chain.

What is organizational architecture?

Organizational architecture is the engine of every enterprise and the source of what makes it distinctively capable and effective in several critical ways.[cliv] First, all enterprises are made up of the same essential organizational ingredients in the form of different types of 'capital', all of which are necessary to function well.[clv] These represent the organizational 'form' of an enterprise and include:

- the aggregated skills, behaviours and knowledge that reside within an enterprise's people (human resources or capital);
- the value of networks and relationships through which people connect and co-operate formally or informally (social capital);
- formalized structures, systems, processes and organizational cultures (organizational capital);
- physical assets such as real estate, machinery and facilities (physical capital);
- the value of technologies, whether information or production related (technological capital).[cxlviii]

Second, possessing rare, unique or inimitable core organizational components (e.g. a unique set of people capabilities) permits an enterprise to pursue a differentiated market strategy that competitors cannot easily emulate.[clvi] This is the foundational principle behind a strategic approach to organizational design. This can be a focus on people (human capital), values and behaviours (culture), relationships and networks (network leadership), information and knowledge (knowledge), technology (information) or any other variety of basic organization.

Despite its manifest importance, the subject of organizational design is neglected shamefully in management theory and practice. A search on Google for the term 'organizational design' returns a miserly 47.7 million results when compared to a whopping 3.3 billion results for the term 'business strategy'.[21] For relative comparison, a search for the term 'Kim Kardashian' – a television celebrity popular at the time of writing – returns a mere 273 million results! In terms of published

[21] All figures are rounded-up values and correct at the time of writing.

works, a search of books on Amazon.com returns the maximum limit of 60,000 results for 'strategy' and only 2,000 results for 'organizational design' (and only 865 if spelled with a British s).

From a strategic alignment perspective, an enterprise's organizational architecture is as critical as any other link in the enterprise value chain and deserves renewed attention as a matter of strategic importance.

A focus on core organizational components

Organizational architecture, as it is conceived here, focuses on four core organizational components, which, when selected, developed and mobilized together, are what gives an enterprise a competitive edge. These components are the enterprise's *core people*, its *core organizational structure*, its *core organizational culture* and its *core work processes*.[ii] Each is defined as follows:

1. *Core people*: Defined as the ideal characteristics of the human capital (regardless of whether they are employees, contractors or partners) upon which the enterprise relies to perform the work that differentiates it from its competitors. Core people characteristics can include strategically valuable competencies, behaviours, knowledge and effort of both individuals and groups.[(ibid)] These characteristics can be developed in line with shifting strategic and organizational priorities through targeted development.[clvii] Seniority is not a factor determining which roles (or people) are considered core to an enterprise's competitiveness. As a core organizational component, *core people* is concerned with the characteristics of any role, and the individuals that occupy them, which are vital to the successful implementation of the enterprise's business strategy.[clviii]
2. *Core organizational structure*: Defined as the characteristics of the organizational structure that ideally enables an enterprise's core people to perform their best work. This can be through efficient co-ordination or self-directed collaboration, for example. Characteristics of an enabling organizational structure can include the degree of hierarchy (i.e. rigid supervision versus delegation of authority) and management prescription (i.e. reliance upon

defined and non-negotiable rules to inform work or more subjective guides to behaviour, such as values). It can include verticalization (i.e. the structural division of different lines of business) and agility (i.e. how fixed or adaptable organizational structures are required to be to enable the enterprise to keep pace with change in the operating environment).

3. *Core organizational culture*: Defined as the strategically desirable values, beliefs and behaviours that influence how the enterprise's core people (and wider population potentially) act when performing their role.[clix] In contrast to organizational structure, organizational culture is largely intangible. Still, it can be explicit in the form of espoused values (value statements, for example) or implicit in the form of basic underlying assumptions that are tricky to realign but exert a powerful influence on the actions of the enterprise's people.[clx]
4. *Core work processes*: Defined as the designated processes, activities, tasks, measures and workflows that are critical to how the enterprise's core people perform their work.[ii] These include formal objectives, the performance period, workflows and standards, social routines, customs and practice. These features define the aims, priorities and intensity of how individuals and groups act together to perform the enterprise's purpose as effectively as possible.

Two points are worth noting. First, the organizational architecture is a selective focus only on those core organizational components that offer the greatest potential for competitive differentiation. Additional organizational components that could be considered include different varieties of physical resources (e.g. office buildings, workspaces, equipment and machinery) or technological resources (e.g. information systems and robotics performing work). However, both these and other non-core organizational resources are set to one side because they are relatively easily acquired or emulated by competitors. However, rapid advancement in new technologies is changing this equation. For instance, artificial intelligence may soon become an indispensable core organizational resource within an enterprise's organizational architecture, alongside or even instead of people.

Second, the organizational architecture is not concerned with the selection, development and mobilization of *all* of an enterprise's people, but only those who are core to its capability to differentiate itself from its competitors. In other words, the organizational architecture is focused solely on those people, structures, cultures and processes that together give their enterprise a competitive edge. It is not about those who simply sustain business as usual, as important as they may be in that regard.

SECTION 6.3 ALIGNING ORGANIZATIONAL ARCHITECTURE, THE LEADERSHIP CHALLENGE

The ideal form of an enterprise's organizational architecture *depends* (surprise, surprise) upon the type of competitive edge it needs to win customers and beat rivals (i.e. its chosen business strategy and its organizational capability requirements).[ii] When enterprises like Soft Co. fail to choose the appropriate variety of each core organizational component or fail to combine them in complementary ways, the result is a poorly aligned or even misaligned organizational architecture. It either does not support the development of strategically valuable organizational capabilities or frustrates the process entirely. The consequences of misalignment include lack of competitive differentiation, hampered growth, poor customer satisfaction, poorly engaged employees, missed business opportunities and financial wastage.

At this stage in the enterprise value chain, the strategic alignment challenge for enterprise leaders is twofold. First, to select the ideal variety of each strategically important core organizational component. Second, to ensure all components are complementary to form one coherent and strategically aligned organizational architecture, which supports ideally the development of strategically valuable organizational capability. These two enterprise leadership priorities can be expressed in terms of *organizational architecture variety* and *organizational architecture complementarity*.

Organizational architecture variety

From a wide array of options, enterprise leaders must first choose the appropriate variety of each core organizational component that best supports the development of strategically valuable organizational capability.[clxi] Consider again the example of aerospace company

Rolls-Royce (reviewed in Chapter 4). Its extreme high-precision manufacture of the world's most advanced aircraft engines serves as an excellent example of this crucial principle at work. A key challenge for the company in recent years has been the attraction, retention and development of local engineering talent to support global growth and policy of locating the manufacture and servicing of its products (think turbines) close to its customers (think airlines). To service the high-growth Asian airline market, the company set up a new advanced manufacturing facility in Singapore at the cost of $565 million.[xiii] The expansion required Rolls-Royce to recruit 450 engineering and technical staff to produce parts for some of the most innovative aircraft in the market, such as the newly introduced Airbus A350.[(ibid)]

Competing successfully in the aerospace sector requires manufacturing products to the highest of standards. Unlike its home-based engineering workforce in Derby, UK, many of whom have decades of experience manufacturing its highly technically sophisticated products, local engineering talent had no such benefit of experience. Rolls-Royce took the innovative approach of deconstructing its standard manufacturing process into smaller and simpler routines. Deconstruction and simplification made it easier for new staff to learn the manufacturing process. By encouraging high levels of task specialization, Rolls-Royce developed its local engineering staff more quickly to the required level of technical ability to meet volume targets and required quality standards.[(ibid)] Task simplification, routinization and singular focus have become essential *Efficiency Maximizer* characteristics for engineering staff in its Asian operations, even if the wider enterprise is embracing a *Network Exploiter* approach to market competitiveness.

Consider for your own enterprise which variety of each of the following core organizational components supports your chosen strategic approach ideally:

- *Core people*: Which type of people are core to your ability to differentiate your offering(s) to the market in line with your chosen business strategy? For instance, enterprises seeking to compete based on innovation value most highly characteristics such as individual creativity, a long-term performance focus and a willingness to take risks.[clxii] In contrast, firms pursuing a competitive strategy based upon efficiency and cost containment are likely to value employee cost-consciousness, error-reducing behaviour and work intensity.[clxiii] Which roles, occupations, individuals or groups within your extended workforce (including those within outsourced operations or partner human resources) are most strategically important to you? What are their ideal characteristics in terms of skills and behaviour? And why?

- *Core organizational structure*: Which variety of organizational structure best enables your core people to perform their strategically important work? There are many different varieties of structure, each suited to the pursuit of a range of different competitive strategies and the organizational capabilities required to implement them successfully. Organizational structures can be hierarchical or flat; tangible or intangible; impermeable or porous; centralized or decentralized; vertically integrated or horizontally integrated; stable or flexible.[clii] Each different attribute supports a different way of working and produces different organizational outcomes. For example, hierarchical supervision, divisions of labour, procedures and the enforcement of rules are associated with operational efficiency. Adaptability, informality and little hierarchy (or management compression, as it is sometimes called) are associated more with employee empowerment and innovation capability.
- *Core organizational culture*: Which variety of organizational culture is most likely to influence your people to behave in a strategically desirable way? Influential management literature highlights the importance of developing a 'strong' organizational culture – one where there is widespread commitment to the values and beliefs that are important to the organization.[clxiv] An enterprise's core organizational culture can embody these values and influence employees to behave in a way that is consistent with them. For example, an organization's culture can be open to outside influences or remarkably self-contained. Organizational culture can also emphasize individual effort or collective enterprise-wide interests. It can influence the degree

to which risk-taking is embraced or something to be avoided. All characteristics are valuable but to different degrees on an enterprise-by-enterprise basis according to its organizational capability requirements.

- *Core work processes*: Which variety of work processes are critical to aligning your core people's work to what is most important to the enterprise in performance terms? Objectives, for instance, can be programmed well in advance of the performing of work, in circumstances where we know what 'good' looks like in objective terms, or they can evolve, especially in conditions of high uncertainty. The direction given to people determines their focus, as does the time period. Do you emphasize planning and performance over the near term or the longer term? Are workflows highly defined in advance or left open to evolve and benefit from prior experience? Are measures of performance output-based in the form of hard metrics (such as the number of unit sales or the financial value of the new business), or input-based (such as the skills required)?

The answer to any of these questions should be, of course, *it depends* (don't groan). The ideal variety of each core organizational component depends principally upon the enterprise's organizational capability requirements.[ii] The value of an enterprise's core organizational components – its people, for example – is determined by the degree to which they support the development of strategically valuable organizational capabilities, e.g. efficient execution in the case of the *Efficiency Maximizer* or horizontal connectivity in the case of the *Portfolio Integrator*.[(ibid)]

The danger is that, frequently, enterprise leaders fail to exercise strategic choice over their core organizational components, as in the case of Soft Co., or they apply the outcomes of their choices inappropriately. For example, different lines of business within the same company may each require a different organizational architecture according to their different strategic requirements. Applying a one-size-fits-all approach to selecting, developing and mobilizing organizational components in different business operations (within a multi-divisional company, for example) is a sure-fire way of creating misalignment and destroying value.

Equally, not refreshing core organizational components creates the potential for misalignment. Enterprise leaders should regularly review their organizational architecture to ensure it remains fit for purpose in the context of changing strategic requirements. In the absence of a regular review, an enterprise's organizational capabilities can become 'core rigidities', which limit competitiveness over time (as noted in Chapter 4).[clxv]

Which organizational outcomes are the centrepiece of your business strategy, and which combination of different varieties of core people, structure, culture and processes are best fit for purpose? Your answer defines the form, function and value of your enterprise's organizational architecture.

Organizational architecture complementarity

As noted in the introduction of this section, strategically valuable organizational capability cannot be developed from any one core organizational component alone, no matter how rare, unique or inimitable it might be. For example, the oft-repeated mantra *'People are our most important asset'* may be true for some enterprises, but in reality, an enterprise's people – no matter how talented – cannot alone propel it to success on a sustainable basis. What really matters is how all four core organizational components combine to form an organizational architecture that supports the development of organizational capabilities that give the enterprise a competitive edge.[clxvi]

Investments in selecting, developing and mobilizing an enterprise's core people must be supported by complementary investments in the other three core organizational components, such as core organizational structures that enable effective co-ordination and collaboration with other individuals and groups. Additionally, investments in fostering complementary core organizational cultures, which guide strategically desirable behaviour, should be aligned to support core work processes, which in turn support an enterprise's core people to perform their work as productively as possible. If any one of these four core organizational components is in conflict with the others, the organizational architecture overall is likely to be a poor fit for purpose.

Misalignment of one or more core organizational components introduces harmful friction into the engine room of the enterprise.

For example, attempts to generate a culture of inter-departmental collaboration to support product and service synergies will fail utterly if the enterprise's rigid organizational structure frustrates any attempts by its people to connect with those outside of their individual line of business or function. Similarly, elaborate work processes designed to promote efficient working will be rendered useless if those performing the work – the enterprise's people – are not capable of complying with rules or procedures. An enterprise's core organizational components in the form of its people, culture, structure and processes need to be designed to work in finely tuned synchronicity – as beautifully ordered as the instruments of any symphonic orchestra – if they are to be effective.

Consider the example of Oracle Corporation (Oracle). Developing internal network connections is a critical knowledge management activity at Oracle and a source of its competitive advantage. Historically, it pursued aggressive expansion in the enterprise software and 'on-premises' data processing and storage market. In a major realignment of its business in the early 2000s to keep pace with rivals, including the other global market leader SAP, Oracle introduced additional enterprise software solutions to complement its core database business, including bespoke applications and consulting services.[clxvii] To successfully monetize this new portfolio of client propositions required a significant investment in horizontal connectivity between different lines of business within the company internationally.[clxviii]

One such mechanism intended to support close collaboration and global connectivity is the Oracle Community of Practice (COP). COPs are staff networking forums that complement the formal organizational structure. They provide a means of sharing essential customers insights, exchanging technical knowledge, brainstorming potential innovations and achieving common educational and developmental outcomes between what would otherwise be separated lines of business.[(ibid)] COPs support the creation, transfer and integration of new knowledge on an enterprise-wide basis, cross-cutting different lines of business and geographies in the global company.

As described by an Oracle executive, COPs enable Oracle to '*Become a more efficient and effective organization by using knowledge management concepts, processes and tools*.'[clxix] More specifically, the benefits of COPs are described as building required knowledge where it is needed in the business; developing skills; transferring professional know-how; driving innovation; enabling community problem solving; and sustaining a positive organizational climate.[(ibid)]

COPs, then, facilitate the creation of valuable knowledge 'flows' and knowledge 'stocks', i.e. through enterprise-wide knowledge management mechanisms like COPs, knowledge flows to where it is required organizationally and enhances the overall stock of unique knowledge within the company.[clxx] Staff self-nominate on a 'pick and choose' basis where to devote their time between various projects and initiatives.[clxxi] COPs also foster a sense of a company-wide culture – a strong set of Oracle beliefs, values and behaviours. Senior leaders regularly participate in COP activities and reward noteworthy contributions and performance.[(ibid)]

A COP is an example of a mechanism by which to integrate the different elements of the company's organizational architecture to produce value that is difficult for competitors to acquire or emulate. These different core organizational components – people, culture, structure and processes – work in harmony to create strategically valuable organizational outcomes in the form of service innovation at Oracle.

Considered thus, and illustrated in Figure 6.1, the whole of an enterprise's organizational architecture is more valuable than the sum of its individual components when they are selected, developed and mobilized to be complementary.

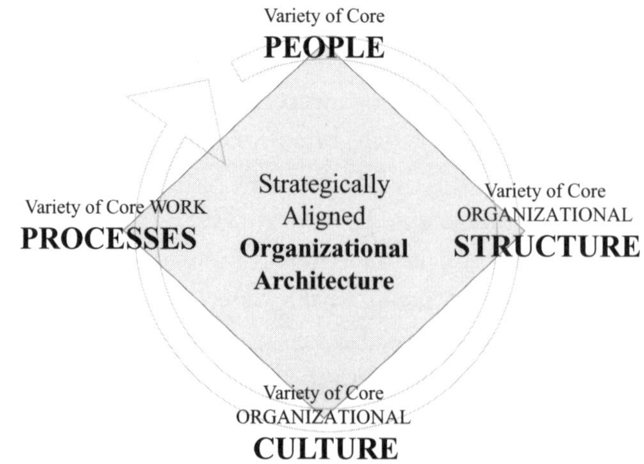

FIGURE 6.1 The organizational architecture

Consider for your own enterprise: how well do your individual core organizational components complement each other to form one coherent and strategically aligned organizational architecture? Specifically:

- How well does your organizational structure support your core people (the talents that are most essential to the implementation of your strategic approach) to co-ordinate their activities, either stably or flexibly, and collaborate where desirable?
- How well does your organizational culture influence your core people (and more widely if necessary) to behave in a way that is most strategically advantageous, whether focused on efficient execution or exploratory innovation, for example?
- How well do your work processes support the type of work that is strategically important to the enterprise, either over the near term or the longer term and in ways that are either known in advance or evolving, for example?

And:

- Which individual core organizational components – either your people, structure, culture and/or work processes – might you need to realign to ensure all of your core organizational components are complementary and strategically aligned?

As simple as baking a cake?

To summarize the strategic alignment challenge in practical terms, consider the metaphor of baking a cake. One must first choose the type of cake one is trying to prepare. Is it a chocolate cake or a fruit cake? Both are equally delicious but in different ways. They each require different ingredients used in different proportions in their preparation if they are to turn out well. This is analogous to our organizational capability requirement. What type of organizational architecture are we trying to build to implement our market-winning business strategy? What does our enterprise need to be capable of?

Back to the cake. Both chocolate cake and fruit cakes are baked using the same essential ingredients of flour, eggs, sugar, butter and so on. However, there are many different varieties of each of these essential baking ingredients. The different varieties of sugar include granulated sugar, caster sugar, pearl sugar and demerara sugar, to name but a few. Choose the wrong variety of sugar, or flour, or any other of the essential ingredients from which the chosen cake is made, and it will likely end up a flop. When thinking about your enterprise, which people characteristics are core to your strategy? Which organizational structure will enable your core people's best performance? Which organizational culture is most likely to produce strategically desirable behaviour? Which work processes drive critical performance?

Bakers, whether amateur or professional, must exercise careful forethought and deliberate planning to ensure they have assembled the necessary ingredients to a high level of specification. They need to understand the process by which the ingredients combine to produce what is expected in the form of the intended variety of cake. It is no different for enterprise leaders – they must exercise careful forethought about the type of organizational capability they are seeking to develop (that of either the *Efficiency Maximizer*, *Enterprising Responder*, *Portfolio Integrator* or *Network Exploiter*, to use the concepts of Chapters 4 and 5) and design their organizational architecture accordingly, by selecting, developing and mobilizing appropriate varieties of each core organizational component.

Not as simple as baking a cake

Where the metaphor with baking cake falls down is that, unless we are experimenting in the kitchen, we know precisely in advance of baking a cake what the required ingredients are and the proportions in which they should be used. Thanks to helpful recipes and cookbooks, we know beforehand what a good cake should look like (complete with attractive pictures) and how precisely it should be made. The result of a baker's efforts should be predictable, assuming the baker has the requisite level of skill and follows instructions faithfully.

If only leading a complex and dynamic enterprise were so easy. In the turbulent and complex reality of 21st-century business, enterprise leaders rarely always know in advance what 'good' looks like strategically or organizationally. Nor are there readily available instructions for them to follow. In my consultancy and executive education work, I have observed that enterprise leaders often do not know what to do or how to think about the organizational design of their enterprise. The danger is that they look to influential external examples of perceived best practices and seek to emulate their success by importing those same practices on the false presumption of a similar beneficial effect in their own enterprise. This is a phenomenon organizational theorists refer to as 'mimetic isomorphism'.[clxxii] It can lead enterprises to adopt practices that are a poor fit for their circumstances and create damaging misalignment.

Choosing the appropriate variety and combination of all an enterprise's organizational components – especially its core components – should be the bread and butter of boards and corporate functions, such as information technology, finance, operations, human resources, real estate and facilities management. However, these functions often operate independently of each other. Consequently, the organizational components over which they exercise stewardship may align poorly either to the business need overall or to the priorities of other functions (more on this in the next chapter).

Regardless of role or remit, enterprise leaders need a framework to collectively determine the ideal variety of each of their enterprise's core organizational components and combine them to form an organizational architecture that is fit for purpose and gives the enterprise a competitive edge.

SECTION 6.4 THE STRATEGIC ALIGNMENT FRAMEWORK, ORGANIZATIONAL ARCHITECTURE

The SAF helps leaders at this stage of the enterprise value chain identify four distinct forms of organizational architecture. Each supports the development of different organizational capabilities. The complementary varieties of each of the four core organizational

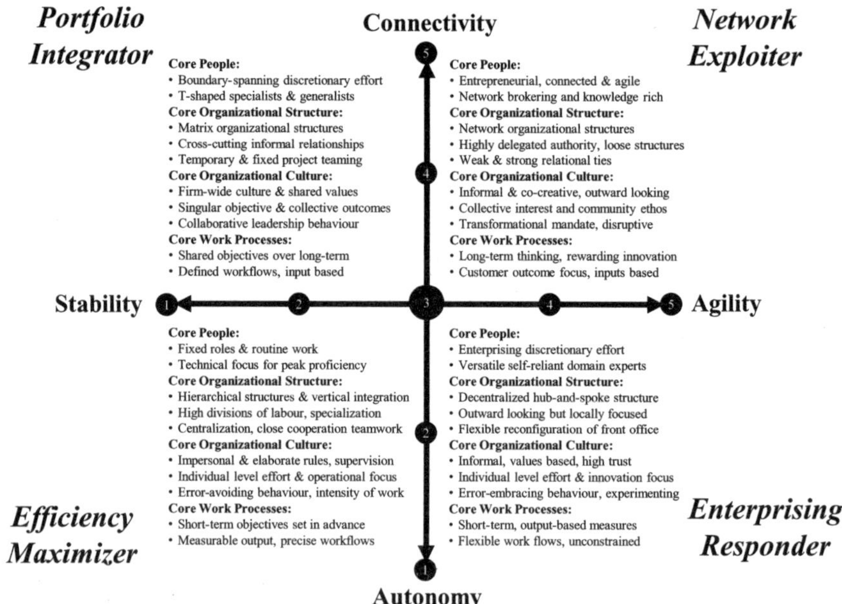

FIGURE 6.2 The Strategic Alignment Framework; organizational architecture

components that make up these distinctive organizational architectures are described according to the strategic approach they support best (illustrated in Figure 6.2).[22]

[22]A note on methodology. The organizational architecture characteristics described in this section are derived from primary action research. This included principally:

a) A comprehensive review of literature permitted the synthesis of core people, core organizational structure, core organizational culture and core work process characteristics.
b) A series of related diagnostic scales were developed to 'map' the current and ideal state of an enterprise's organizational architecture through desktop research, executive interviews and opinion surveys.
c) A pilot enterprise was selected for mapping. The prototype characteristics were used to diagnose its current state and ideal future state organizational architecture. Refinements were made to both characteristics and scales over the course of the engagement.

In addition to validating the characteristics and scales (following refinement), the findings permitted personnel within the pilot company to make better evidence-based decisions at the corporate function level. It informed realignment initiatives by helping to identify gaps between (a) how they were organized and (b) how they should have been organized ideally. The characteristics and scales were then applied to a variety of additional enterprise settings in multiple sectors. I am grateful to Dr Barry Varcoe for his collaborative input. Some of the organizational architecture characteristics described in Section 6.4 are derived from our collaboration and jointly authored unpublished works.

Which strategic approach resonated with you most when considering your business strategy and organizational capability in Chapters 4 and 5, respectively? Accordingly, which organizational architecture is the best fit to support your strategic approach and give you a competitive edge in the market(s) in which you are competing?

The Efficiency Maximizer organizational architecture

Efficiency Maximizers succeed by efficiently exploiting scalable market opportunities. Their market competitiveness is a function of their ability to execute their intended strategies more efficiently than competitors. What gives *Efficiency Maximizers* a competitive edge are the following organizational architecture characteristics:

- *Core people*: An *Efficiency Maximizer*'s core people are central to the efficient execution of the enterprise's intended business strategy. They enable it to operate at scale in the often highly commoditized markets in which it is competing for customers. Core people occupy fixed posts typically, whether supervisory or performative, to facilitate mastery of applied skills and a narrow focus on the specific competencies required for role proficiency. People development is geared towards knowing new tactics or techniques to enable continuous improvement and peak operational efficiency. Routine performance against known standards is the name of the game for *Efficiency Maximizers*. Tight supervision, adherence to formalized procedures and intensity of work are the hallmarks of core people characteristics. Indeed, the management of the *Efficiency Maximizer*'s core people resembles the features of its products – simple, standardized, separated (i.e. working alongside, but not necessarily dependent upon the discretionary collaboration of others) and, crucially, efficient.
- *Core organizational structure*: At the enterprise level, the core organizational structure of the *Efficiency Maximizer* is typically that of a vertically integrated hierarchy. There is a high level of division of labour across the enterprise, manifest in the arrangement of separate verticals representing specialized

divisions, functions, business units (e.g. individual lines of business) and teams. The organizational structure is also typically top-down in terms of the distribution of authority, with an enterprise's most senior managers enjoying the most influence over strategic planning and work co-ordination. The organizational structure ensures effective co-ordination through close supervision, with integration only occurring at the senior management level. Structurally, *Efficiency Maximizers* primarily rely on their internal resources, and there is a discernible boundary between the internal and external environment. At the team level, *Efficiency Maximizers* emphasize close co-operation teamwork (e.g. within a designated unit, such as a restaurant or a factory) and not between units – something that would be more common to a *Portfolio Integrator*.

- *Core organizational culture*: The *Efficiency Maximizer*'s core organizational culture is inward facing by design. Work is geared around the enterprise's inner mechanics and operations to ensure the efficient execution of the intended strategy. Culturally, the climate is tightly regulated to ensure conformity against desired standards. The focus of employee effort is typically centred around the individual, albeit en masse. Individuals are highly incentivized to perform their work as intensively as possible. There are clear benchmarks for what constitutes good performance established by relative comparison to colleagues. Routinization and formalization of ways of working are intended to discourage variation from established norms. Rules are elaborate, and conformity is expected.
- *Core work processes*: Core work processes typically incorporate objectives set well in advance of the work itself and prescribed across large numbers of employees tasked with performance against fixed standards. The planning period is usually near term and focused on the maximal exploitation of known opportunities. Ways of working are carefully designed, something akin to the Taylorist approach to scientific management – every step, action and duration of task completion is measured, refined and then prescribed

> as the standard against which individual performance is assessed. Therefore, ways of working are highly defined, and the outputs of individuals' efforts are carefully measured to ensure the required levels of work intensity and productivity. Core work processes are essential to the efficient execution of intended strategy within *Efficiency Maximizers*. They reduce deviation from established norms and standards and enable the maximization of economies of scale.

Japan Rail provides an excellent example of the *Efficiency Maximizer* organizational architecture. Japan is home to one of the world's most complicated but high-performing rail systems, moving an estimated 12 billion passengers per year. In the last 10 years, the annual average delay was 0.9 minutes per operational train, including delays due to uncontrollable causes (e.g. natural disasters).[clxxiii] For its high-speed Shinkansen (bullet train) service between Tokyo and Osaka, which runs 19 trains per hour over 560km (348 miles), the figure is an astonishing 0.4 minutes per train.[clxxiv] By comparison, figures comparing the punctuality of subway services between Tokyo and London are stark. The percentage of days when the Tokyo Metro Ginza Line was delayed by more than 10 minutes was 6 per cent in 2017. The equivalent figure for London's Central Line was 68 per cent (and that was for delays of more than 15 minutes).[clxxv]

A wide variety of factors are responsible for Japan Rail's enviable track record (pun intended!). Core work processes supporting the efficient execution of its highly elaborate timetable are critical. One such core work process that is common to all of Japan's rail-operating companies is the practice of 'pointing and calling' (P&C), or *shisa kanko*. It is immediately observable in the behaviour of train conductors, drivers and station staff for anyone riding the rails in Japan. P&C requires staff to express the completion of a task, such as checking a signal or speed gauge, with a physical movement (pointing typically, although saluting co-workers is also common) and calling out, even if alone, to *'Raise the consciousness levels of workers'* to promote reliable and accurate completion of tasks.[clxxvi]

The routinization of P&C is credited with reducing workplace errors by up to 85 per cent.[clxxvii] Other management systems that are common features of *Efficiency Maximizers* include Lean Thinking, Six

Sigma and total quality management. All are intended to maximize efficient implementation by reducing errors, improving reliability and eliminating wastage, and require worker conformity to be effective.

Japan Rail's success is no accident. It is the best-performing rail system in the world because its enterprise leaders have purposefully and systematically designed their organization to be highly formalized, defined and process driven – all of which are required to manage complex mass transportation operations safely, punctually and efficiently.

The Enterprising Responder organizational architecture

Enterprising Responders differentiate themselves from their competitors by offering their customers novel products and services, whether in the form of wholly new offerings or the customization (or even personalization) of existing offerings. This requires high levels of *customer agility*. What gives *Enterprising Responders* a competitive edge are the following organizational architecture characteristics:

- *Core people*: Core people within the *Enterprising Responder* lead the development of new products and services in response to changing market preferences. They are at the forefront of market innovations and are highly enterprising when identifying new opportunities for competitive differentiation. Core people are comfortable with role ambiguity and loose measures of success. Affording high levels of delegated authority to the core people of *Enterprising Responders* is typical, providing them with the freedom to operate without constraint or regard to the prevailing status quo. Extremely adaptable, *Enterprising Responder* core people need to be highly independent, self-motivated and self-reliant. They are domain masters typically – they often have in-depth professional or expert 'field' knowledge aligned to what is in demand in the marketplace and the ability to realign it as required. *Enterprising Responder* core people are like cats if a metaphor helps. They respond to incentives and not instructions, typically.
- *Core organizational structure*: The core organizational structure within *Enterprising Responders* typically resembles a

hub-and-spoke style arrangement. Within the hub, a central co-ordinating group function provides a degree of necessary administrative infrastructure, often in the form of a shared balance sheet and shared corporate functions. Management discretion resides within the spokes, which, as individual lines of business, teams or functions, operate largely autonomously of each other and focus on their particular market and customer base. At the front line, work structures are typically highly flexible. Teams are built around a field of expertise and the rapid and creative application to client opportunities. Like its market offerings, the structure of units within the *Enterprising Responders* are configured around customer/ client engagements and reconfigured in step with changing customer preferences and market opportunities.

- *Core organizational culture*: The core organizational culture of the *Enterprising Responder* is highly entrepreneurial at the point at which work is performed (interaction with the customer, for instance) and highly unconstrained. The culture emphasizes focus and self-reliance to support high levels of creativity and autonomy. Core people are typically freed from constraint as much as possible to focus on identifying and exploring the development of the next opportunity. Error-embracing cultures are standard. Experimentation is an essential part of the innovation process, and failure is a regular occurrence and is treated as an opportunity for learning. For the same reason, a significant emphasis is placed on organizational learning and the development of an entrepreneurial mindset in addition to requred technical or field expertise. Core people are encouraged to be risk-takers. The use of incentives provides the focus of effort. The loose organizational culture permits a high degree of individuality and discretion in how that individual effort is applied day to day.
- *Core work processes*: The core work processes of the *Enterprising Responder* incorporate objectives over a short-term period, typically. Objectives are loosely defined and represent targets against easily measurable financial outputs (e.g. chargeable

> hours in professional services firms or unit profit in the case of new product development). *Enterprising Responders* are typically highly incentive driven to support individual initiative and self-reliance. Individuals and the small teams they gather around them lead the exploration of market opportunity and deliver innovative (often premium) products and services. The focus is on performance, but the workflow is improvised. Individuals have a large amount of discretion to determine how they might work best. The combination of defined targets, incentivization and adaptability enables maximum agility around customer needs.

An example of the *Enterprising Responder* logic at work is the software developer, Valve. Founded by former Microsoft software developers, the company has become a market leader in video games, including genre-defining hits like 'Half-Life' and 'Counter-Strike'. More recently, its Steam software platform has become the world's biggest digital distribution platform for its own games and those of other developers. When measured on a per employee basis, Valve is the most profitable company in the world (gaming is one of the fastest-growing sectors in the world, with games now commonly making more money than big-budget Hollywood movies).

The company affords its people almost total freedom to decide how to meet and exceed customer requirements. Valve lets its people *'Create or self-select into projects and opportunities that they, the employees, rather than managers, find most promising.'*[clxxviii] It operates a simple working practice known as 'the rule of three'. A project originator, who can be anyone in the company, is required to recruit at least two other employees on to the project.[(ibid)]

This serves as a useful discipline in several ways. First, the originator must persuade their peers of the potential value of the project, with new ideas subject to scrutiny and testing before any commitment of time or resource is made. Second, three heads (or more) are better than one. The rule of three ensures that the collective wisdom of the talent within the firm is mobilized, even if only on a small scale, to help to get any new project or product off the ground.[(ibid)]

The Portfolio Integrator organizational architecture

Portfolio Integrators differentiate themselves by offering to the market different combinations of their products and services, either in the form of enhanced choice, or novel combinations, or easy access for customers to its portfolio via a one-stop-shop channel to market. They succeed by exploiting *horizontal connectivity* and the potential of synergies between their different lines of business, functions and geographies. What gives *Portfolio Integrators* a competitive edge are the following organizational architecture characteristics:

- *Core people*: Core people within the *Portfolio Integrator* lead the formation and maintenance of horizontal connections across the different lines of business, divisions, functions and teams of the enterprise to realize value greater than the sum of the parts. Their unique contribution is to promote connectivity and collaborations between individuals and groups operating within the rigid organizational structure of individual domains (e.g. lines of business) that would not otherwise be connected structurally. This is either to share knowledge, co-create new business ventures or pool resources. This 'boundary-spanning' behaviour is enabled by *Portfolio Integrator* core people being 'T-shaped'.[clxxix] They possess in-depth knowledge about a critical area of the enterprise's business portfolio and a broad knowledge of other business areas. *Portfolio Integrators* I work with describe their core people as 'collaborative leaders', the idea being that their leadership contribution is to form new connections between otherwise structurally separated teams, cross-fertilize ideas and lead productive and novel collaborations.
- *Core organizational structure*: The overall organizational structure of *Portfolio Integrators* resembles a matrix. The first layer of the structure enables unconstrained horizontal movement and collaboration between different individuals and groups. The second layer resembles typically a more formal vertical structure representing the enterprise's established lines of business, divisions and functions. These unconstrained

horizontal structures take the form of relational (for which read 'social') ties. These are either weak or strong. Weak ties facilitate the simple exchange of knowledge between individuals and groups, such as customer intelligence, which is applied to particular areas to improve their management practice and performance. Strong ties are the crystallization of interdependent working relationships. Success requires a joint commitment to a shared goal and the pooling of resources (e.g. human or financial resources) for success. It enables the efficient spanning of multiple boundaries by the *Portfolio Integrator*'s core people, minimizing the risk of structural friction posed by turf wars, narrow interests or structural inertia.

- *Core organizational culture*: A *Portfolio Integrator* core organizational culture typically espouses enterprise-wide values, encouraging its core people to identify with the interests of the enterprise overall and not any one single part of it. Many *Portfolio Integrators* use the language of 'one firm' or describe themselves as a 'one-firm firm' – the idea being there is a single set of values that permeate the entire enterprise and its activities. Strategically valuable behaviours include those that facilitate collaborative effort and the breaking down of structural silos. Core organizational cultures embrace empowered networking and the voluntary forging of new connections. The enterprise-wide culture remains inwardly focused (i.e. within the enterprise). It is intended to be as homogenous as possible to reduce barriers to collaboration and the transaction costs of integrating the enterprise's product and service portfolio in novel ways that appeal to customers.
- *Core work processes*: *Portfolio Integrator* core work processes are typically collaborative because the focus of the effort is exploring potential synergies. Core work processes provide the *Portfolio Integrator*'s core people with sufficient adaptability to realize the potential for making new connections and pursuing novel combinations of products, services, teams and technologies over the longer term. Nevertheless, *Portfolio Integrators* rely upon relatively stable and established processes

to transact day-to-day business to support the scalability of its core product and service offerings (i.e. creating a novel product through collaborative leadership and then scaling it).

The Chinese telecommunications company Huawei is a good example of *Portfolio Integrator* thinking in action. It is the world's largest telecoms equipment manufacturer with more than $90 billion sales, 66 per cent of which originate outside of China via its operations in 145 countries.[clxxx] Huawei retains a strong hierarchy through which its senior executives exercise close management over dedicated lines of business and functions, including manufacturing, product development, sales and finance.[xiii] As diverse enterprise capabilities (think know-how), these functions are capable of being reconfigured rapidly around specific commercial opportunities or challenges. For example, a team from across the company's functions can be quickly assembled to service a new customer opportunity or explore the potential of a new technology.[(ibid)]

Horizontal connectivity provides the company with a strategic advantage in three key respects. First, under the guidance of top leadership, cross-functional teams from Huawei's global operations regularly take a new product initiative from idea to product development, manufacturing to final installation and after-sales service. This outcomes-based approach delivers end-to-end value to clients and efficiently spans what would otherwise be separated divisions.

Second, technical or commercial talent can be added or reassigned at any stage of the process to flex resourcing requirements on an as-needed basis. Talent reconfigurability is key to forming valuable connections across the entire portfolio of Huawei's functions and lines of business. This is valuable for meeting customer demand for choice and integration, serving global clients and markets (which include substantial capital expenditure infrastructure projects, such as national 5G networks), or identifying the potential for product and service innovation.[(ibid)]

Third, and more practically, solving problems within Huawei relies upon a tried-and-tested methodology of *'huddle and act'*.[(ibid)] When confronted with a problem, such as a customer challenge or a new technical requirement, project teams solicit help from anyone within the company to tap into the 'wisdom of the crowd' and the collective intelligence that resides in the company's human capital. Following the successful resolution of the problem, the 'huddle' disbands, and members return to regular duties.

The robust vertical hierarchy is flexible at all levels horizontally to convene and mobilize its cross-cutting talent to focus on any nascent opportunity or challenge. This ability to flexibly configure and reconfigure its talent has helped propel Huawei to a global market-leading position in just a few decades since its founder and CEO, Ren Zhengfei, started the company with an initial investment of just $5,000.[clxxxi]

The Network Exploiter organizational architecture

Network Exploiters differentiate themselves by offering customers more choices of products and services, with many novel combinations that permit a high level of market customization or even customer personalization. They need to be superior at *network leverage* to capitalize upon the diverse capabilities of their external network connections in ways that would otherwise be too costly to replicate by relying upon in-house resources alone. What gives *Network Exploiters* a competitive edge are the following organizational architecture characteristics:

- *Core people*: The *Network Exploiter*'s core people combine the best characteristics of both the *Portfolio Integrator* and the *Enterprising Responder*. Organizationally, *Network Exploiters* are highly collaborative (for superior connectivity) and enterprising (for superior agility) in equal measure. Their core people occupy roles responsible for designing and managing their enterprise as a network of external partners. They broker relationships between network actors, whether internal or – more likely – external. They mobilize the network overall to offer customers highly differentiated products and services. Core people within the *Network Exploiter* need to be capable of high levels of creativity and initiative. They need to act according to their judgement to steer their enterprise towards opportunity and away from threats. They typically possess wide-ranging knowledge. They need to know a little about many things, especially regarding exploiting the 'economies of association' within their network of partners and how that diverse capability might align with new or novel customer opportunities. In addition to their 'polymathic' knowledge and ability to think at the ecosystem level, they must also be highly adaptable. When required, they need to shift speed and focus from one network opportunity to another and switch roles regularly.

- *Core organizational structure*: The *Network Exploiter* core organizational structure resembles a network or a relationally rich community bound by a common purpose. It consists typically of a central commissioning enterprise and various internal and (more likely) external innovation and delivery partnering enterprises. Beyond contracting and business transacting simply, the structure of the *Network Exploiter* is highly flexible to enable near-continuous reconfiguration of the network around new market opportunities. *Network Exploiters* are 'shapeshifters' – the form and composition of their network are constantly in flux as partners are swapped in and out according to the changing market environment and their performance. The boundary of the *Network Exploiter* is highly porous. It is an extended system (think thousands of interdependent network actors potentially) with high levels of horizontal connectivity (think relationships and collaborations). This is especially true within the central commissioning enterprise and between network partners to support exchanging knowledge, building shared interests and values, and co-delivering integrated customer propositions. Network partners located within multiple fields present the opportunity for the *Network Exploiter*'s core people to harness the collective power of a diverse set of capabilities that can potentially be mobilized rapidly and at scale.
- *Core organizational culture*: For the enterprise to thrive, the *Network Exploiter*'s core people must constantly scan the external environment to identify market opportunities and threats and potential new partners who may bring additional strategically advantageous capabilities to the network. The core organizational culture of the *Network Exploiter* encourages an outward-facing focus, therefore. Its core people need to understand the needs

and preferences of their customers and external partners to perform effective and efficient brokering between the two to produce highly differentiated products and services. Authority is highly delegated based on considerable levels of trust between the enterprise's core people and their relationships with partnering employees. Beyond simple transactions and contracting, a great deal of emphasis is placed upon developing valuable social capital and the strong ties that bind a diverse set of network actors together behind shared opportunities. The focus of all effort is the enrichment of the network as a whole.

- *Core work processes*: Consistent with cultural and structural characteristics, the *Network Exploiter*'s core work processes support high adaptability, connectivity and the exploratory nature of the work performed by its core people. Work is measured by its inputs more than its outputs in preliminary stages – the focus is upon the resources that can be brought to bear in business ventures from the collective pool of all partners. Objectives are typically loosely defined, centred around opportunities as they arise from the network (e.g. new product ideas) or external pressures, such as customer demands for greater choice and personalization. The planning horizon is typically longer term, with the return on investment of many partnership ventures (or innovations) taking several years to mature, primarily if representing a new or untested business model. Rolls-Royce's Power-by-the-Hour and the Amazon platform are two such examples.

Let us revisit the example of ARM reviewed in Chapter 1 and delve a little more deeply. ARM purposefully set out to avoid being a '*hand-to-mouth chip design consulting business*'.[xiii] The founding vision of ARM was to '*become the global standard for Reduced Instruction Set Computing (RISC) chips with a target of embedding ARM designs into 100 million chips by the year 2000*'.[(ibid)] Today, the ARM RISC architecture is the gold standard for chip design worldwide.

This success did not occur by accident or by chance. ARM is designed organizationally with three critical points of structure in mind. The first and perhaps most important from an innovation perspective is the project organization. Strategic projects built around new technologies, problems or market opportunities are formed quickly and efficiently. They draw upon the full range of the firm's human capital value (think skills, knowledge and experience). Second, ARM is organized into five lines of business, with projects cross-cutting each of the divisions to connect innovation to execution. Third, there is a corporate superstructure in which different boards oversee the integration of divisional activity and workflows across the company and ensure they align with overall group strategic priorities.[(ibid)]

Projects are boundary spanning, and senior leaders act in a supporting capacity to ensure barriers to this strategically important 'horizontal connectivity' are kept to a minimum. Their role is to integrate capabilities and knowledge drawn from across the internal organization *and* the external ecosystem of more than 3,000 business partners to push projects forwards, solve complex problems and ensure customer delivery.[clxxxii] Its 'core people' span multiple organizational boundaries, both internal and external, and provide a bridge for valuable knowledge and capability exchange throughout the ARM ecosystem. As 'T-shaped' talent, they typically have in-depth knowledge of one domain and a broad understanding of other areas to establish and nourish valuable connections.

The drive for connectivity to fuel innovation capability is profound. ARM embeds its 'Partner Managers' in partnering enterprises to manage the relationship and ensure effective knowledge exchange. It also regularly seconds its people to its customers and even its customers' customers.[(ibid)] Chapter 1 described ARM as a neural network – a mind made up of cells (network nodes, expertise) and synapses (connections). Its relationships span all aspects of the company, its external partners, customers and customers' customers, all of which is essential to support its position as one of the world's most innovative companies of the last decade.[clxxxiii]

Even so, some industry analysts claim ARM's core mobile computing market has matured, and the company risks becoming *'stuck in the mud'*.[clxxxiv] New markets in automotive computing and high-performance servers offer higher growth potential, but there are significant barriers to entry. A report commissioned by rival chipmaker Nvidia, which agreed to buy ARM from its parent, Softbank, in September 2020 (and discussed in Chapter 1), recommended a pivot towards these new markets and funding the required research and development by cutting costs and trimming investment in ARM's core business.[ibid] Success comes in cycles, or so it seems.

ARM, just like Shell and Foxconn reviewed in Chapter 2, needs perhaps to realign its core markets (as part of its business strategy), its organizational capability and its organizational culture, structure, processes and people (its organizational architecture) if it is to continue to be as successful in future. As noted earlier, strategic realignment is a considerable challenge for an enterprise's leadership. It is also an opportunity for the far-sighted and brave in today's dynamic and disrupted business environment.

SECTION 6.5 REALIGNING ORGANIZATIONAL ARCHITECTURE, THE LEADERSHIP OPPORTUNITY

So far, so much theory. In practice, how can we apply a strategic alignment perspective to designing (and redesigning) an enterprise's core organizational components? We noted previously that within the overall strategic alignment logic, the critical question at the organizational architecture stage is: which ideal form of core organizational culture, structure, processes and people will give us a competitive edge in our chosen markets? There is a part B to the question: how much of an edge do we have currently?

More specifically, how do we know if we have the right core people in terms of their skills, focus and behaviour? How do we know if our enterprise's core organizational culture encourages the correct type of behaviours that support how we are trying to be different from our competitors? How do we know whether our core organizational structure enables our people to co-ordinate and organize to be super-efficient, or the opposite, if that is what is required?

Equally, in the context of a changing environment, or when faced with disruption to the status quo, how should we realign our enterprise's organizational architecture to be ideally fit for purpose for the next, say, five to 10 years? Whether to improve performance or overcome disruption, the realignment of an enterprise's organizational architecture is a critical factor in sustainable business performance and competitive advantage.

In the context of your organizational capability requirements for either efficient execution, customer agility, horizontal connectivity or network leverage, consider the following questions for your enterprise:

1. *Core people*: Thinking forward, which skills, knowledge, experience and behaviours will be key to your enterprise successfully implementing its chosen strategic approach in future? Again, our principal interest is not the entirety of the workforce (although it can be) but on the groups, roles and tasks that set your enterprise apart and make it superior to competitors.
2. *Core organizational structure*: Which type of organizational structure is best for your enterprise in the future? The question is principally a choice between hierarchy, hub-and-spoke, matrix and network-based forms of work organization. Different lines of business within the same enterprise may each require a separate structure. Operating across multiple different structures can add considerably to the complexity of leading such an enterprise. What form should your enterprise take overall to accommodate the variety of its operations?
3. *Core organizational culture*: Which type of organizational culture will best fit how you are trying to succeed in the longer-term future? Which values, beliefs and behaviours are most strategically desirable? For example, where do you wish your people to focus primarily – on external innovation or internal operations? Both are required, but one takes priority over the other, typically.
4. *Core work processes*: Which processes will be core to supporting your enterprise's most important work? Will financial performance require a high level of focus on granular and tangible targets? Or a focus on broad targets and measures intended to support and enable employee empowerment, creativity and innovation capability? Should the priority of your enterprise's future work processes be on long-term value creation or short-term results?

The previous sections of this chapter provide you with a guide to answer these questions. In the context of these strategic requirements, consider further:

5. *Core component complementarity*: When looking forward, how well does each of the core organizational components of your enterprise's organizational architecture support each other? Do they form a coherent and integrated superstructure that makes sense? For instance, does your organizational structure (i.e. how your people co-ordinate and co-operate) complement your organizational culture (i.e. what they value and how they behave) or do they operate in opposition? Do your core work processes enable the performance you require from your people? Is there one core organizational component that is misaligned, creating instability within your enterprise or acting as a break on performance? What should you prioritize in your realignment efforts to bring your organizational architecture into line?

And finally:

6. *The realignment requirement*: How closely do your reflections on the above align to the current state? Can you chart a journey to realign your enterprise's organizational architecture (or on a component-by-component basis) using the SAF?
   a) What is the degree of realignment required? How urgent and important is realignment according to the framework reviewed in Chapter 2, Section 2.2?
   b) Is there one core component that deserves special attention?
   c) What are likely barriers to meaningful realignment? What might derail your best efforts to realign one or all of your enterprise's core organizational components?
   d) What are the implications of failing to realign your organizational culture, structure, processes and people as per strategic requirements?

Of course, there are no right or wrong answers to these fundamental questions about the function and form of how you organize your enterprise. Merely good and bad answers. The first goal of such considerations is to make sense of 'what to realign' about how your enterprise is organized. The second is to make sense of 'realign to what' according to strategic requirements. The SAF is your guide to answering this second question.

An illustration of these considerations in practice is outlined by the following case study, Logistics Co.

Realigning to drive efficiency at Logistics Co.

'Logistics Co.' had been around for years. It was the bluest of blue-chip European companies. If there is a corporate aristocracy, Logistics Co. was it. It enjoyed status as a national institution in its home country. Serving consumers and businesses alike, Logistics Co. was an international household name, principally due to its highly recognizable vehicles rumbling their way across thc world, carrying every conceivable type of freight.

Walking around the corporate HQ was illuminating. The strong corporate culture was manifest in the office layout and people's behaviour. The first order of business was for my host to advise me on etiquette. *'Use the elevator if you must, but better to use the stairs, please – just like the founder did all his career. Lunch is free, but socializing is expected. Sitting is the new smoking, so work standing up if you can – here, your desk is adjustable to chest height. Do you need assistance…'* And so on. The open-plan office was unnaturally quiet. It had a library feel, with people working head down intently on furniture of hues of grey, blue and green. An allusion to the sea, I wondered. It felt like a ship. Big and stately.

Despite its storied past, the company was struggling. Its performance was sub-par compared to the industry average. It wasn't obvious it had fully sunk in internally. Industry analysts were in no doubt. Logistics Co. simply wasn't efficient enough. Its prices were too high, and rivals could match it in virtually every other respect. The company was struggling significantly to match the pricing of new competitors from emerging economies, China especially. Rivals could offer the same global reach, logistics capacity and service reliability but at a much lower cost. For sure, initially, there was low-hanging fruit that could be plucked to find savings to pass on to customers. One easy fix was to limit the speed of its vehicles, thereby reducing the consumption of expensive fuel. But the ease of the fix meant it was also easily emulated by competitors.

No, the urgent strategic priority for Logistics Co. was to find value in economies of scale – to maximize the potential of its distribution channels by increasing the volume of goods transported globally while reducing costs as much as possible. To sustain its performance in the medium- to long-term future, Logistics Co. needed to undergo a *vision-led* realignment of its business strategy, its organizational capability and, most important of all from the perspective of implementation, its organizational architecture. This was the strategic realignment requirement for the company to succeed.

Organized for agility

Beyond easy fixes, the more challenging task was to realign the company to be as operationally lean as possible in two respects. First, to devise and enforce strict operational standards globally to limit local variation of business practice (corporate standardization, in other words). Second, to improve the quality of execution across the company's operations to reduce errors, lower costs and minimize waste. Efficiency was the order of the day, and operational centralization and standardization were the pathways to achieving it. However, the reality of how the company was organized could not have been more different.

Figure 6.3 illustrates the results from a mapping exercise using the SAF a few years ago that plotted the current and ideal variety of Logistics Co.'s organizational architecture. It explains why Logistics Co. had struggled historically to find the efficiencies it needed to match its competitors' lower prices and high freight transport rates. It provides an insight into the realignment journey – the transition from the current state to a strategically aligned 'ideal' state – and the likely changes required along the way.

Mapping data were based upon the responses of a representative sample of managers from across the business. These data indicated that Logistics Co. was organized for high levels of localized agility. It was a decentralized, separated and highly agile organizational structure in which there were high levels of delegated authority at the local operational level. These characteristics ran contrary to the strategic

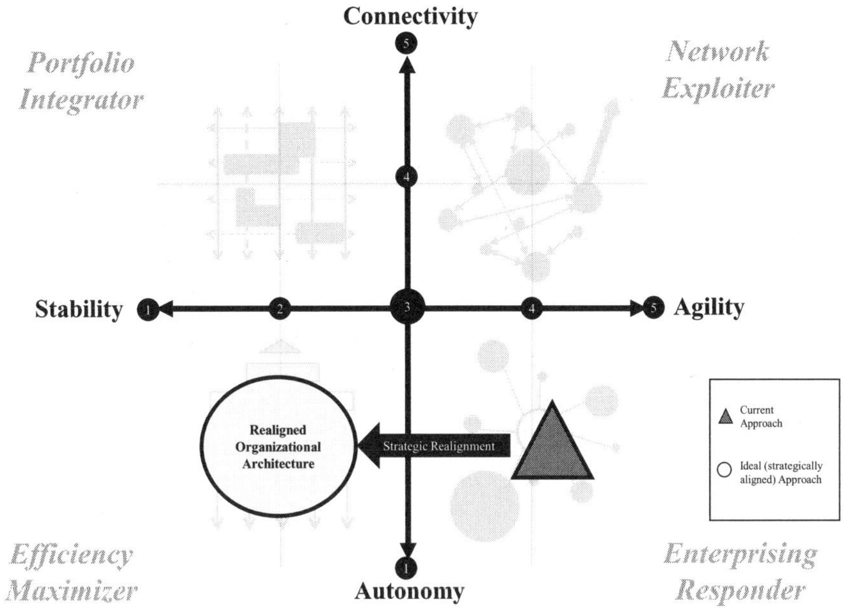

FIGURE 6.3 Strategic realignment to improve efficiency

requirements envisaged by executive-level enterprise leaders for maximizing economies of scale through standardization and consistency.

However, Logistics Co.'s established organizational culture, structure and working processes were long-standing and deeply embedded. They reflected its origins before it encountered intense global competition from low-cost rivals. Its home-country culture also emphasized individual autonomy and egalitarian values. These shared values bound up in its national culture had been what had guided employees' everyday behaviour historically. Certainly not rules or rigid impersonal procedures.

Its established organizational architecture had its advantages, of course. Its organizational culture was quite entrepreneurial. A lot of authority for business decision-making had been decentralized and delegated to front-line operators. It produced exciting innovations, albeit on a local basis, and this meant high levels of local customer loyalty. However, there were also downsides. Localization meant that the quality of implementation and ways of working varied considerably between Logistic Co.'s various end markets and regions, even within the same line of business.

There were few standard processes, and each operating line had its own culture, which they protected fiercely from 'outside influence', even if that meant corporate HQ. It was challenging to scale up such an operating model. Moreover, global customers complained that they had the impression of working with a different company in each case when they transacted with Logistics Co. in more than one market.

Logistics Co. was a conglomerate of autonomous cells, not the finely calibrated machine it needed to be. To suggest it should be otherwise was counter-cultural. Nevertheless, its path to winning customers and beating rivals in a cost-conscious market was to maximize the potential for economies of scale. It was a big business, literally and figuratively, but it was run as a series of small businesses. It was unsustainable in the long term.

Realigning for efficiency

The obvious (but not easy) solution was to focus on the core business and run it as consistently and efficiently as possible. The analysis indicated further that Logistics Co. should invest in creating clear hierarchies of authority. Realignment also required implementing enhanced supervision; strict limits on local authority; fostering a high-performance culture reinforced through extrinsic incentives and penalties; standardized objective setting and performance criteria; close monitoring of local staff; routinization of workflows; and imposition of tangible, measurable and stretching targets.

Hierarchy, supervision, routines, rules and high divisions of labour were the new definition of 'good' in the company. Corporate functions rallied to translate these principles into operational plans. A significant barrier to implementation would be, of course, resistance from local managers and their staff. Local managers were fiercely loyal and rightly proud of working for the company and the heritage it bestowed. However, as the *'bosses'*, they were accustomed to calling the shots, at least on their own turf. Toeing the corporate line would not be an easy transition, but it was necessary. Unless it could realign to be more efficient, Logistics Co. would become less and less competitive in future, losing ground to its competitors on cost, reliability and consistency of service.

Fast-forward to today, and Logistics Co. has undergone a dramatic realignment in recent years, illustrated further in Figure 6.3. For its operating companies, the drive is to '*stick to the knitting*'[23] and focus on the efficient execution of its *Efficiency Maximizer* strategy. It is leaner, more focused and forward-looking in its vision to compete in its chosen markets. Deciding what to prioritize strategically when designing its organizational architecture required a clear focus on the needs of customers and the capabilities of competitors, followed by purposeful and systematic decision-making. Above all, it is more efficient.

In summary, a strategically aligned organizational architecture is a vitally important link of the enterprise value chain. The next challenge for enterprise leaders is to work out how best to manage their core organizational components for value. In particular, which *management systems* will maximize enterprise performance in line with stated performance ambitions? Management systems is the fifth and final link in the enterprise value chain and the subject of the next chapter.

[23]The phrase 'stick to the knitting' was popularized in business and management by Peters & Waterman in their 1982 book *In Search of Excellence*. It means to stick to what you know and be the best you can be at it.

7

MANAGEMENT SYSTEMS

SECTION 7.1 NEITHER STRATEGIC NOR INTEGRATED

'Group Corp.' was a well-established market leader in sectors ranging from precision engineering to retail and everything in between. Its founder had started the company at the beginning of the last century out of the back of his car. Today, the company employed almost 100,000 people in more than 120 countries and delivered over $100 billion in annual revenue. The structure of Group Corp. was a case study of the classic conglomerate. Dozens of operating companies (Op Co.s) sat under the one group brand.

Many were big companies in their own right with their own headquarters, divisional structures and teams. Sitting atop the operating companies was 'Group'. Group was home to the CEO, the board and the company's central management support functions. These included a powerful finance function overseeing the shared balance sheet and treasury, procurement, marketing, strategy, IT and human resources. Group was itself a large organization employing thousands of people.

On paper, the structure seemed to make a lot of sense. In reality, it was hugely complicated, and few inside or outside the company claimed to understand how it worked. Beyond the company brand, there was very little in common between the operating companies. Each had its own culture and way of going about its business. The lack of integration had severe consequences. Group Corp. was suffering from unsustainable conglomerate discount – the whole of the company was valued at less than the sum of its parts (for which read 'operating companies'). Breaking the company up was the obvious but unthinkable consequence unless it could realign to become a more integrated whole and improve its performance.

There were several practical obstacles to successful strategic realignment. First, there was a strong 'them and us' mentality between two critical levels of management: Group management and Op Co. management. Group managers gave an impression of assuming an air of seniority in Op Co. meetings because they sat higher in the corporate pecking order, or so they thought. Op Co. management on the other hand, described Group managers and their functions as *'out-of-touch bureaucrats'* and *'cost centres'*, respectively. *'They [Group] just don't get it'* was a common refrain. Conflicting priorities, assumptions and ways of working between the two levels of management created harmful misalignment and barriers to change and improved performance.

Second, to improve group-wide integration and performance, Group Corp.'s Board centralized decision-making. Previously, Op Co.s had been left mainly to their own devices, as long as they hit their numbers. But now, wave after wave of one-size-fits-all management policies was issued from on high. Centralization and standardization were very evident in human resources. 'Group HR' assumed responsibility for designing and managing the company's people management systems, including its newly introduced and deeply unpopular Management Incentive Programme (MIP). The MIP was originally poached from Group Corp.'s banking business and then rolled out to all operating companies. It aimed to drive a high-performance culture by paying individuals according to their performance against stretching measurable targets set in advance.

However, many Op Co.s complained that the MIP was a poor fit for their purposes. For them, good performance required team collaboration and long-term innovation. The MIP promoted short-termism and punished collaboration, they argued, by encouraging staff to compete with each other to get a larger slice of the pie (for which read 'bonus pool'). It became readily apparent that the other one-size-fits-all people management systems were also a poor fit for the entire company's multifaceted workforce. Contrary to intentions, Group HR policies had resulted in further disintegration, high attrition of valued staff, wasted effort and energy-sapping conflict. It wasn't just HR, though. The same was said of the misaligned interventions of virtually every other corporate function.

Third, there was also perceived misalignment *between* the various Group management functions, with the potential to introduce value-destroying dysfunctions to all levels of the company. For example, despite inhabiting the same HQ office (but on different floors, of course), Group HR and Group IT rarely co-ordinated their thinking or decision-making. This was most obvious in the botched introduction of hybrid working – a favourite complaint of Op Co. management. Even before the Covid-19 global pandemic, Group Corp. had ambitiously tried to introduce hybrid working on an enterprise-wide basis. Group HR had crafted policies providing employees globally with much more flexibility to work from home or the office and at hours that suited their lifestyles. It was a bold proposition intended to increase employee engagement and help Group Corp. stand out as an employer of choice for top talent.

However, implementing these new working arrangements required a considerable realignment of IT systems and support. First, and most basically, the company had to move away from desktops to providing employees with laptops – no easy task for tens of thousands of employees operating worldwide. The capital outlay was enormous, and Op Co.s bore the brunt financially, whether they liked it or not. Second, more than merely providing hardware, remote working necessitated implementing new security protocols, including 'zero trust' policies to enable employees to securely work anywhere and at any time. Group IT complained that Group HR had not factored in the necessary lead time to ensure the security infrastructure was adequately set up. Third, remote working required a much greater reliance upon collaboration platforms, such as Slack, Zoom and Teams. The trouble was that individual Op Co.s had traditionally used different systems. Rationalizing dozens of different working systems under one provider and one set of protocols was a mammoth task.

For all these reasons, IT wasn't ready, and despite much fanfare, Group Corp.'s hybrid working policy failed to launch. The status quo of office-based work persisted. The lack of alignment between HR and IT meant that neither function was serving the needs of the business well. People managers located at the front line in Op Co.s commented that it seemed as if the right hand didn't know what the left hand was doing. How could that be so?

Interestingly, at the early onset of the global pandemic in 2020, and despite their earlier (even first-mover) attempts to introduce hybrid working, Group Corp. was caught off guard and seemed woefully unprepared to transition its workforce to remote working compared to its rivals, partners and even business customers. Evidently, things had not improved since the initial failure to launch.

The company was as poorly integrated and as misaligned as ever in three crucial respects:

1. misalignment between the two critical Group and Op Co. management levels;
2. misalignment between the diverse strategic requirements of individual Op Co.s and the standard policies of Group functions;
3. misalignment between Group functions themselves, resulting in poorly integrated management systems.

The functional management of Group Corp. as a complex, diverse, multinational enterprise of many moving parts was, in reality, *neither strategic nor integrated*. The consequence was confusion, faltering corporate realignment and continued conglomerate discount. But for how long?

SECTION 7.2 MANAGEMENT SYSTEMS

Management systems are the final link in the enterprise value chain and are a critical aspect of implementation. Management systems are the functional policies, procedures, practices and activities used by an enterprise to manage the core components of its organizational architecture – its core people, core organizational structure, core organizational culture and core work processes.[ii] Management systems are how enterprise-level leaders *manage* their enterprises strategically to achieve competitive performance levels in their chosen markets.

Consider the strategic use of people management systems (also referred to as 'human resources systems' in this context). People management systems are how enterprises recruit, select, develop, progress, performance manage and reward their employees. When designed in a particular way, illustrated below, they can foster distinct employee values, beliefs and behaviour, all of which produce a distinctive organizational culture:

1. *Recruitment and selection:* Selecting employees already predisposed towards strategically desirable values, beliefs and behaviours (e.g. hiring, selection panels, sourcing talent).
2. *Exit*: Removing employees who do not lend themselves towards what is desired (e.g. reorganization, redundancy).
3. *Development*: Socializing employees according to what is considered strategically vital and developing their technical and behavioural competencies accordingly (e.g. training programmes, leadership development, executive education, secondments, on-the-job training).
4. *Succession*: Progressing employees who demonstrate leadership potential and exemplify cultural values (e.g. promotion, either vertical or horizontal).
5. *Performance management*: Setting objectives and assessing employee performance in such a way as to establish required standards, guide effort and reinforce desirable behaviour (e.g. 360-degree appraisal, recognition schemes).
6. *Reward*: Incentivizing desirable behaviour and levels of effort against essential goals (e.g. short- or long-term incentive programmes, performance-related pay, battlefield bonuses, share options).

The logic is that, when strategically aligned, distinct varieties of organizational culture contribute to developing equally distinct types of strategically valuable organizational capability. This in turn permits the effective implementation of the enterprise's chosen business strategy. Thus, strategically aligned people management systems are as crucial as any other link in the enterprise value chain. Management systems enable all preceding links of the enterprise value chain to take form.

These considerations should give us pause to consider an important principle related to strategic realignment. While management systems are the fifth and final link in the enterprise value chain, they are most likely to be the first to be the focus of realignment efforts to overcome disruption and improve performance. However, management system redesign is contingent upon the desired form of the organizational architecture, which is itself contingent upon the enterprise's organizational capability requirement, and so on. Enterprise leaders can only make sense of the design (and redesign) of their management systems in the context of the requirements of the preceding link.[24]

Here is the rub. From a strategic alignment perspective – and illustrated by the enterprise value chain – our visioning and planning are linear. The form of each link of the enterprise value chain is defined by its function of supporting the preceding link. Simply put, form follows function (covered in detail in Chapter 1, Section 1.2). Therefore, the enterprise value chain runs from *the left to the right*. Such linearity is typical in Western thinking and has limitations, perhaps. Nevertheless, it is rooted in logic, cause and effect. However, the *implementation* of any strategic realignment effort runs from *the right to the left,* starting with management systems.

In summary, the enterprise value chain is bidirectional. 'Left to the right' enterprise leadership establishes a vision of the ideal form of an enterprise for every link of its value chain. 'Right to the left' enterprise leadership brings the vision to life – it implements the idealized enterprise in practice. Enterprise leaders must be sensitive to this notion of bidirectionality and encompass both directions of travel in their strategic realignment thinking, planning and action.

It is important to note that management system redesign applies to many functional areas and not just people management. Enterprises typically use different management systems corresponding to different functional areas, such as operations, finance and information technology. Financial expenditure associated with functional management systems by corporations is considerable. For example, the average annual enterprise investment in information technology in the banking and

[24]Operationally, a whole raft of essential considerations also applies at this stage in proceedings. These include legal and regulatory compliance, health and safety, risk management and accounting practice, for example. However, these are not factors in securing competitive advantage typically and not the focus of our attention here. They have the potential to destroy value if mismanaged or poorly executed, not create it.

securities sector is more than 7 per cent of annual revenues.[clxxxv] By 2025, the global outsourced market in facilities management services will exceed $1 trillion.[clxxxvi] Employee payroll costs vary by industry but can exceed 70 per cent of total annual operating costs in service-based companies.[clxxxvii] Whether as investments to be managed for value or costs to be managed as risk, an enterprise's management systems are a matter of strategic importance.

There are myriad different ways in which to design each of an enterprise's management systems. Workplaces, for example, can be designed as partitioned offices or as open-plan or co-working spaces. Contrary to prevailing fads and fashions, or prescribed 'best practices', no one design of a workplace, or any other functional management system, is better than another in the abstract. They are different, with each supporting a different style of working, which may or may not be strategically desirable, depending upon the enterprise's circumstances.

The leadership challenge is choosing the appropriate form of each functional management system and integrating them to form one 'total management system'. To meet this challenge, enterprise leaders need to be strategic and cross-functional in their outlook and decision-making. Good choices will best support the management of their enterprise's organizational architecture and deliver desired enterprise performance levels.

Strategically aligned management systems

Regardless of function, what matters for performance is *how well* each management system supports the management of the enterprise's organizational architecture to deliver the level of performance it needs to succeed.[ii] The ideal form of any of an enterprise's management systems depends upon which type of core organizational culture, structure, processes and people are core to the enterprise's capability to implement its chosen business strategy.[(ibid)]

The streaming service Netflix is a good example of a company that designed a distinctive approach to employee evaluation (as an example of a people management system). In place of its formerly industry-standard annual appraisal system, it instituted an informal 360-degree process. In addition to manager feedback, other staff are asked to relay what they think their peers should stop, start or continue doing to perform their work as best as possible. Performance evaluation is now a continuous process at Netflix, rather than occurring annually. It does not rely upon the views of a single manager but on those of the whole team to emphasize the strategic value of collaboration and mutual accountability.[clxxxviii]

By contrast, a poorly aligned management system (or subsystem) can limit or even destroy value. As a counter to Netflix, consider the example of Microsoft's now discontinued 'stack-ranking' approach to evaluating employee performance. Stack ranking (also known as 'forced ranking' or 'forced distribution') is the practice of ranking all employees on a bell curve according to their individual performance and sorting a specified quota into a rating as either a top performer, good performer, average performer, below-average performer or poor performer.

Critics claim its stack ranking system ran contrary to the collaborative organizational culture required by Microsoft to implement its services-based business strategy.[clxxxix] Introduced under former CEO, Steve Ballmer, it created *'An incentive for star Microsoft workers to avoid working with other stars since they knew it could hurt their chances of getting a top rating when it came time for employee reviews.'*[(ibid)] Additionally, it produced negative behaviour generally, as staff developed tactics to stay out of the bottom 'bucket', including allegedly sabotaging the work of others, withholding important information from colleagues and focusing only on short-term performance.[(ibid)] In other contexts, such as in sales-force management, stack-ranking systems have proved very effective when designed and managed carefully. However, it was not suitable at Microsoft, given its strategic approach requiring collaboration between staff and not competition.

From a strategic alignment perspective, two key principles should be observed. First, no one form of any management system is best in all situations. To apply this principle to the different strategic approaches within the SAF, an operations management system (for example) used to support the management of an *Efficiency Maximizer*'s organizational architecture – that emphasizes tight regulation of work, internal focus and individual effort – should be designed very differently from one used in an *Enterprising Responder*, *Portfolio Integrator* or *Network Exploiter*.

This principle applies to all functional areas of management, from real estate and facilities management to procurement and people management. How enterprise leaders design their functional management systems should depend, above any other consideration, upon strategic requirements. The best management system is the one that best supports the management of the enterprise's organizational architecture, in whatever form that may take.

Second, there is no one functional management system, no matter how sophisticated or well resourced, that can alone deliver the performance needed to succeed. It requires the combined power of all of the enterprise's management systems working in concert. Illustrated by Group Corp. in the previous section, an enterprise's people management system, for example, cannot alone engender positive organizational realignment or produce superior performance. It needs to be complemented by equally well-designed IT management, financial management, operations management, and real estate and facilities management systems. These different functional management systems have to be complementary.

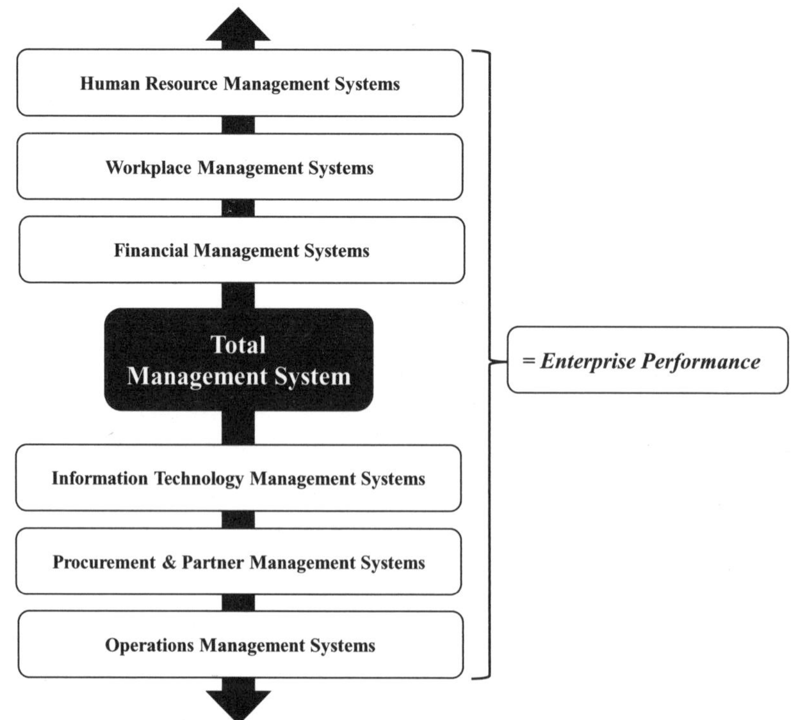

FIGURE 7.1 Integrated management systems

I frequently observe the performance-damaging consequences of disintegrated or, even worse, conflicting management systems. More often than not, it is because an enterprise's corporate functions design their management systems independently of each other. This is understandable, even if regrettable. Functional management systems are often very complex, and many require high levels of technical knowledge and proficiency to be designed and managed effectively. Specialization makes it difficult to develop a general appreciation of the complexity of other areas, even if they are – or should be – complementary to be strategically aligned (as illustrated in Figure 7.1).

SECTION 7.3 ALIGNING MANAGEMENT SYSTEMS, THE LEADERSHIP CHALLENGE

Which form should each of your management systems take ideally to deliver competitive performance? Yep, you're probably fed up of hearing it, but *it depends!* For this final link in the enterprise value chain, the leadership challenge is to choose, first, which form of each management system best supports the mobilization of the enterprise's core organizational components for maximum strategic value. Second, to ensure that all management systems, whether people, facilities or technology related, are complementary and not operating in conflict.

To address the leadership challenge, consider the following in the context of your own enterprise or one of its strategically important functions or business lines:

- Which management systems do you require to manage your enterprise's organizational architecture – the organizational cultures, structures, processes and people that are core to making your enterprise capable of succeeding in the markets in which it is competing? Even in small entrepreneurial start-ups, you will need different types of functional management systems to grow your enterprise.

Consider further:

- First, which form of each management system is best fit for purpose? Which form of information technology management

system, say, will deliver organizational outcomes consistent with your chosen strategic approach? How different in principle are your ideally envisioned management systems when compared to current practice?
- Second, how well do each of your functional management systems support each other? How well integrated are they? Each should be part of an integrated and strategically aligned portfolio, which flexes and morphs in step with the changing strategic requirements of the enterprise. What steps could you take in the future to ensure they are better aligned?

From a strategic realignment perspective, your answers to the questions set the scene for redesigning your management systems to overcome disruption and improve enterprise performance.

SECTION 7.4 A TALE OF REDESIGNING THREE MANAGEMENT SYSTEMS

This section refers to the SAF again to illustrate a case study of the redesign of three functional management systems – workplace, people management and information technology – to support the management of two different lines of business and two very different approaches to market success within the one enterprise, 'Choc Co.'.

Choc Co. was a well-established confectionary company headquartered in the US. It had substantial marketing and production operations in more than 20 countries and served many more markets worldwide. A market leader, its past success was based upon its capability to efficiently execute its *Efficiency Maximizer* business strategy and maximize the potential for economies of scale in each of its markets. Its core products – a variety of global-brand chocolate and candy products – had once been considered luxury items sold individually and eaten sparingly. Today, they were typically sold in multipacks. They were often heavily discounted in the form of 'buy one, get one free' offers by mega-retailers using their huge purchasing power to drive down supplier prices (while offering their own economy house-brand product alongside).

It was recognized internally that Choc Co. had to move with the times, not least to respond to unprecedented public scrutiny and regulation. In addition to the commoditization of its core market, concerns over health and nutrition were disrupting consumer buying behaviour. Significant resources were being diverted into building a new and high-potential line of business around novel lifestyle and health offerings. The new business would have to rely upon the close involvement of a network of partners because the expertise required for innovation was too costly to develop in-house. Where Choc Co.'s established consumer confectionary business conformed to the *Efficiency Maximizer* strategic approach, its new business was based on the radically different *Network Exploiter* strategic approach.

To succeed in its market, Choc Co.'s established *Efficiency Maximizer* business needed to be highly efficient. Its high level of operational efficiency was the result of, first, the routine work performed by its core people operating at peak proficiency. Second was its focus on defined task and transparent lines of performance accountability within its hierarchal core organizational structure. Third was its formal and rule-bound core organizational culture, which encouraged maximum intensity of individual effort, stable operations and error-avoiding behaviour. Fourth was its core work processes, which channelled employee effort (augmented by automated processes) through elaborate workflows aligned to short-term and detailed objectives set in advance.

By contrast, Choc Co.'s fledgling *Network Exploiter* business needed to be good at *network leverage* to power its business model innovation and delivery to market. What gave it the potential to succeed was the entrepreneurial mindset of its core people and their ability to connect and broker relationships with partner enterprises. It needed a relationally rich and agile network-based organizational structure in which authority was highly delegated. Its informal core organizational culture emphasized collaboration, adaptability and collective shared interest. Core work processes supported long-term performance measured in the quality of business inputs principally (the vibrancy and diversity of the business's network, for example).

The burning question was: which management systems would best support the management of these two distinct organizational architectures and deliver the required levels of performance for Choc Co.? A one-size-fits-all approach surely could not work, everyone agreed. To address this strategic alignment challenge, the company's leadership adopted a novel approach to decision-making. It convened a cross-functional working group of senior executives from the two business units and a range of corporate management functions. These included real estate and facilities management (RE&FM), human resources (HR) and information technology (IT).

The purpose of the working group was to choose the ideal design of the future workplace, people management and information technology management systems for the two different lines of business. Alignment was the order of the day.

Redesigning Choc Co.'s workplace management system

When considering 'what to realign to', and illustrated in Figure 7.2, the working group envisaged that the ideal design of the *Efficiency Maximizer* workplace should be an *open* layout. This was to provide efficient workspaces, management visibility and oversight over activities. It would be composed of *modular* units so that the physical workplace layout could be reconfigured rapidly to match changing capacity requirements. It would also be based on the *internal* needs of Choc Co. operations solely and in *dedicated* fashion, with the company's work being performed there and nowhere else.

Similarly, the working group envisaged that the ideal design of the *Network Exploiter* workplace should also be an *open* layout but to support ad hoc co-working and not for productivity monitoring. In all other respects, the ideal *Network Exploiter* workplace should be designed significantly differently. Workplaces were envisaged as needing to be highly *integrated* with information technologies to support non-routine knowledge work and permit important communication activities such as teleconferencing, virtual and mobile working. Hot-desking would be the norm to support individual *activity* and mobile working. All workplaces would be designed as co-working spaces to facilitate collaboration and made available to the staff of *external* partners and even customers in the style of a serviced 'drop-in' workplace.

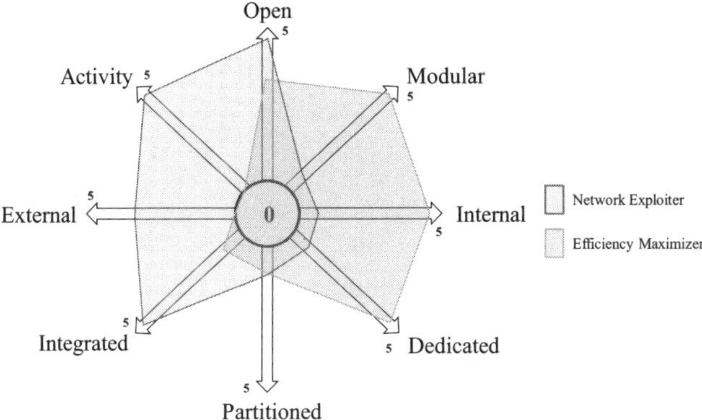

FIGURE 7.2 Redesign of Choc Co.'s workplace management system

Regardless of the business line, all workplaces were to be decked out in Choc Co. colours (consistent with its logo and branding), albeit in different styles, and serviced to a very high level by the RE&FM function. Beyond these superficial matters, however, it was apparent the two businesses required very different approaches to how their workplaces were designed and managed according to strategic requirements.

The follow-up challenge for the RE&FM function was to convert these ideal design principles into practical management policies and lead their implementation to become realized management practice. It was also apparent that any workplace, no matter how well designed, could not alone deliver superior enterprise performance. To be considered effective, the workplace management system needed to be designed to complement other functional management systems and vice versa.

Redesigning Choc Co.'s people management system

Illustrated in Figure 7.3, the working group envisaged that the ideal design of the *Efficiency Maximizer* people management system should maximize the *individual* effort and performance of each employee. It should focus on the development of individuals' *technical* skills to ensure peak proficiency in the role as rapidly as possible. The requirement should be for *specialist* knowledge relating to employees' tasks and essential operations. The emphasis on *performance* should be defined by peak productivity and the fewest possible errors as the primary measure of individuals' success in role.

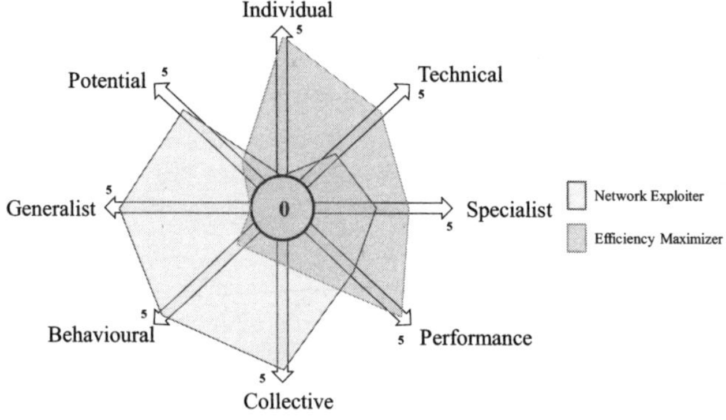

FIGURE 7.3 Redesign of Choc Co.'s people management system

The ideal design of the *Network Exploiter* people management system should also include a (moderate) focus on performance, specialist knowledge and technical skill, in common with the design of the *Efficiency Maximizer* people management system. However, in all other respects, the ideal *Network Exploiter* people management system differed significantly. Instead, it should incentivize *collective* effort and performance reflected in group goals and bonuses based upon team or company performance. The aim was the development of *behavioural* competencies primarily – focused on collaborative and flexible leadership and the ability to cope with uncertainty. It required *generalist* knowledge of other parts of the Choc Co. enterprise and its external partners. This was to enable the forging of novel network connections and an emphasis on the fulfilment of individuals' *potential* to lead realignment for enhanced organizational agility around customers.

Choc Co.'s HR function was responsible for maintaining a common set of minimum standards to apply to all employees' behaviour and conduct (and grievance and disciplinary case work if necessary). It also looked after management processes such as payroll and compliance with employment law. Beyond these 'hygiene' factors, and just as with the design of the workplace, the different people management requirements of the *Efficiency Maximizer* and *Network Exploiter* businesses were obvious. The opportunity for strategic contribution by the HR function was to lead the development of differentiated designs of people management subsystems for the two different businesses.

And yet, even the combined power of workplace and people management systems designed to be complementary were not enough to deliver the performance each business needed to succeed. Other strategically important functional management systems were also required, including information technology.

Redesigning Choc Co.'s information technology management system

Figure 7.4 illustrates the ideal design of the *Efficiency Maximizer*'s IT management system according to the deliberations of the working group.

To support the management of the *Efficiency Maximizer* business, the ideal design of the IT management system needed to be based upon the use of highly *customized* end-to-end software processes to support the seamless and efficient performing of tasks and activities against exacting standards. It needed a focus on the use of software and hardware developed for purely *proprietary* use and dedicated to serving the one specialized purpose in the *Efficiency Maximizer* business (i.e. supporting specialist but routine tasks). The business required *transactional* information technologies to support efficient routine work as much as possible. It needed standardized *enterprise-led* hardware and software prescriptions.

By contrast, the ideal design of the *Network Exploiter* IT management system needed to be focused on the idiosyncratic needs of the individual *user* (and not their business overall, for example). Multiple different computing systems being used simultaneously according to user preference were required. For example, some staff liked Windows

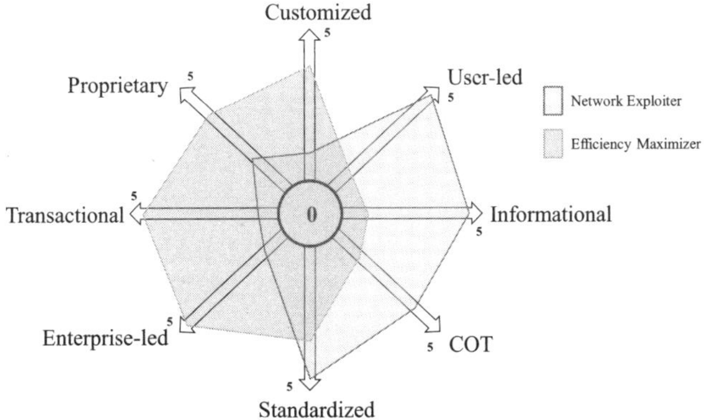

FIGURE 7.4 Redesign of Choc Co.'s information technology management system

PCs, and others preferred Macs. Choc Co. wished to support both if that is what its *Network Exploiters* wanted. Furthermore, it needed to support non-routine discretionary and *informational* work (e.g. creative or relational work) that could not be automated. The design was to use *commercial off-the-shelf technologies* (COT) software systems and capabilities, ported in-house to support remote and flexible working and the safe sharing of the enterprise's IT resources with external partners and networks. Finally, the requirements of individual users called for little more than *standardized* IT solutions, which could be realigned easily and cheaply to support individual activity-based working. Indeed, individuals were to be given a budget to procure their own software, as long as it did not pose a security risk.

The challenge for the IT department was to support the management of these two very different designs of IT systems. The *Efficiency Maximizer* requirement of the IT function was to design and implement (and support on an ongoing basis) a proprietary enterprise IT management system geared around the efficient performing of routine work. Conversely, the *Network Exploiter* business required the design and maintenance of a user-led commercial off-the-shelf IT management system, designed around the individual (including external partners and contractors) and their discretionary style of virtual and flexible working.

Choc Co.'s CIO summarized the challenge well by describing his function's role as being to

> *Support the needs of two very different customers, one in the style of a B2B (business to business) relationship, and the other more like a B2C (business to consumer) relationship.*

The strategic function and capabilities of the IT department needed to be twofold, therefore – just as in the case of HR and RE&FM and Choc Co.'s other corporate functions.

The Choc Co. case illustrates that to fulfil a strategic function, each corporate management function, regardless of area, has to be both strategic and integrated in its outlook and decision-making. There is no other way to secure a seat at the table in a strategically aligned enterprise.

CONCLUSION

As a bridge between theory and practice, one of the key objectives of this book is to provide readers with the concepts, insights and frameworks to consider the confusing and changeable world of enterprises more critically. By understanding this world better, it is hoped the book will help you as an enterprise leader (or an aspiring one, perhaps) to ask good questions, have better conversations and make the best choices possible in future about how to align and realign your enterprise's purpose, strategy and organization.

Before signing off, it is worth considering a key underlying message of the book (in addition to the rejection of universalism in favour of contingency, as described in the introduction). There is an enormously diverse and ever-expanding body of published material on competitive strategy, HR, marketing, IT, operations, innovation, culture management, digital, leadership, customer and many other business and management topics. Each topic represents a specialist niche within what should be a broad concern for designing and managing enterprises of any variety to function better in the future.

As much as new material is to be welcomed, the volume can be just overwhelming. The more information we have, the more specialist we need to be as scholars and managers to make sense of it. With specialization comes sophistication but inevitably also separation. With separation comes the increased risk of misunderstanding and conflict (or misalignment, you might say) between increasingly fractured fields, functions, groups and individuals. Put simply, how we approach the design and management of enterprises is becoming increasingly niche and disconnected. This process of fragmentation is a feature of our Information Age and afflicts every sphere of our socially constructed world.

And yet, a strategic alignment perspective on business and management demands precisely the opposite qualities of our scholarship and leadership. After all, all enterprises are value chains consisting of interdependent linkages that can only be as strong as their weakest link.[ii] The same is true of our political, economic and social systems and the global value chains they rely on. They are as vulnerable to disruption as any complex system of many moving parts. The events associated with the Covid-19 global pandemic are a stark example of this.

I wrote this book partly to be an antidote to the increasing fragmentation of the subject in theory and practice. It has laid down a practical blueprint for how to think strategically and comprehensively as an enterprise leader. Alignment as an end state does not occur naturally or by accident. It occurs purely as a result of reasoned strategic choice (and perhaps a dash of luck) – hence the reference to strategic alignment and strategic realignment throughout this book.

In the final analysis, the quality of leadership decision-making makes all the difference to whether an enterprise is aligned or not and whether it is a success or a failure. Our unique ability as a species to choose a course of action as a result of rational deliberation and set apart from our compulsions is the highest pinnacle of the human experience (in the author's opinion, at least). To make a positive difference to the lives of others, whoever they are and in whatever form that may take, is the highest calling.

Both of these sentiments should be a cause for celebration, not anxiety. In truth, this is the ultimate motivation behind the writing of the book: an earnest belief that enterprises, which are vital to our lives and well-being economically and socially, should and can function better and that it is within our unique gift as people to make it so.

If you are successful in implementing positive realignment in your own enterprise or a future endeavour, and if this book has helped even in a small way, I would be delighted. Thank you for reading and *bon courage*.

ACKNOWLEDGEMENTS

Both editions of this book have been a long time in the making. None of this work would have been possible without the generous support over many years of a small army of colleagues, students, collaborators and friends, spanning academia and practice.

On the academic side, I am immensely grateful to my colleagues at the University of Oxford, Oxford Saïd Business School (the School). The School is a highly collegial and supportive environment in which to debate new ideas, seek advice and receive instruction on robust approaches to the subject matter and research methods. Special thanks must go to members of my subject group (Technology, Operations Management and Organizational Studies – TOPOS), in addition to the wise counsel and the generous personal and institutional backing of Dr Andrew White, Associate Dean for Corporate Relations, and the school's former dean, Professor Peter Tufano.

I have also drawn widely upon the support of a close network of colleagues at other institutions. Very special thanks must go to my former doctoral supervisor, and long-term mentor, Dr Philip Stiles, University of Cambridge, Cambridge Judge Business School. Philip has remained a constant source of the most invaluable guidance and moral support throughout the entire journey, of which this book is a single but major milestone. Professor Scott Snell, University of Virginia, Darden School of Business, also deserves special recognition for challenging me to think critically about the foundational concepts behind the *Strategic Alignment Framework*.

Other scholars who generously gave of their time include Professor Kazuhiro Asakawa, Keio University, Keio Business School; Professor Jusuke Ikegami, and the late and very much missed, Professor Emeritus Masataka Ota, both of Waseda University, Waseda Business School;

Professor Peter Williamson, University of Cambridge, Cambridge Judge Business School; and Professor Sandy Pepper, Department of Management, London School of Economics and Political Science.

On the practice side, I am sincerely grateful to the thousands of talented students who entrusted me with their education on matters relating to strategy and organizational behaviour. Whether undergraduate, graduate or executive, their critical but always constructive feedback over the course of 15 years of teaching, in which I have always sought to teach original content derived from my research, has been a major source of the energy I required to write this book. I am also grateful to the dozens of research subjects/case studies, executive education clients and consultancy clients who collaborated with me in long-term relations to apply very practically my strategic alignment concepts to inform change within their leadership teams and enterprises more widely. Each represented a laboratory of sorts for the purpose of experimenting with introducing a strategic alignment approach to improve their enterprise performance. In addition to practical outcomes, each generously provided the access necessary to derive publishable research insights.

Many individuals from industry have provided encouragement and support for the writing of this book – they are too many to mention, but they all have my thanks. I wish to offer special thanks to Dr Barry Varcoe and acknowledge his valuable contribution to the development and refinement of some of the concepts in the book. Barry is an experienced practitioner and thoughtful scholar in the field of business and management and was hugely supportive in collaborating extensively to grounding the body of work. The following also deserve special mention for acting as critical friends to keep me honest and relevant for the world of practice – and for being at the end of a phone whenever I needed it, despite leading incredibly busy lives. In alphabetical order, they are Nina Bjornstad; Nicola Downing; Shingo Kobayashi; Clara Mohl Schack; Paul Nanninga; Phil Riman; Shin Shinozaki; Jonathan Trimble; and Victoria Wright.

I am very grateful to Toby and Vicki Roe of Roe Communications for proactively and conscientiously assisting me throughout the drafting of the book, acting as copy-editors and a general sounding board for my writing ideas and plans, whether good, bad or ugly. I am also extremely grateful to the team at the publisher, Bloomsbury. Ian Hallsworth, Editor-in-chief, has been terrifically supportive, from the inception of the book through to its publication, very ably supported by Allie Collins, Editor, and Matt James, Assistant Editor.

Many thanks go to my loving parents, who are always so supportive. Since the first edition's publication, they have, without fail, made it their business to seek it out in every bookshop on every holiday and dutifully report back. Finally, my most profound thanks must go to my wife, Clara. Much more than simply putting up with my distractedness (and I am sorry to say, occasional grumpiness) while in the thick of writing, Clara read and proofed every word on every page of every one of the 30 or so eventual drafts of both editions, and nurtured and cajoled me as required to get me over the line to completion.

This book would not have been possible without you all. Thank you.

REFERENCES

i. Trevor, J. & Varcoe, B. (2016). 'A Simple Way to Test Your Company's Strategic Alignment'. *Harvard Business Review*. 16 May. Harvard Business School Publishing.

ii. Trevor, J. & Varcoe, B. (2017). 'How aligned is your organization?'. *Harvard Business Review*. 7 February. Harvard Business School Publishing.

iii. Trevor, J. (2020). 'How to align your organization in times of change'. Oxford Answers: www.sbs.ox.ac.uk/oxford-answers/how-align-your-organization-times-change

iv. Gallup (2020). 'Align Your Purpose, Brand and Culture for a Winning Employee Experience': www.gallup.com/workplace/242240/employee-experience-perspective-paper.aspx

v. Lawrence, P.R. & Lorsch, J.W. (1967). 'Differentiation and integration in complex organizations'. *Administrative Science Quarterly*, pp. 1–47.

vi. Trevor, J. (2013). 'From New Pay to the *New*, New Pay?' *WorldatWork Journal*, *22*(1): pp. 19–28.

vii. www.macrotrends.net/stocks/charts/MCD/mcdonalds/revenue

viii. www.businessinsider.com/amazing-facts-mcdonalds-2010-12?r=US&IR=T

ix. Sponsorship Research International (2014).

x. www.arm.com/company/arm-30-anniversary

xi. www.arm.com/why-arm/partner-ecosystem

xii. Williamson, P.J. & De Meyer, A. (2012). 'Ecosystem advantage: How to successfully harness the power of partners'. *California Management Review*, 55(1), pp. 24–46.

xiii. Trevor, J. & Williamson, P. (2019). 'How to Design an Ambidextrous Organization'. *European Business Review*, March–April, pp. 34–43.

xiv. www.bbc.co.uk/news/technology-54142567

xv. www.reuters.com/article/us-arm-holdings-m-a-nvidia-elon-musk-idUKKBN2FU02N

xvi. www.arm.com/blogs/blueprint/arm-30-years

xvii. Project Management Institute. (2017). 9th Global Project Management Survey.

xviii. Economist Intelligence Unit. (2017). 'Closing the Gap: Designing and Delivering a Strategy That Works'.

xix. Sharp, B. (1991). 'Competitive marketing strategy: Porter revisited'. *Marketing Intelligence & Planning*.

xx. Thompson, E.P. (1967). 'Time, work-discipline, and industrial capitalism'. *Past & Present*, *(38)*, pp. 56–97.

xxi. Simon, H.A. (1990). 'Bounded rationality'. *Utility and Probability*, pp. 15–18. Palgrave Macmillan, London.

xxii. Varcoe, B. & Trevor, J. (2017). 'Leading the Aligned Enterprise'. *Developing Leaders Quarterly (26)*, pp. 35–40.

xxiii. www.home.barclays/content/dam/barclayspublic/documents/news/471-392-250413-salz-response.pdf

xxiv. www.ft.com/content/0bc94580-7466-11e8-b6ad-3823e4384287

xxv. www.gallup.com/workplace/321032/employee-engagement-meta-analysis-brief.aspx

xxvi. Hope, J. & Fraser, R. (2001). 'Beyond Budgeting: Questions and answers'. *CAM-I, BBRT, Dorset*, pp. 1–28.

xxvii. Ferlie, E., Fitzgerald, L., McGivern, G., Dopson, S. & Bennett, C. (2011). 'Public policy networks and "wicked problems": A nascent solution?'. *Public Administration, 89*(2), pp. 307–324.

xxviii. www.bbc.com/worklife/article/20200608-what-is-the-competency-trap?ocid=ww.social.link.linkedin

xxix. www.cnbc.com/2021/06/24/microsoft-closes-above-2-trillion-market-cap-for-the-first-time.html

xxx. www.forbes.com/companies/xerox/

xxxi. Heracleous, Loizos Th., Papachroni, A., Andriopoulos, C. & Gotsi, M. (2017). 'Structural ambidexterity and competency traps: Insights from Xerox PARC'. *Technological Forecasting and Social Change (117)*, pp. 327–338.

xxxii. www.bbc.co.uk/news/business-56937428

xxxiii. www.bbc.co.uk/news/business-56910255

xxxiv. www.bbc.co.uk/news/business-54112461

xxxv. Picoult, J. (2021), 'Peloton's Predicament: What to Do When Demand Outstrips Supply'. *Forbes*, January 2021.

xxxvi. www.oag.com/coronavirus-airline-schedules-data

xxxvii. www.airport-technology.com/news/all-nippon-trial-commonpass-digital/

xxxviii. Darwin, C. (1909). *The Origin of Species,* pp. 95–96. New York: PF Collier & Son.

xxxix. Megginson, W.L., Byrd, M.J. & Megginson, L.C. (2000). *Small Business Management: An Entrepreneur's Guidebook*. McGraw-Hill, Irwin.

xl. www.bbc.co.uk/news/business-56022908

xli. www.bbc.co.uk/news/business-46424830

xlii. www.ft.com/content/340501e2-e0cd-4ea5-b388-9af0d9a74ce2

xliii. www.ft.com/content/b229250d-5d9e-4bb1-bb91-e57888233a98

xliv. www.foxconn.com/en-us/press-center/press-releases/latest-news/456

xlv. Ewenstein, B., Smith, W. & Sologar, A. (2015). 'Changing change management'. *McKinsey Digital*, pp. 1–4.

xlvi. Handy, C. (2016). *The Second Curve: Thoughts on Reinventing Society*. Random House.

xlvii. Aguilar, F.J. (1967). *Scanning the Business Environment*. New York: Macmillan.

xlviii. www.bbc.co.uk/news/world-57368247

xlix. Christensen, C., Raynor, M.E. & McDonald, R. (2013). 'Disruptive innovation'. *Harvard Business Review*.

l. Panel Article. (2020). '15 Technologies That Will Disrupt the Industry in the Next Five Years'. *Forbes*.

li. Purdy, C. (2020). *Billion Dollar Burger: Inside Big Tech's Race for the Future of Food*. Penguin.

lii. Estabrook, B. (2020). '"Billion Dollar Burger" Review: Wherefrom the Beef?'. *Wall Street Journal,* 8 June2020.

liii. Browne, A. (2021). 'Golden Nuggets: The Fake Meat Revolution Is on Its Way'. *The Spectator*, June 2021.

liv. *Meat Global Industry Almanac 2015–2024.*

lv. Dent, D. (2020). 'The Meat Industry Is Unsustainable'. IDTechEx Research Article.

lvi. Gratton, L. (2021). 'How to Do Hybrid Right: When designing flexible work arrangements, focus on individual human concerns, not just institutional ones'. *Harvard Business Review*, May–June 2021.

lvii. Smith, J.H. (1998). 'The enduring legacy of Elton Mayo'. *Human Relations*, *51*(3), pp. 221–249.

lviii. www.forbes.com/sites/jackkelly/2021/04/01/google-wants-workers-to-return-to-the-office-ahead-of-schedule-this-looks-like-a-blow-to-the-remote-work-trend/

lix. Silver, N. (2012). *The Signal and the Noise: The Art and Science of Prediction.* Penguin UK.

lx. www.bbc.co.uk/news/business-51499776

lxi. www.economist.com/podcasts/2021/02/17/hard-reboot-can-intels-new-boss-turn-the-chipmaker-around

lxii. www.bbc.co.uk/news/technology-53142989

lxiii. www.ft.com/content/51f63b07-aeb8-4961-9ce9-c1f7a4e326f0

lxiv. www.bbc.co.uk/news/business-52462660

lxv. www.bbc.co.uk/news/business-53605691

lxvi. www.bbc.co.uk/news/business-56020650

lxvii. Campbell, P., (2021), 'Jaguar Land Rover lays out electric plans in radical overhaul', Financial Times, February 2021: https://www.ft.com/content/4a7f386b-121b-450e-936c-e7935daab089

lxviii. Donaldson, L. (2001). *The Contingency Theory of Organizations.* Sage Publications, California.

lxix. Paauwe, J. & Boselie, P. (2005). '"Best practices ... in spite of performance": Just a matter of imitation?', *The International Journal of Human Resource Management 16*(6), June 2005, pp. 987–1003.

lxx. Trevor, J. (2016). 'Future Work: Changes, Choices and Consequences'. *European Business Review.*

lxxi. Hamel, G. & Zanini, M. (2018). 'The end of bureaucracy'. *Harvard Business Review*, 96(6), pp. 50–59.

lxxii. Heckscher, C. & Donnellon, A. (1994). *The Post-Bureaucratic Organization: New Perspectives on Organizational Change.* Sage Publications, California.

lxxiii. Chesbrough, H., Vanhaverbeke, W. & West, J. (eds.). (2006). *Open Innovation: Researching a New Paradigm.* Oxford University Press on Demand.

lxxiv. www.pgconnectdevelop.com

lxxv. www.fastcompany.com/3003448/when-co-creation-becomes-beating-heart-marketing-companies-win

lxxvi. Facebook Briefing (2018): https://newsroom.fb.come/company-info/

lxxvii. Taneja, H. (2019). 'The era of "move fast and break things" is over'. *Harvard Business Review* (21).

lxxviii. Reeves, M., Wesselink, E. & Whitaker, K. (2020). 'The End of Bureaucracy Again?', *Boston Consulting Group*, July 2020.

lxxix. Rigby, D.K., Sutherland, J. & Takeuchi, H. (2016). 'Embracing agile', *Harvard Business Review*, *94*(5), May 2016, pp. 40–50.

lxxx. Winter, R. 'Mass customization and beyond – evolution of customer centricity in financial services'. In Rautenstrauch, C., Seelmann-Eggebert, R. & Turowski, K. (eds.). *Moving into Mass Customization*, pp. 197–213. Springer, Berlin/ Heidelberg.

lxxxi. Wright, S. (ed). (2014). *Competitive Intelligence, Analysis and Strategy: Creating Organizational Agility*. Routledge, Abingdon.

lxxxii. Jarillo, J.C. (2013). *Strategic Networks: Creating the Borderless Organization*. Routledge, Abingdon.

lxxxiii. Landsberg, M. (2003). *The Tools of Leadership: Vision, Inspiration, Momentum*. Profile Books.

lxxxiv. Leider, R.J. (2015). *The Power of Purpose: Creating Meaning in Your Life and Work*. Berrett-Koehler Publishers.

lxxxv. White, A. (2016). 'Lessons from Companies That Put Purpose Ahead of Short-Term Profits', *Harvard Business Review*, June 2016.

lxxxvi. Collins, J. & Porras, J.I. (2005). *Built to Last: Successful Habits of Visionary Companies*. Random House.

lxxxvii. https://thewaltdisneycompany.com/about/#our-businesses

lxxxviii. 'How Disney Encourages Employees to Deliver Exceptional': hbr.org/sponsored/2018/02/how-disney-encourages-employees-to-deliver-exceptional-customer-service

lxxxix. Herbert, F. (1969). *Dune Messiah (Vol. 2)*. Hodder, London.

xc. www.wholefoodsmarket.com/our-mission-values

xci. www.cnbc.com/2018/06/15/a-year-after-amazon-announced-whole-foods-deal-heres-where-we-stand.html

xcii. Kular, S., Gatenby, M., Rees, C., Soane, E. & Truss, K. (2008). 'Employee engagement: A literature review'.

xciii. www.nytimes.com/2014/06/01/opinion/sunday/why-you-hate-work.html?_r=1

xciv. news.gallup.com/reports/189830/e.aspx?utm_source=gbj&utm_medium=copy&utm_campaign=20160830-gbj

xcv. www.forbes.com/sites/simonmainwaring/2013/07/16/marketing-3-0-will-be-won-by-purpose-driven-social-brands-infographic/#418f50751886

xcvi. Zingheim, P.K., Ledford, G.L. & Schuster, J.R. (1996). 'Competencies and competency models: Does one size fit all', *ACA Journal*, 5(1), January 1996, pp. 56–65.

xcvii. Roche, W.K. (1991). 'Trust dynamics and organizational integration: The micro-sociology of Alan Fox', *The British Journal of Sociology*, *42*(1), March 1991, pp. 95–113.

xcviii. White, A. (2016). 'Lessons from Companies that Put Purpose Ahead of Short-term Profits'. *Harvard Business Review*, pp. 56–65.

xcix. www.telegraph.co.uk/technology/2021/07/15/revolut-becomes-valuable-british-fintech-company/

c. www.businessinsider.com/facebook-actually-paid-3-billion-for-oculus-vr-2017-1?r=US&IR=T

ci. www.telegraph.co.uk/technology/2019/02/25/microsoft-betting-augmented-reality-future-workplace/

cii. www.bbc.co.uk/news/business-47336304

ciii. www.statista.com/statistics/301735/tomato-ketchup-usage-frequency-in-the-uk/

civ. Porter, M.E. & Advantage, C. (1985). 'Creating and sustaining superior performance'. *Competitive Advantage*, *167*, pp. 167–206.

cv. Porter, M.E. (1997). 'Competitive strategy', *Measuring Business Excellence*, *1*(2), 1997, pp. 12–17.

cvi. www.ibm.com

cvii. Sky News, 'Perfect storm for retailers,' March 2018.

cviii. www.coutts.com

cix. Kaplan, R.S. & Norton, D.P. (2006). *Alignment: Using the Balanced Scorecard to Create Corporate Synergies*. Harvard Business Press.

cx. Cooper, R.G., Edgett, S.J. & Kleinschmidt, E.J. (1999). 'New product portfolio management: Practices and performance'. *Journal of Product Innovation Management*, *16*(4), July 1999, pp. 333–351.

cxi. uk.reuters.com/article/uk-byd-results/chinas-byd-expects-2018-profit-to-fall-by-a-third-as-competition-rises-idUKKCN1N31MK?utm

cxii. www.economist.com/node/18441175

cxiii. Cohen, W.M. & Levinthal, D.A. (1990). 'Absorptive capacity: A new perspective on learning and innovation'. *Administrative Science Quarterly*, March 1990, pp. 128–152.

cxiv. Williamson, P. J. & De Meyer, A., 2012, 'Ecosystem Advantage: How to Successfully Harness the Power of Partners'. *California Management Review*, 55(1), pp. 24–46.

cxv. Heckscher, C., Heckscher, C. & Donnellon, A. (eds.). (1994). 'Defining the Post-Bureaucratic Type'. *The Post-Bureaucratic Organization: New Perspectives on Organizational Change*. Sage, Thousand Oaks.

cxvi. Prahalad, C.K. & Ramaswamy, V. (2000). 'Co-opting customer competence'. *Harvard Business Review*, *78*(1), pp. 79–90.

cxvii. www.rolls-royce.com/products-and-services.aspx

cxviii. Trevor, J. & Stiles, P. (2007). 'GHRRA Case Study Report, Rolls-Royce Plc'. Cambridge University.

cxix. www.economist.com/node/18073351

cxx. Rogoway, T. (2020). 'Northrop Grumman's Plan to Replace the MQ-9 Reaper with Stealthy Autonomous Drones'. *The Warzone, The Drive*: www.thedrive.com/the-war-zone/37498/northrop-grummans-plan-to-replace-the-mq-9-reaper-with-stealthy-autonomous-drones

cxxi. Adner, R. (2013). *The Wide Lens: What Successful Innovators See That Others Miss*. Penguin.

cxxii. Donaldson, L. (2001). *The Contingency Theory of Organizations*. Sage Publications, California.

cxxiii. Goold, M., Campbell, A. & Luchs, K. (1993). 'Strategies and styles revisited: Strategic planning and financial control'. *Long Range Planning*, *26*(5), pp. 49–60.

cxxiv. Schneider, M. & Somers, M. (2006). 'Organizations as complex adaptive systems: Implications of complexity theory for leadership research'. *The Leadership Quarterly*, *17*(4), pp. 351–365.

cxxv. Raisch, S., Birkinshaw, J., Probst, G. & Tushman, M.L. (2009). 'Organizational Ambidexterity: Balancing exploitation and exploration for sustained performance'. *Organization Science*, *20*(4), July–August 2009, pp. 685–695.

cxxvi. Aversa, P., Furnari, S. & Haefliger, S. (2015). 'Business model configurations and performance: A qualitative comparative analysis in Formula One racing, 2005–2013'. *Industrial and Corporate Change*, *24*(3), June 2015, pp. 655–676.

cxxvii. 'Why General Electric Is Struggling'. *The Economist*, 30 November 2017.

cxxviii. Prahalad, C.K. & Hamel, G. (1990). 'The core competence of the corporation'. *Harvard Business Review*, May–June 1990, pp. 79–91.

cxxix. Kang, S.C., Morris, S.S. & Snell, S.A. (2007). 'Relational archetypes, organizational learning, and value creation: Extending the human resource architecture'. *Academy of Management Review*, *32*(1), pp. 236–256.

cxxx. Hindo, B. (2007). 'At 3M, a Struggle Between Creativity and Efficiency'. *Business Week*.

cxxxi. Nahapiet, J. & Ghoshal, S. (1998). 'Social capital, intellectual capital, and the organizational advantage'. *The Academy of Management Review*, *23*(2), April 1998, pp. 242–266.

cxxxii. https://blog.ongig.com/job-titles/c-level-titles/

cxxxiii. www.mckinsey.com/business-functions/organization/our-insights/building-capabilities-for-performance

cxxxiv. Delery, J.E. & Doty, D.H. (1996). 'Modes of theorizing in strategic human resource management: Tests of universalistic, contingency, and configurational performance predictions'. *The Academy of Management Journal*, *39*(4), pp. 802–835.

cxxxv. Powell, W.W. & DiMaggio, P.J. (eds.). (1991). *The New Institutionalism in Organizational Analysis*. University of Chicago Press.

cxxxvi. Hamel, G. & Prahalad, C.K. (1990). 'The core competence of the corporation'. *Harvard Business Review*, *68*(3), May–June 1990, pp. 79–91.

cxxxvii. Prahalad, C.K. (1993). 'The role of core competencies in the corporation'. *Research-Technology Management*, *36*(6) 1993, pp. 40–47.

cxxxviii. Grant, R.M. (1999). 'The resource-based theory of competitive advantage: Implications for strategy formulation'. *Knowledge and Strategy*, April 1999, pp. 3–23.

cxxxix. Horowitz, B. (2003). 'It's Back to Basics for McDonald's'. *USA Today*, 2003.

cxl. Taneja, H. (2018). 'The End of Scale'. *MIT Sloan Management Review*, *59*(3), Spring 2018, pp. 67–72.

cxli. Burton, D & DeLong, T. (2000). 'Morgan Stanley: Becoming a "One-Firm Firm"'. Harvard Business School, Case Study 9-400-043, May 2000.

cxlii. www.morganstanley.com/about-us-governance/businesssegments

cxliii. Davis, S. & Lawrence, P. (1978). 'Problems of Matrix Organizations'. *Harvard Business Review*, May 1978.

cxliv. Collins, J. & Porras, J.I. (2005). *Built to Last: Successful Habits of Visionary Companies*. Random House.

cxlv. www.aboutamazon.com

cxlvi. www.brucebnews.com/2018/08/the-amazon-ecosystem-the-company-that-wants-to-sell-everything-to-everyone/

cxlvii. Thietart, R.A. & Forgues, B. (2011). 'Complexity science and organization', in *The SAGE Handbook of Complexity and Management*, Allen P., Maguire S. & McKelvey, B. (eds.). Sage, London, 2011, pp. 53–64.

cxlviii. www.bbc.co.uk/news/uk-england-northamptonshire-45124215

cxlix. Schein, E.H. (1991). 'What Is Culture?'. In Frost, P.J., Moore, L.F., Louis, M.R., Lundberg, C.C. & Martin, J. (eds.). *Reframing Organizational Culture*. Sage Publications, California, pp. 243–253.

cl. Nahapiet, J. & Ghoshal, S. (1998). 'Social capital, intellectual capital, and the organizational advantage'. *Academy of Management Review*, *23*(2), pp. 242–266.

cli. Nadler, D.A. and Tushman, M.L. (1980). 'A model for diagnosing organizational behavior'. *Organizational Dynamics*, *9*(2), pp. 35–51.

clii. Nadler, D.A. and Tushman, M.L. (1980). 'A model for diagnosing organizational behavior'. *Organizational Dynamics*, *9*(2), pp. 35–51.

cliii. Beer, M. & Nohria, N. (2000). 'Cracking the code of change'. *HBR's 10 Must Reads: On Change Management*, *78*(3), pp. 133–141.

cliv. Nadler, D., Tushman, M., Tushman, M.L. & Nadler, M.B. (1997). *Competing By Design: The Power of Organizational Architecture.* Oxford University Press.

clv. Barney, J.B. (2001). 'Resource-based theories of competitive advantage: A ten-year retrospective on the resource-based view'. *Journal of Management*, *27*(6), December 2001, pp. 643–650.

clvi. Barney, J. (1991). 'Firm resources and sustained competitive advantage', *Journal of Management*, *17*(1), March 1991, pp. 99–120.

clvii. Dess, G.G. & Picken, J.C. (1999). *Beyond Productivity: How Leading Companies Achieve Superior Performance by Leveraging their Human Capital*. American Management Association.

clviii. Lepak, D.P. & Snell, S.A. (1999). 'The human resource architecture: Toward a theory of human capital allocation and development'. *Academy of Management Review*, *24*(1), pp. 31–48.

clix. Smircich, L. (1983). 'Concepts of culture and organizational analysis'. *Administrative Science Quarterly*, pp. 339–358.

clx. Schein, E.H. (2010). *Organizational Culture and Leadership (Vol. 2)*. John Wiley & Sons.

clxi. Donaldson, L. (2001). *The Contingency Theory of Organizations*. Sage Publications, California.

clxii. Schuler, R.S. & Jackson, S.E. (1987). 'Linking competitive strategies with human resource management practices'. *Academy of Management Perspectives*, *1*(3), August 1987, pp. 207–219.

clxiii. Arthur, J.B. (1994). 'Effects of human resource systems on manufacturing performance and turnover'. *Academy of Management Journal*, *37*(3), June 1994, pp. 670–687.

clxiv. O'Reilly, C. (1989). 'Corporations, culture, and commitment: Motivation and social control in organizations'. *California Management Review*, *31*(4), pp. 9–25.

clxv. Kang, S.C., Morris, S.S. & Snell, S.A. (2007). 'Relational archetypes, organizational learning, and value creation: Extending the human resource architecture'. *Academy of Management Review*, *32*(1), January 2007, pp. 236–256.

clxvi. Delery, J.E. & Doty, D.H. (1996). 'Modes of theorizing in strategic human resource management: Tests of universalistic, contingency, and configurational performance predictions'. *Academy of Management Journal*, *39*(4), August 1996, pp. 802–835.

clxvii. www.nytimes.com/2004/12/14/technology/oracle-to-acquire-peoplesoft-for-103-billion-ending-bitter-fight.html clxviii. Trevor, J. & Kotosaka, M. (2017). 'Strategic human resource management: an agenda for Japanese companies in the 21st century'. *Harvard Business Review.*

clxix. Oracle Presentation at Cambridge Judge Business School (2004).

clxx. Morris, S., Snell, S.A. & Lepak, D. (2006). 'An architectural approach to managing knowledge stocks and flows: implications for reinventing the HR function'. In *Reinventing HRM,* pp. 67–90. Routledge.

clxxi. Trevor, J & Stiles, P. (2007). Oracle Case Study, Global Human Resource Research Alliance, Cambridge Judge Business School Working Paper Series.

clxxii. DiMaggio, P.J. & Powell, W.W. (1983). 'The iron cage revisited: Institutional isomorphism and collective rationality in organizational fields'. *American Sociological Review*, pp. 147–160.

clxxiii. english.jr-central.co.jp/about/punctuality.html

clxxiv. Fujiyama, T. (2018). 'Comparing railway systems in the UK and Japan from the view of their punctuality'. Daiwa Foundation Seminar, May 2018.

clxxv. Ministry of Infrastructure, Land and Tourism (2017). 遅延の「見える化」を開始 downloaded from www.mlit.go.jp

clxxvi. www.jniosh.go.jp/en/

clxxvii. www.atlasobscura.com/articles/pointing-and-calling-japan-trains

clxxviii. Felin, T. (2016). 'When strategy walks out the door'. *MIT Sloan Management Review*, *58*(1), August 2016, p. 95.

clxxix. Hansen, M.T. & Von Oetinger, B. (2001). 'Introducing T-shaped managers. Knowledge management's next generation'. *Harvard Business Review*, *79*(3), pp. 106–116.

clxxx. www.huawei.com/uk/about-huawei

clxxxi. Tao, T., De Cremer, D. & Chunbo, W. (2016). *Huawei: Leadership, Culture, And Connectivity*. Sage Publications, California.

clxxxii. Parsons, B. (2013). 'ARM Case Study, Future of Reward Conference'. Downing College, Cambridge.

clxxxiii. www.businessweekly.co.uk/news/hi-tech/15787-arm-world's-top-five-innovators

clxxxiv. Ralph, A. (2021). 'Chipmaker ARM "stuck in the mud"'. *London Times*, 27 July.

clxxxv. deloitte.wsj.com/cio/2018/03/12/it-spending-from-value-preservation-to-value-creation/

clxxxvi. (2017). 'Top trends in facilities management: How society, demographics and technology are changing the world of FM'. CBRE.

clxxxvii. Trevor, J. (2010). 'Can Pay Be Strategic?'. In *Can Pay Be Strategic?*. pp. 168–199. Palgrave Macmillan, London.

clxxxviii. McCord, P. (2014). 'How Netflix reinvented HR'. *Harvard Business Review*, *92*(1), pp. 71–76.

clxxxix. Wingfield, N. (2013). 'Microsoft abolishes employee evaluation system'. *New York Times*.

INDEX